SKYWARD

ALSO BY RICHARD E. BYRD

Alone: The Classic Polar Adventure

Discovery: The Story of the Second Byrd
Antarctic Expedition

Little America

To the Pole: The Diary and Notebook
of Richard E. Byrd, 1925–1927
(Raimund E. Goerler, Editor)

SKYWARD

Man's Mastery of the Air as Shown by the
Brilliant Flights of America's Leading
Air Explorer. His Life, His Thrilling
Adventures, His North Pole and
Trans-Atlantic Flights, Together
with His Plans for Conquering
the Antarctic by Air

Richard E. Byrd

ADMIRAL, U.S. NAVY

Jeremy P. Tarcher/Putnam
a member of
Penguin Putnam Inc./New York

Most Tarcher/Putnam books are available at special quantity
discounts for bulk purchase for sales promotions, premiums,
fund-raising, and educational needs. Special books or book excerpts
also can be created to fit specific needs. For details, write
Putnam Special Markets, 375 Hudson Street,
New York, NY 10014.

Jeremy P. Tarcher/Putnam
a member of
Penguin Putnam Inc.
375 Hudson Street
New York, NY 10014
www.penguinputnam.com

First published by G. P. Putnam's Sons 1928

Library of Congress Cataloging-in-Publication Data

Byrd, Richard Evelyn, 1888–1957.
Skyward: man's mastery of the air / Richard E. Byrd.
p.   cm.
Originally published: New York: Putnam, 1928.
ISBN 1-58542-010-7
1. Byrd, Richard Evelyn, 1888–1957.   2. Air pilots—United States—
Biography.   3. Explorers—United States—Biography.   4. Aeronautics—
Flights.   I. Title.
TL540.B8A3   2000   99-37617 CIP
629.13′092—dc21
[B]

Printed in the United States of America
1   3   5   7   9   10   8   6   4   2

This book is printed on acid-free paper. ∞

Book design by Jennifer Ann Daddio
Frontispiece photo © AP/Wide World Photos Inc.

To those who have stuck by me through thick and thin: among the front rank of whom are Floyd Bennett, Edsel Ford and my always splendid shipmates

Contents

Foreword

Skyward is a chronicle of achievement for the twenty-five years following the Wright Brothers' first powered flight. Written by then Commander Richard Evelyn Byrd in 1928, the book is amazing for its foresight during the formative years of the aviation-dominated twentieth century. It is of particular interest for its primary account of key long-distance flight and aviation exploration efforts by one of America's first and most adventurous pilots.

Rear Admiral William A. Moffett, who wrote the foreword to the 1928 edition of *Skyward,* was the architect of the U.S. Navy's Bureau of Aeronautics, the organization that made possible the rise to preeminence of U.S. Naval Aviation. In his foreword, Rear Admiral Moffett gives credit to Richard Byrd for personally helping to engineer the establishment of that Bureau in those turbulent days following World War One.

Prematurely retired from active duty as an ensign because of an athletic injury suffered while attending the U.S. Naval Academy, Richard Byrd was recalled to active duty in 1917 when the United States entered the war. He then gained his coveted Navy wings and subsequently excelled as a true aviation pioneer. Byrd candidly records his pilot and explorer views in that wondrous post–World War One period of great aviation experimentation when we still had not completed our discovery on earth.

What is astounding is the prescience of the author in defining the rudiments for aviation safety. Surrounded by those who were having accidents, Commander Byrd first recognized the key elements needed for air safety. His wisdom in defining the then-dreaded spin as well as the discovery of its recovery is a classic bit of aviation history, and his view that accidents are an unwelcome but factual initial part of any new form of transportation says a great deal for those pioneering in flight. His words on air safety still ring true today.

Constantly on the leading edge of discovery of more efficient flying procedures, Byrd faced many disappointments in his aviation career, but he resolved and rose above challenge after challenge. It is a trait that made him the consummate explorer. His early and determined goal of flight across the Atlantic was set first during World War One when he wanted, without success, to deliver a Curtiss-built U.S. Navy seaplane to Europe. When administrative hurdles of that time proved too much, he sought a position on one of the post-war Navy Curtiss flying boats intending to fly the Atlantic, based on his early and appreciable knowledge of air navigation. This too was not to be, but he flew on the first two legs in the NC-3 flying boat.

Undaunted and determined to cross the Atlantic in any way he could, he volunteered to be a crew member of the ill-fated English-built U.S. Navy lighter-than-air craft, the ZR-2, but was fortuitously denied the opportunity. This set in motion his quest to fly over the North Pole in the three-engine monoplane Fokker *Josephine Ford.* Flying over land and ice never before crossed by air, Byrd credited the new National Geographic–developed sun compass and intuitive dead reckoning that led to his goal, but it was really his indomitable spirit as he relentlessly pursued his goal. Seventy years later, with navigation improvements that include the Global Positioning System, the feat seems deceptively easier and some have even challenged his accuracy. Given the air navigation tools and the state-of-the-art airplanes and engines of 1925, this was a magnificent achievement and he was recognized by his nation. His efforts and adventurous spirit led many into aviation and to follow in his footsteps.

Richard Byrd believed in the ability of air transport airplanes to carry passengers cross the Atlantic. Positioned to make such an attempt with several others in May 1927, their efforts were eclipsed when Charles Lindbergh made the flight to Paris in his single-engine Ryan. Again undaunted, Byrd felt his goal was loftier. He wanted to show the flexibility, safety, and passenger-carrying capability of a larger multiengine airplane. This ability was demonstrated the following month, on June 30, 1927, when he and three others flew their three-engine airplane across the Atlantic without visual reference to sea or land to prove that passengers soon would be commonly carried in international air travel. Always the visionary, Byrd believed that great airplanes would course the skies in the twentieth century.

Richard Byrd foresaw much of what was to come in aviation. His book catalogues true adventure in a time when aviation was young and we had so few answers. It was a time when there were still a few places in the world to be discovered. Commander Richard E. Byrd's inquisitiveness and spirit in *Skyward* demonstrates that when a person pursues the unknown and conquers it, he or she will excite the young to follow and to excel in their own right.

—DONALD D. ENGEN

VICE ADMIRAL,

UNITED STATES NAVY (RETIRED)

Vice Admiral Engen was director of the Smithsonian Institution's National Air and Space Museum at the time of his death in 1999. He was a former administrator of the Federal Aviation Administration and Deputy Commander-in-Chief of the U.S. Atlantic Command and the U.S. Atlantic Fleet, as well as a recipient of the Navy Cross, the U.S. Navy's highest award for valor.

Foreword to the
Original Edition

I wish I were writing this book instead of only its foreword. I would put in much that I know Byrd will leave out—much of his own life and achievements. After years of association with this young flyer I find he makes light of what most of us would weigh heavily.

Byrd's polar and trans-Atlantic flights were but incidents in many years of high adventure. He went around the world alone at the age of twelve. After graduation at Annapolis he helped put down two revolutions in the West Indies. He distinguished himself by years of splendid service with our battleship fleet.

Not the least of all this unwritten record is the fact that he has been officially cited twenty times for bravery or conspicuous conduct. He has received the thanks of Congress as well with the four highest medals the country can give: Congressional Medal of Honor, Congressional Life Saving Medal, Distinguished Service Medal and the Flying Cross. Probably no other man has all of these decorations.

These are but a few of the larger items that Byrd modestly omits from his yarn.

Some of the more specific details that occur to me as regards the great part he has played in promoting aviation are equally important and should be printed between these same covers.

For instance, I attribute to Byrd a very large part in having achieved a Bureau of Aeronautics for our Navy. The formation of this bureau has greatly advanced the development of aviation in the Navy.

Byrd thrilled the world by reaching the North Pole by air and, not content with this success, navigated the North Atlantic by air through two storms when for over twenty hours he saw neither land nor sky nor sea. Yet he arrived over Paris only to find there the centre of another storm area, with the visibility so low he could not see the landing field. To have tried to land would have resulted in the death of others. So he set out for the sea. In spite of storm and darkness he was able to navigate a true course to the lighthouse over a hundred miles away.

It is worthy of especial note that in every case his exploits have been in the name of science. Two of many facts prove this: Last year he could have taken enough extra fuel to keep him in the air over France until morning had he not insisted on eight hundred pounds of scientific equipment and two extra men to make observations and to demonstrate that passengers could be carried. He accepted the hazard of flying in bad weather, realizing the increased opportunity for helpful meteorological research.

Byrd's generosity and unselfishness have never received full credit. I happen to know that he gave up a chance to make $100,000 in connection with the newspaper serial rights to his Atlantic flight because the offer did not properly assure financial reward for the three men who accompanied him.

It was not generally known that Byrd very generously coached the navigators of some of the entries in the trans-Atlantic air race, without any thought of the effect on his own chances of being the first to cross the ocean to France.

It is not generally known that Byrd has steadfastly refused to commercialize his expeditions.

I remember years ago when he and I discussed the hazards of such a flight. He said:

"The worst possible thing that can happen is for the pilot to reach Paris in darkness and fog and storm."

This combination is exactly what happened on the night of June 30, 1927: a situation that would have been fatal to a leader with less skill and courage, and who had prepared less carefully.

Foreword

I am glad we have Byrd. It is his idealism, modesty, unflagging industry and devotion to the scientific advance of flying that combine to make him so immeasurably valuable to aviation today.

WILLIAM A. MOFFETT,

REAR ADMIRAL, U. S. NAVY,

CHIEF OF BUREAU OF AERONAUTICS

SKYWARD

I.

The Flyer's Viewpoint

ONE OF MY FIRST and most striking impressions of aviation came the day a man rushed into my stateroom aboard the battleship waving a newspaper that had just been brought us by the pilot.

"For God's sake, listen to this!" he exclaimed. "Jack Towers has fallen fifteen hundred feet in an airplane and lived to tell the tale."

I couldn't believe it.

"He was thrown out of his seat." (In those days the flyer sat right out in the open on a little bench.) "But he caught by a brace and dangled in mid-air. On the way down he kicked at the control wheel. Apparently he righted the plane just before it hit. *Think of the nerve of the man!*"

I did think of his nerve; and many times since I've admired the courage of those early pilots who flew thousands of feet in the air with defective machines about which they knew almost nothing. And it's good to feel that my friend, Commander John W. Towers, U.S.N., the hero of the incident, is alive today and still a flyer of note.

The horror people felt fifteen years ago in reading about Towers' escape is still felt when newspapers print tragic details of some aeronautical accident without regard for technical reasons behind the accident. As a result the average citizen still looks on flying as one of the most attractive forms of suicide.

If I had a son twenty years old today and he should come to me with the question: "Is it all right for me to fly?" I'd answer: "Go to it. And I hope you get your pilot's license soon because I want you to do a lot of flying before you're through."

He might break his neck. But also he might be run over by a taxi, burn up, catch pneumonia or be struck by lightning. Those things happen to people every day.

I would like any young man who likes the idea of flying to go into aviation today first because I believe that, given reasonable perfection of equipment and training that is available today, it is thoroughly safe to make other than pioneer flights. Secondly, I know of no other profession, trade or industry that in the coming fifty years is likely to exert a more profound or far-reaching influence on civilization.

The point I want to emphasize is that flying can be made safe. That is, ordinary every day flying for pleasure and business. But the public is forever being confused by accidents from careless flying, pioneer flights, or military maneuvers in the air.

When I entered aviation my father told me good-bye. It was his impression that he would never see me alive again. The other members of my family felt about the same; all except my mother. She was the one who let me go around the world alone at the age of twelve. To her, flying didn't seem to have any more danger in it; just a different kind.

My mother was about right about ordinary routine flying. By statistics it is possible to demonstrate that the dangers of the air aren't anything like what they are supposed to be. Else so many young men and women wouldn't be struggling to enter aviation. Nor so many bankers eager to invest their money in it.

I can remember as a boy hearing discussion about which was the safest railroad on which to travel. None of them was considered very safe. Railway casualty lists of the day were often like those of wartime. Now people discuss not which is the safest railroad but which is the most comfortable. Safety is taken for granted.

Probably the outstanding cause of big railway wrecks in this country has been the presence of another train on the track ahead. Probably the outstanding cause of airplane accidents has been forced landings from a stalled engine. Ten years ago we often held our breath until a pilot climbed several hundred feet to an altitude from which he could glide safely to the ground. Nowadays the chances of having a motor stall that has been properly cared for are reaching the vanishing point.

Of course it isn't always a stalled motor that brings a plane down. Not many months ago a pilot was flying above New York. Suddenly he caught the pungent odor of burning gasoline. Flames were shooting out of a crack in the fuel line.

This is one of those situations that still come to every modern form of transportation. Scarcely a week passes that I do not read of fatal accidents to automobiles, railways and elevated trains that rose from just such sudden and almost unmanageable emergencies.

In the case I am reciting the pilot escaped more safely than some of the passengers on the trains or motors. He sideslipped for hundreds of feet in such a way as to blow the flames away from his main fuel supply; and he managed to worm his machine into a vacant lot through a maze of poles. He wrecked it but did not hurt himself or his assistant.

Railways advertise their safety by publishing statistics. Aviation can do the same. British commercial airlines have flown over 5,000,000 miles in seven years with only four fatal accidents. German airlines in 1926 carried 56,268 passengers for a total of 3,838,425 miles with only one fatality. Our own national airways maintained by the Army Air Corps have in one period to their credit 1,200,000 miles with but one serious accident. Twelve planes of our Navy's bombing squadron have flown 216,000 miles without a single accident that amounted to anything.

It is interesting, in this connection, that I have recently come across a *London Times,* dated June 14, 1842, which contained the following statement: "In 1841 the number of passengers carried on the eight railway lines numbered 10,508, the distance 3,562,338 miles yearly. In this time only 56 passengers were injured, of whom 22 were killed."

Two kinds of fatal accidents undo, in the unreflecting public mind, much of the good that fine records achieve. One kind comes from experimental or pioneering work; the other from unorganized flyers who work independently and often lack proper repair and inspection facilities.

My recent flights to the Pole and across the Atlantic were in the nature of experiments. Every research worker takes the same sort of chances as we took whether he be boiling an unknown chemical in his test tube or pushing out across geographical frontiers.

By unorganized flyers I refer to private owners of planes, of which there is a rapidly growing number in this country. Some of these fellows have more enthusiasm than they have caution and are without sufficient funds to properly equip themselves. Such flyers help aviation a lot. They often bring enthusiasm and capital and public sympathy to the science of aeronautics. But often they hinder as much as they help.

I know a young flyer who had got his pilot's license in the Reserve Corps. He was so passionately fond of flying that he could hardly wait to have his own machine and set up a taxi service near his home town. He didn't have enough capital to buy an expensive plane.

About that time he met a man who had bought up a lot of wartime junk from the government. Among the junk was a discarded plane of ancient vintage.

"I'll let you have it for $300," said the junk dealer, "provided you take it out of here this week."

The youngster closed the deal and set about tinkering on the old crock. Just as his time was up he hopped off. He flew safely to his home town, and managed to start business there taking passengers up for rides at five dollars a head.

Then one morning he went aloft in a gusty breeze. As the machine wasn't designed as well as later models it soon became unmanageable and crashed. The passenger was killed and the young pilot badly hurt. Next day the morning papers carried glaring headlines of "ANOTHER FATAL AIRPLANE ACCIDENT!"

Whereupon there ensued the following conversation at thousands of breakfast tables all over the country.

"Heavens, here's another horrible airplane accident! 'Passenger crushed to death; pilot escapes with painful injuries'!"

"Too bad it wasn't the pilot. There ought to be a law against flying!"

It is interesting to record that almost exactly this same sort of opinion was once held about railroads. In 1845 Sir Samuel

Hoare seriously made a report to his country that "The largest item in railway returns bids fair to be the list of killed."

Flying also suffers from the fixed idea in the public mind that it is just a new species of human lunacy. The Wright Brothers are said to have invented or discovered flying in 1903. This is not so. To deny it in no sense reflects on that pair of gifted pioneers, who certainly were the first to fly, even if they didn't actually discover the art.

The idea and some knowledge of mechanical flight is as old as man. Before the dawn of written language man captured birds and saw that enough speed with proper "kite" surface would keep a body aloft. This is not encyclopedic romancing on my part. I was for a time with the Smith Sound Eskimos of North Greenland. This little tribe is still in the Stone Age. Well do I remember Nucarpingwaq freezing a huge dead burgomaster gull with outstretched wings, then tossing it off a cliff to show me how it could fly. "Had I material, White Man," said the native hunter, "I am sure I could build wings big enough for a man to fly with."

As early as 400 B.C. a flying chariot was constructed of a balloon and paddles. Leonardo da Vinci who died in 1519 left behind him not only the Mona Lisa but a series of sketches that showed a knowledge of the principles of aeronautics.

Engineers for three centuries have declared that human flight merely awaited a power plant light enough to carry itself and a pair of wings aloft.

Swift improvement of the steam engine in the nineteenth century awakened new hopes in those who knew how near flight was. Langley actually built and flew a small model plane in 1896, using a 1½ horsepower engine. He might have flown a full-sized machine of the same design shortly afterwards had it not been damaged by accident and his own death hastened by ridicule. His machine with some changes was years later actually flown by a pilot, Glenn Curtis.

In the meantime an obscure device had been developing that carried the final factor for achieving human flight. This was the internal combustion gas engine. Its distinguishing feature lay in the fact that its fuel burned in its cylinder and not in a furnace. The first one was built about 1850. It weighed more than 500 pounds per horsepower. Advent of the automobile in 1900 gave this much-despised form of power a terrific impetus. In a few years engines were being built by Ford and others at weights as low as 25 pounds per horsepower.

At almost exactly this point flight becomes theoretically possible. Immutable physics created by the Almighty before the earth was born fix from 25 to 30 pounds per horsepower as the maximum weight an engine can lift off the ground, provided adequate wings are used.

Now the Wrights had ingeniously developed appropriate wing surfaces in their gliders. So in a sense their fine industry was rewarded by a great piece of luck; it was exercised just at the time the gas engine reached the arbitrary point of which I have just spoken.

With magnificent skill the brothers put together an engine that weighed only 13 pounds per horsepower, thus giving them about 12 pounds per horsepower, to be used on wings and body. This proved enough. And on December 17, 1903, near Kitty Hawk, S. C., the first true flying machine rose with a pilot, Wilbur Wright, and driven by a six-bladed propeller attached to a gas engine, flew 852 feet in 59 seconds.

Meanwhile the first great patron of the gas engine, the automobile, was galloping ahead. In 1900 newspaper editorials literally prayed to the Almighty for deliverance from the curse that was upon us in the shape of the horseless carriage. In 1910 accidents to racing cars alone were enough to make one's blood run cold.

I remember going to a big automobile race in the early days when the cars did not even drive on an enclosed track, but hurtled around a course many miles long laid off on sections of regular highway. As a result there were both paved and dirt portions to cover. Car after car skidded on the worst dirt section of the road where a large and morbid crowd of thrill-seekers was gathered to watch for accidents.

This sort of thing focussed public attention on automobiles. There was no condoning it. I do not intend to, even by implication. I merely want to bring out the fact that we have irresistibly gone through the same phase of aviation; are still going through it, I believe. Subconsciously the minority who fly are eager to impress the wonder and profit of it on the majority who don't. In 1905 those who drove motors worked just as hard to get their friends and family to drive. One couldn't say there was any intrinsic sense in the fever for motoring that sprang up. It just sprang up.

Isn't it possible that this irresistible spirit is nothing more nor less than the *spirit of human progress* that defies nature, peril and death with a blind fury not to be denied?

At any rate, whatever have been the metaphysical truths behind flying, this "madness" as many nonflyers are wont to call it, we are at just about the same point in flying today that we were in automobiling in 1905. We should tithe our tolerance to suit.

War injected another factor into flying. Military exigency stood for speed at the expense of safety. The fastest plane was the best fighter. The idea of high flying speed is still a strong one. Some of our prize races have been as tragic as the early automobile races were.

It would not be fair for me to make a blanket condemnation of speed contests. They have brought out many defects in engine and fuselage and have helped to develop our fast combat planes. But I am profoundly pleased to find that they are gradually giving way in popularity to reliability and endurance contests, which will ultimately do for the plane what they did for the automobile; establish its feasibility for use by the average man or woman.

It is true that in England and the United States there have been apparently an unreasonable number of casualties in army and naval flying; but it must be remembered that this work is largely experimental and pioneering and that the flyers must engage in dangerous tactical maneuvers. On top of all this there is the very important fact that the army and navy flyer cannot, in the nature of his work, put safety first, as the commercial flyer must do.

Take just one sample of mass misfortune from my own service. This came in the 1926 race for the Schneider trophy, one of the most important air meets ever held.

The Schneider trophy is given for seaplanes only. The great interest in the 1926 contest rose chiefly from the fact that Italy was a close contender for the cup which had been won twice in succession by Americans.

The U. S. Navy team suffered its first loss when my friend Lieutenant Frank Conant, U.S.N., was drowned just before the contest in a service pursuit plane. He was flying low over Hampton Roads which in places is filled with fish-nets during the season of the race. It is believed that one of his pontoons struck a net mooring stake.

To condemn flying in Conant's plane on the basis of such an accident would be like condemning a make of car because the driver was unfortunate enough to strike a hidden stump in the road.

A week later the preliminary trials for the main event were held. They were marred by a number of unfortunate accidents of a minor nature leading up to a complete wreck of the navy's most promising entry, a fine Packard-engined racer piloted by Lieutenant Tomlinson. In landing on choppy water he had the luck to capsize his ship and was nearly drowned. It is possible his pontoons were too small.

The important point I want to make is that this contest was one for speed. Therefore, every item of weight and air resistance was cut to the bone. But much of the public saw only a group of deplorable accidents resulting from a number of seaplane flights and at once was ready to condemn flying even more heartily than before.

Flights made for the promotion of aviation are for the sole purpose of ascertaining where and how the happy air traveler of the future will go. When I say flying is safe I speak of the performance of ships that have been tested in design, cruising, radius, maneuver ability and lifting power until these factors have been established, and the ships used in good weather over known routes where there are plenty of landing fields; in other words, with normal commercial flying conditions. To judge safety of aviation by experiments in which both pilots and designers are frankly and openly taking risks for the sake of aeronautic progress is like saying that a new breakfast food is poison because in the chemical experiments leading up to its invention one of the research workers had a violent attack of indigestion.

Bernt Balchen, the fine young Norwegian who went to Spitzbergen with me and was on the *America* with us when she flew to France, is a test pilot for a big airplane manufacturing company. When I asked him how he felt about his work he said:

"I like it because I take up planes that have never been flown before. Half the excitement is not knowing what is going to happen."

Pioneering work in every field of science has been done under conditions that men would not repeat commercially. When Peary set off for the pole his steamer was loaded to the point where she wallowed deeply in the ground-swell. When the first steamer set out to cross the Atlantic Ocean she was reported as "exceedingly awkward to handle because of the weight of machinery she carried." Our planes were dangerously heavy and unwieldy when they attempted to take-off for the trans-Atlantic flight. I have seen a lot of this sort of thing in recent years. René Fonck bravely ventured a take-off with his three-engined Sikorsky plane with a bigger load of gas than such a ship had ever attempted to carry before. Very little indeed was known about the performance of three-engined planes. It was understood in advance by all concerned that a large risk was taken. Two men burned to death in this attempt.

When my old friend and shipmate Noel Davis crashed last spring in his three-engined plane, killing himself and Wooster, the tragedy was explained to me by another pilot:

"They were so near the limit of the load they could carry that when they banked and reduced their lifting surface they could no longer stay aloft."

Again here was pioneering with a three-engined plane.

But it was a necessary development and we must learn about it even at the sacrifice of lives. We knew all about one-engined planes.

Then our plane, the *America*, crashed with three of us injured—Floyd Bennett critically. Our crash marked, I believe, the turning point. We were learning more about the three-engined plane. We repaired the *America* and carried on some very careful scientific experiments.

When we hopped off on our trans-Atlantic flight we did not know just how far our plane would go with the fuel aboard. We simply made as many preliminary tests as possible and gradually increased the load until our figures indicated that we should make our destination. We had learned what we could about the maximum load such a three-engined plane would lift. It was pioneering and we knew it was risky.

If we had crashed on our take-off or suddenly run out of fuel before we got to France the only just conclusion would have been that our experiment was a failure. But when we got into the air and crossed the ocean we proved for the first time that a big plane with three motors designed like ours could do the trick.

A large percentage of accidents comes from testing and pioneering in a thoroughly proper way; such accidents are part of the progress of any form of science. It is the great misfortune of aviation that the public receives more news about this sort of work than from any other flying done.

Few people have any idea how many airplane accidents in

the past have had nothing at all to do with the pilot or his machine. They were the sole result of the motion of the invisible air about him.

Non-flyers often fail to realize the impossibility of landing on rough areas. It can be readily understood if one should visualize an automobile with wings on it going nearly a mile a minute and landing in a field full of rocks or ditches.

The Wrights had not been flying long before they recognized what are still termed "pockets" and "bumps" in the atmosphere. Accurately speaking there is no such thing as a pocket or a bump in the air. These sensations which the pilot feels are the result of meeting currents of air flowing up and down. When the plane enters an up-current it is yanked upward, and the flyer feels as if he had ridden over a bump. When entering a down-current he naturally goes down with it as long as it lasts, with the feeling that he is falling in a vacuum.

One of the best pilots in the world who was flying across South America not long ago nearly came to grief while leaving a small town located in a valley. He did not know that the air entering the valley with the afternoon winds fell from the heights of land in a regular Niagara Falls. The worst of it was, as always, that this vast Niagara of air was absolutely invisible. *It had to be discovered by the aeronautical pioneer.* When the pilot took off he fought his way upward for a long while only to be carried downward with equal speed. He finally escaped, missing a fatal accident almost by inches.

A most terrible experience in my life was the two thousand miles we spent storm tossed in the *America* on our cross-ocean flight without seeing ground or water beneath us, followed by hours of a similar experience in a storm at night over France. I think my companions cheerfully subscribe to this statement. For over twenty-four hours of that flight we saw nothing whatever beneath us. I sincerely hope no other flyers ever have that experience.

Hour after hour the notations in my log of that journey declare that it was utterly impossible to navigate. We could not tell which way the winds were blowing, which way we were drifting, or what sort of land or water was below us.

Our chief safety lay in watching our instruments closely so that we should not be carried so close to the surface of the land or sea that we might crash without warning. Had we done so we should have been killed instantly. Our lives hung on our altimeter. As night closed in we could not even see the ends of our wings. At this critical time there was a leak in our gasoline tank.

I mention these points not to emphasize the hazards of such a flight but because I wish to lay stress on the peculiar nature of the perils and show how far they were removed from normal conditions of flying.

We were traveling in a territory as new as the dreaded polar regions were to Hendrik Hudson and his tiny vessels four centuries ago. Once when we fought our way above the fog around 10,000 feet we came out upon a weird view. Towering peaks of vapor surrounded us. Below was a gray murk that clutched at our plane. There was no horizon.

For ten years prior to my trans-Atlantic flight I had been studying weather conditions over the North Atlantic. In the course of these studies I learned many things that helped us on the way. However, it wasn't long after I hopped off for France that I discovered our information was still defective.

It is necessary that an ocean flyer know meteorological conditions for each zone through which he will pass before his passage. He must know the barometric pressure and the temperature for various altitudes. Fog and cloud conditions are equally important.

Study of air disturbances is a life work in itself. Gradually we are becoming familiar with the general movements of those of the North Atlantic. Already we know that the movement of storm centers is north and east, that storm areas are circular and that their movement is cyclonic; that is to say, anti-clockwise.

Often these storm areas overlap and sometimes they are elliptical. Sometimes they seem to contract or expand as they move. This is possibly because they come into contact with other similar disturbances.

On our first night after leaving Newfoundland we were flying in a fog until we climbed to an altitude of over a mile. The temperature fell as we mounted and ice began to form on our wings. It was quite possible for us to take on enough ice to pull us down into the sea. Thus comes the need for advance information on fog area and depth not only from ships on the ocean but also from aeroplanes flying at points along the flyer's route. Only in this way will it be possible to know whether one should try to climb beyond the clouds or to out-flank the storm area.

It must be understood that as matters stand now there is only a relatively slight system for instructing the ocean flyer. The United States Weather Bureau does enormously good work and went out of its way many times this summer to see that our pilots had the best possible weather information. But these data were based on more or less desultory reports from ships plying between Europe and America. These ships were often some distance from our air route and were, of course, on the surface of the sea.

The great volcanoes Kilauea in Hawaii and Vesuvius in Italy are sights that few tourists care to miss. It is quite safe to proceed along a certain trail to the vicinity of the craters. But while first investigators took risks in ascertaining where and how to go, the safety of the present visitor can in no way be measured by the perils of early prowlers.

Few pilots have not had their turn at a landing crash. Every pilot recalls vividly the dizzy time he brought down his plane after his first solo flight when training. At this critical moment in flight comes another great fraction of air accidents.

But this isn't a very damaging fact in the consideration of air safety. In the navy we always have to forget a crash or two that we made in the early days of learning to bring a boat alongside a battleship or a dock. And there will come a time when a young pilot will fly successfully the first time.

When we first took the *America* up for test last spring we knew that she was an untried machine. We knew that there would be problems of balance and weight and landing speed that would have to be solved before she could be taken on a long flight.

After a few minutes in the air we started down. Floyd Bennett, Noville and I were up in the cockpit with Anthony Fokker, the designer, who was doing the piloting. Floyd and the rest of us were passengers.

When Fokker stopped the engine to come down for a landing we found that a combination of five or six things had made the *America* very nose heavy. We went up again but when Fokker finally tried to land we crashed. My arm was broken, Noville internally injured, and Bennett was smashed up so badly that he was in the hospital for months and out of the Atlantic flight.

The next day the following statement was made:

"It is patent from the accident to Byrd's plane that we as yet have far from reached any dependable safety in aviation."

This statement was altogether unfair to aeronautics. I mention the incident because it so effectively illuminates what friends of aviation are up against every day in the year. The accident was to a truly experimental type of plane and under conditions that opened us all to risks that no passenger would ever be asked to face. Even the average pilot would not fly under such circumstances. Yet the safety of flying was impugned on the basis of our private test that bore but indirectly on practical aviation of the moment.

The test pilot in a sense faces death every time he puts a new plane through its paces. The pioneer in aeronautics takes chances at every new venture he essays. It is part of the game.

But the passenger or pilot flying in a tested plane under normal and proper conditions can certainly nowadays do so with the comforting assurance that at last *it is reasonably safe to fly.*

The degree of this safety is increasing daily with increase of safe landing fields throughout the country. In areas where there are not sufficient landing fields, there is a gradual swing to the multi-engined plane for passenger service that will fly with at least one engine dead. Nor has commercial aviation yet done all it can to bring greater safety. Weather predictions are being made gradually more reliable, landing fields, beacons, and other lights are ever increasing in number; landing speeds are getting lower; brakes are being installed on the wheels. Three-engined planes are being built that will fly with but one engine. This gives practically no danger of a forced landing from engine trouble.

Finally aviation's great enemy "fog" is gradually being conquered by radio, beacons, and direction finders, and amber colored lights that will to some extent penetrate it. Until fog is thoroughly conquered the flyer must have sufficient good weather predictions to evade it.

The Flyer's Viewpoint

With safe flying, strong public air-consciousness, a multitude of planes and pilots, aviation is gradually coming into its own. It is with this viewpoint the true flying enthusiast enters his work. He is not blind to the danger any more than is the careful automobile driver. But he is spurred on by a vision of the priceless agent for great achievement that is now at our command.

So it is that I believe in flying and commend it to the country's youth as a pursuit worthy of a man's devotion. And I hope that those who take up the game will experience the same pleasure I have had with the great good fellowship I have found among my shipmates of the air.

II.

Learning
to Fly

MY FIRST AERIAL ADVENTURE was in the Annapolis gymnasium. I was captain of the Navy Gym Team which was out to win the intercollegiate championship of the year. In line with this ambition I devised a hair-raising stunt on the flying rings. My plan was to get a terrific swing, high enough to be able to count on an appreciable pause at the end of it.

I figured I could at this moment do what was called "dislocate," which meant swing completely head over heels without changing grip, with arms at full length—unbending, forcing my shoulders through a quick jerk, that made it look as if they were put out of joint. In addition, I was going to make another complete turn, legs outside, letting go with my hands as my ankles passed my forearms, and catching again as I fell.

About a week before the big meet came off I mustered up my courage and gave this risky stunt a try. To my relief, as much as to my pleasure, I did it without breaking my neck.

The day before the meet the gym was crowded with people watching practice. As the contest would be close all hands were much excited. I felt secretly elated because I was sure my stunt would give us the points needed to win. Never before had I reached the altitude I reached that afternoon when my last turn came on the rings. I was conscious of the dead silence as I swooped through the air for my final effort.

With a quick whirl I "disclocated." It felt all right. The next second I was spinning into the second turn. I let go; caught—but only with one hand. For an instant I strained wildly to catch the other ring. But it had gone. People afterwards told me a queer sharp sigh went up from the crowd at this moment.

I fell. It was a long way down even for a flyer. Luckily it wasn't a nose dive. I came down more or less feet foremost. The crash when I struck echoed from the steel girders far above me, and there was a loud noise of something snapping. I tried to rise, but fell back stunned. The effort told me, though, that I was far from dead. I noted there was no feeling in my right leg. I glanced down as willing hands came to lift me and saw that my ankle and foot was badly crumpled; the same foot I had broken playing football against Princeton.

My team not only won the meet next day without me, but

captured the intercollegiate championship to boot. Never again, I felt, would I attach any undue importance to myself.

That was December 1911. I missed the semi-annual examination. I was due to graduate in June. For five months I wrestled with nature on one hand and with the spectre of academic failure on the other. The Navy made no allowances for me and wanted me to go back a class. After a great struggle I managed to graduate. I don't believe I could have pulled through but for my great desire to go out in the fleet with my classmates. They were a very splendid lot and it made me rip-snorting mad whenever anyone suggested my going back to the next class below us. But I was still—confidentially, of course,—something of a lame duck. The bones in my foot and leg had all knit but one. The boney knot on the outer side of my right ankle was still in two pieces. It clicked when I walked. Someone told me if I walked a lot I would grate the fragments together and induce flow of osseous fluid. I did this for weeks. It hurt; but it apparently worked.

This terrific struggle I had made to graduate taught me a great lesson—that it is by struggle that we progress. I learned concentration during that time I never thought I possessed.

Five futile years followed. Futile in the sense that they contributed so little to my life's work, aviation. My game leg was a nuisance. Sometimes it worked, sometimes it didn't. Long hours of watch-standing aboard a man-of-war proved too much for it. Certain kinds of deck duty left me aching all over from the pain that began in the old mangled ankle. One day, after I had fallen down a gangway the surgeons decided to nail that last knob of bone together. For some time I thought they used a silver nail and felt set-up by so precious a finish to my anatomy. But when I found it was just a plain old-fashioned galvanized nail they had used I lost even that thrill.

The Navy regulations would not allow my promotion on account of my injury. I was retired on three-quarters pay; ordered home for good. Career ended. Not enough income to live on; no chance of coming back; trained for a seafaring profession; temperamentally disinclined for business. A fizzle.

Then war. War did a lot of things for a lot of men. In a sense it saved me. For a willing cripple suddenly became to a mad world as valuable as a whole man who might be unwilling. Washington used me to mobilize the Rhode Island State Militia. Thence I was promoted to a "swivel chair" job in the Navy Department. I transferred enlisted men from station to station, and official papers from basket to basket. Secretary Daniels added me to the Commission on Training Camps as its Secretary. There I came in close touch with Raymond B. Fosdick, Chairman of the Commission, one of the most brilliant men with whom I have ever come in contact and as agreeable as he was brilliant. This gave me a bigger desk and deeper baskets. But I didn't want furniture; I wanted to fight.

For several years I had known my one chance of escape from a life of inaction was to learn to fly. For years I had wanted to fly but my leg and obligations had prevented. Now that even willing cripples were looked upon to do their bit perhaps I would be permitted to fly. But the doctors said, "No, not with that leg." To which I was impelled to burst out angrily, "But you don't fly with your legs!" Only I didn't; I'd been schooled never to do any bursting out.

After a while desire got the better of my schooling. I lost twenty-five pounds worrying over the uselessness of what I had become—just a high-class clerk—when I had been trained to go out and fight—fight wind and seas and the country's enemy. And here I was, a big desk, deep baskets, reams of official papers, and I still in my youth. Hundreds of army and naval officers were chafing at swivel chair jobs. By conspiracy I went up again before the medical board. "You'll have to take leave, Byrd," they said. "You're in terrible condition."

Truly I was on the verge of a breakdown. In addition to my worry I had worked day and night to help organize the Commission so that I could fight and fly—do my duty. Yet that short half hour in the Board Room was the turning point of my life.

"Give me a chance," I begged them. "I want to fly. Give me a month of it and if I don't improve to suit you I'll do anything you say."

They were sports, those surgeons. So does war do away with much of the vexing formality of peace. They decided to give me one short month of my heart's desire. Ultimately they gave me two. Fresh air, zest of flight, the deep joy of achievement, compounded a tonic that fattened and strengthened me at once. When the time came I passed all tests with flying colors, was pronounced in perfect health and have been so ever since. Surely a feather in the cap of aviation, this quick cure of a run-down man. Moreover, I haven't been off active duty since.

I was ordered to Pensacola for instruction. This was the fall of 1917. Congress had declared War. The country was seething with excitement. Our first destroyers had gone over to join the British Grand Fleet. Every edition of the newspapers was full of gory horrors. The Western Front was one grand riot of organized murder. I reached Pensacola ready to loop-the-loop that day if national emergency required.

Glistening Florida sunshine brought all the details of the station out in sharp relief. Men in whites and in khaki were hurrying to and fro. Big open hangars gaped like reptiles that had disgorged the birds they had swallowed and found indigestible. The birds themselves—Navy seaplanes—were drawn up along the sea ramp; some were in the water; some roared overhead. Men were hauling them up and down, starting engines, taking off and landing. A hive of activity, typical of the thousand military hives buzzing about the country.

Brilliant sunshine; such blue water. And how full of eagerness all the men seemed. The picture stamped itself on my mind.

Something attracted my attention; a shout, or an uplifted hand. I glanced to a training plane in the azure sky above me. It wobbled as I looked. It hesitated, dipped, then dove straight down. It came leisurely enough at first. I didn't realize its seeming lack of speed was due to its great height. Soon it was dropping like a plummet. Tail skyward, it plunged into the Bay. Across the still water came a terrific crash. I stood rooted to the spot, horror-struck.

A speed-boat dashed out toward the wrecked plane. On its deck, ready for their gruesome task, I saw stretcher bearers, surgeons and divers.

The tail of the wrecked plane and a part of one wing protruded from the surface of the water. Pilot and student were caught in the wreckage below, both unquestionably dead. The speed-boat drew alongside. Divers splashed overboard with pliers and wrenches. In twenty seconds one emerged dragging a limp form after him. I think I must have held my breath while the rescue party struggled for the other flyer. Finally the boat shoved off. Some one near me said in a low voice, "The wrecking barge'll have to get it."

"It." So that's what you were after a crash! Just a body. *It!* I felt downhearted.

After a while I walked away. Perhaps I'd get used to it. Suddenly I was grabbed from behind. The thought flashed through my mind that perhaps I'd been asleep and had had a nightmare. Now some one was waking me up.

"Hello, Dick Byrd!"

It was my old friend and classmate, Nathan Chase. He paused in the middle of his greeting. I suppose my face revealed more than I wanted it to. "Don't mind that," he said and nodded toward where the wrecking barge was moving up to the wreck that contained *it*.

"Have 'em often?" I asked him.

"Oh, every day," he said. "Sometimes two or three times a day." Then in the next breath: "Want to go up, old man?"

I'm frank to say that was not the moment I would have selected to go up. I hadn't suddenly lost my nerve. Nor had I changed my mind about becoming an aviator. All the prime yearning for action was still in me. I was just temporarily nonplussed. I've since learned what the feeling means. And I've found that the best antidote for it is prompt and vigorous action.

Chance had given the action I needed. Still in a bit of a fog I presently found myself wearing helmet and goggles. A plane stood nearby with its engine turning over. Evidently it had been got ready for Chase. Before we climbed in Nat handed me some cotton.

"Stuff it in your ears," he shouted. "You'll be deaf if you don't."

Mechanically I did as I was told. We were in line with the barge grappling for the wrecked plane just ahead of us.

The plane was exactly like a land one, except that its wheels had been replaced by a pontoon which now rested on a truck. When we had taken our seats mechanics pushed the truck down a concrete ramp into the water. As our pontoon floated Chase gave her the gas. We skidded thunderously away and swerved into the wind for a take-off. I felt the whole body rear back and spray flew high all around us. Gradually we assumed an even keel, the spray lessened, waves began to slap bumpily against the bottom of the float. We were in the air.

My pilot pointed to an instrument in front that read in hundreds of feet. I gathered this told our altitude. When the pointer read 4000 feet he turned and smiled at me. Fortunately I could not interpret this sign and the motors prevented talk. As a result I had a few seconds more of reasonable complaisance before the worst began.

I suppose Chase knew how I was feeling about the fatal crash I had just witnessed. The medicine he chose was to go through all the stunts he knew. And stunting in those days, years ago, wasn't what it is today. We had a cumbersome seaplane under us, too.

We dived and rolled and slipped. We did a tail-spin until I could almost see the rescue boat on its way out to us. There weren't even names then for some of the things Chase did. For minutes I couldn't tell which was sea and which was sky.

Suddenly we came out of a spin. He nudged me with a nod towards the stick. The next instant I realized I had control of the plane. That was Nathan's idea of a joke on me. The responsibility cleared my brain. It was perfectly idiotic for me to try to fly. I knew that. But this was no time to argue. I managed to keep our course straight ahead; nothing but common sense. But soon we were headed downward, judging from the roaring of the engine and the wind singing through the wires. I glanced at the altimeter; it showed a loss of a thousand feet already. Luckily Chase took her back before it was too late and brought us safely to earth.

I do not recommend such a method as a means to teach the novice. True, the passenger is more likely to grow dizzy than the pilot, for responsibility and the effort to control the plane have a steadying effect. Further, the pilot knows at all times in just which way the plane is going to dip or swing and so automatically prepares himself for the centrifugal forces set up. But too sudden a plunge into piloting may dampen the candidate's ardor.

My training now began in earnest, groundwork as well as flying. I remember taking apart my first airplane engine. The vast number of cams, valves, rods, screws, bolts and other pieces fascinated me. They all seemed so *dead,* so unrelated when spread around on the greasy canvas at my feet. They were dead. To the novice they were as meaningless as so many cobble-stones.

I remember that same afternoon we reassembled the engine. The mechanic with me became a little feverish as we neared completion of the job. At first I thought he had the knock-off whistle on his mind. He puffed and panted over a Stilson wrench; he cut his finger and let it bleed unnoticed.... The whistle blew. He seemed not even to hear it.

We finished. A small crane panted up and swung the engine into place. Suddenly I had a streak of apprehension across the back of my neck, as if I had been touched with a cold finger. Did we have all the parts in place? Would the engine run? Would it hold up the plane? Would it *live?*

The moment came. Tired, greasy, silent, the mechanic and I stood and watched our engine roar into life, the plane it pulled slide across the field, crop the daisies and soar into the blue.

In that moment a new understanding of aviation came into my life; in watching that plane rise, fly, devour space, I felt that I had helped create something alive; I had contrived a creature that by widening the vista of human life and quickening the processes also thereby lengthened life; that by conquering the forces of wind and gravity had added to man's triumph over Nature.

I made my first solo flight after about six hours' flying with an instructor. I had got the "feel" of the plane and was now confident that I could do as well alone as with the licensed pilot along. The rub was whether I would know how to handle my machine if trouble came.

First flight alone is probably the greatest event in an aviator's life. Never again does he feel the same thrill, the same triumph, as when he first eases back the controls and lifts his airplane clear of all natural support. Then there is that special and extra little sensation when one banks and lands alone for the first time. It is at this point that the new hand so often loses his nerve or lets his judgment slip and crashes. Nowadays such accidents happen less frequently. Much more instruction is given before soloing. But in the war I have known new pilots to hop off alone with less than three hours in the air.

"Twenty minutes flying is enough," warned my instructor, Ensign Gardiner. This was the usual warning given on account of the strain of the first solo hop. As my plane was shoved into the water I glanced back. The poor fellow could not hide his anxiety. I knew he felt that if I lost my life it would be as much his fault as mine.

As the machine bobbed up I shot my throttle wide and pulled the controls back to ride high on the waves. When I had some speed I shoved the controls forward again to make the float coast. A minute or so later I figured I could lift. With a fine feeling of elation I took off.

For what seemed a long time I flew straight ahead. It was too good to be true. I was flying at last. I glanced down at the water. It looked dark and sparkling in the fresh seabreeze just picking up. The station seemed very *hard* and *dead* by comparison. Quickly I glanced back at my instruments. Nothing was wrong yet.

I began to think what I'd do next. I concluded that I should try some landings. After all, if I could land safely I might then call myself a flyer. Any one could get a plane up into the air. I nosed down gradually. But when I leveled off I was going too fast. As it had been drummed into my head not to lose flying speed, I was taking no chances. I struck the surface with a big splash and porpoised—that is, leaped out—

some distance beyond where I hit. But I didn't smash anything, which was a comfort. I tried three more landings in quick succession. In all I kept at it for an hour and twenty minutes on that first flight. Gardiner got pretty worried about me. But when I finally taxied up to the landing I felt a confidence that was the pleasantest sensation I had ever known. The big thing about flying is to come down safely.

As I came alongside the mechanic in charge of my plane called out to me: "How'd she go?"

"Couldn't have been sweeter," I told him.

Instantly his rugged face melted into the sticky satisfaction of a man who has inherited a million dollars. And right away he began to nuzzle his engine like a mother cat who's just taken her own blood back. The Commandant happened along at that moment. "Attention!" barked some one, "according to Hoyle." It was a secret joy to me to see the ill-concealed scowl of impatience on the mechanic's face. I knew at last how he felt. I had flown; had come down safe; I had him to thank for an engine that kept on running. What was military frumpery beside that?

In the ensuing period of my training I specialized in landings. I made hundreds a week. I made them from every altitude and in almost every position the plane could assume, with and without power. I tried stopping the engine suddenly a few feet above the water; again in the middle of a bank; and sometimes in midair well up. I knew an engine failure was far more dangerous at fifty feet than at 5000. I wanted to be prepared. I found out at what angle I could climb and get down without a tail spin in case my engine stalled. I landed on smooth water and on rough waves. I found both difficult. Over glassy water it is hard to find the surface. All this practice saved me from at least three fatal crashes in the early weeks of my flying, and a number of times since then.

As I progressed the fundamentals were continually being dinned into my head. I grasped that I must not try to stunt under 3000 or 4000 feet; that I must keep high enough, if possible, always to be within gliding distance of a landing plane; to be certain to keep the flying speed of the plane at all times; to keep a sharp lookout for other planes; always to land into the wind.

I learned that the majority of casualties, outside a stalled engine, came from the pilot allowing his plane to lose its flying speed. I learned first-hand that when this happened the plane stalled and dropped promptly into a nose dive, or dropped backward into a tail-spin. (This dangerous speed I found to be different for different loads on the same plane.) If on a bank my plane side-slipped and then went into a tail spin.

With the other young pilots I learned that such stalls are generally caused by climbing too rapidly, by making a bad turn, or gliding down at too flat an angle. I soon found that if the turn were not properly made the plane would skid from centrifugal force just as an automobile skids on a slippery street.

After I had made the grade with single pontoon planes I took some lessons in the twin pontoon type and in the big flying boats. In the latter there is no pontoon of any sort. The fusilage is a big boat in itself. Crashes in these machines were the worst because their engines were above and behind the pilot, smashing down on him if the plane made a bad landing.

When my time came for land machines they proved easier in several ways. The chief difference lay in the fact that one can judge distance and landing speed so much better over land than over water.

When the Navy Department through the Commandant, handed me my pilot's wings and a clean bill of health I was sitting on top of the world. Furthermore, the galvanized nail in my leg seemed to be holding tight.

III.

On the Thin Edge
of Eternity

IT FELL TO MY LOT while at Pensacola to try to find out why so many of our pilots were being killed. The conclusion must not be drawn from these accidents I describe that aviation cannot be made safe. It is because of them that we have learned enough to make aviation safe. As I was one of the few regular officers on the Pensacola Air Station in 1917 I was detailed to the "Crash Board." This was really a sort of "Coroner's Jury." Officially, we had to "sit" on the ghastly evidence that came out of each tragedy. Also I had to go out with the rescue boat and help haul the mangled bodies of my friends out of the water. It wasn't exactly what you might call stimulating work; certainly not for the beginner.

I remember my first case came while I was still a student. A plane nose-dived into the Bay a few hundred yards from the landing. Though rescue boat and divers reached the wreckage in a few moments, both victims were dead before we arrived. We examined the wreckage carefully as soon as it could be hoisted to the wrecking barge. We found control wires were in good shape, and enough of the body and wings intact to indicate that the equipment was still all right when the plane took her fatal dive.

Next day the Senior Member of the Crash Board looked around the table after all evidence was in and we had cudgeled our brains to figure out what had happened.

"The only things that really help," he said, "are that a student was aboard and that the plane was up only about six hundred feet when she went into a spin."

The rest of us sat there like dummies. As we were all flyers, we would have given our bottom dollar to know what had killed our friends. The same fate might be ours before the day was out. Moreover, solution of the mystery could possibly save a score of lives that week, taking the whole country into consideration.

"Probably the student was at the controls," went on the Senior Member, but without conviction, "and made a bad turn. The plane side slipped and then went into a spin. Before the instructor could get her out she was down."

Pretty vague; altogether unsatisfying. But the best we could do in those days.

It had been some years before pilots had learned how to get out of tail-spins; that is, spinning towards the earth with tail up. It nearly always ended in tragedy. One day a naval pilot at Pensacola got into a spin and accidentally kicked the high side of the rudder and got out of the spin. That is how the tail-spin was conquered.

When we had signed the formal report of that first crash, I took a walk out into the country. I wanted to be alone. Planes were still humming overhead and I was due to go up at three o'clock. But first I wanted to come to some sort of understanding with myself. What was the sense of all this killing of good men?

After two hours of hard walking and harder thought I decided that it was all just a case of pioneering; more violent than what had gone on with railways, automobiles and radio; but the same in principle. Flying would be worth all the other three put together, once we got it going. Besides it would help to win the war. These views I concluded justified the sacrifice.

Three days later I was standing on the beach waiting for my engine to be warmed up. Suddenly the siren sounded. Another crash.

I ran to the rescue boat, boarding her just as she shoved off. Along the ramp and landing were gathering silent men. Out of the quarters into the unfailing sunshine hurried wives and mothers, children, even servants. "Who now?" was the question every man and woman wanted to ask, but were afraid to.

When we rounded up to the plane's wreck only one wing

was visible above the water. We dove in; our diver followed. As I came to the surface I saw the surgeon preparing his kit, frantic to help, but useless until the diver brought up something.

He finally came up—empty-handed. A gunner's mate said: "Only one man down there. He's gone. Not a chance to get him out here. Got to lift the whole mess."

We looked for the other body. It was never found. When the wrecked plane came up at the end of the crane tackle we saw snarled up in it the student. Both hands had a death-grip on the driving wheel. We needed no more to tell us what had happened. The student had lost his nerve in the air and grabbed the thing nearest him as a drowning man grabs his rescuer, throwing the plane into a spin.

When these disasters happened little was said about them in quarters. No one felt inclined to discuss details of a tragedy that could strike anywhere among us. Sometimes it seemed to me our mess was a little gayer after a crash: probably a subconscious effort to throw off the depression such things brought.

It is hard to realize now how absurd were some of the accidents that happened to flyers in those days, nor how easily a pilot could get into trouble with some of the crude devices then still in use.

One day two good flyers were stunting at an altitude of about 2000 feet. I made it a practice to watch as much trick flying as I could in order to pick up the style of the various pilots. This day I was leaning against a hangar enjoying the antics of my two friends far up in the blue sky above me.

It was considered a feat at the time to get into a tail-spin and then get out; good, insurance too, for one could never tell when this form of descent might be forced upon him unexpectedly. The plane I was watching presently went into a tail-spin. I had half expected it to. She was high enough to be safe; also it was evident that she had been put into the spin deliberately by the pilot in control.

Down the plane came, down, down—revolving in graceful spirals as she fell. When she reached about 1000 feet she was still spinning abruptly. A man behind me exclaimed: *"Good God, another!"* Some one cried a warning to the observation tower. When the plane was at 200 feet and still falling we knew that she was a goner. One ray of hope came to me as I ran to the rescue boat. The plane was not in a tight spin; that is, her spiral was a fairly large one. Even at this the crash when she hit was pretty awful.

As the speed boat raced toward the wreck I puzzled over what might have happened. I knew that as a rule planes didn't fall so leisurely in a tail-spin. Also there was no reason to believe that a good pilot, such as was aboard, would deliberately let his plane get so far down before trying to take her out of the spin. At that moment I had the pleasure of seeing the two dripping occupants of the plane clamber upon their one undamaged wing. Both were bleeding as we came alongside; one had a broken nose, the other a broken thumb; both were badly bruised and shaken up.

"Got my foot caught," grinned one.

"How's that for luck?" asked the other, but did not smile.

It seemed the bigger of the two, a man who weighed nearly two hundred pounds, had got his foot caught under the rudder bar, while the other man was putting the machine through her paces. The rudder had whipped over hard from a left tailspin and had caught and held the poor devil's foot all the way down. This had prevented righting the plane. When the latter struck, the blow released his foot. A narrow squeak, if there ever was one. The Crash Board decided that the only reason the two men lived was because their plane's spiral had been a loose one, and the plane itself had struck on a flat part of her spin.

How little the public at large still knew about aviation in those days was shown when one of our pilots was once flying in a high headwind several thousand feet up. At times strong gusts almost exactly balanced the forward movement of his machine. As a result every now and then he seemed to stand still. An elderly lady happened to glance out of a window and saw the stationary plane. After a few moments of astonishment she hurried to the telephone and made the following report to the fire department:

"I don't know what you can do about it, but there's a plane stuck in the air over my house and can't get down!"

As time passed some of the air tragedies came pretty close

to my heart. Personal friends were killed and families that I had known for years were bereaved without warning. Of course it was all part of war and a part of the progress of the new art which they were helping develop. Only now that those hard days have gone and flying is an established science do I realize under what strain pilots used to work.

Among my best friends I numbered the Morgan Drapers. This ensign and his lovely young wife had come to the station filled with enthusiasm for flying and brimming with excitement over the prospect of getting to Europe for active service in the air. Night after night I dined with the happy pair, while we did nothing but gossip about planes and engines and stunts.

Morgan Draper was a splendid flyer with plenty of nerve. Stunt flying had a peculiar fascination for him. I believe he would have made a great combat pilot had he lived to reach the Western Front. One of the things he wanted especially to do was to shift seats in the air. There was no particular point in achieving this feat at the time. It was just one more of those special tricks which seemed to add a little to a man's perfect confidence in his plane. Of late years planes have actually been developed that are so stable in flight that in calm weather the pilot may leave his controls for a moment and walk about in the cabin. I suppose Draper had in mind that such a thing was not far off for the planes of his day.

One afternoon he took up a new plane which I had just tested. It was in perfect working order and one of the best machines on the station. Its engine was hot, and the controls had stood full test. I doubt if any one could have gone up under safer circumstances than in a warmed-up tested plane in perfect weather.

As the friend he had with him climbed into the front seat Draper winked at me. I gathered this meant he was going to do some of the trick flying at which he had become so skilled. I didn't worry. I had no cause to. But the very fact I knew he was in the air risking his life in a dozen wild ways made it impossible for me to get him out of my mind.

Five hours passed and no word from the plane. In those days people didn't fly five hours without advertising the flight in advance, and making more preparations than we make today for a trans-Atlantic flight. We knew the plane must be down.

A messenger came up and saluted: "Telephone call from Pensacola, sir. Clerk in a clothing store says he saw a plane hit the water in a straight nose dive and that the spray went a hundred feet into the air!"

"When did he see this?"

"About two hours ago, sir."

Two hours! And men drown in two minutes. It was Morgan Draper, I knew. We never learned why the clerk did not make the report sooner. However, it probably wouldn't have changed the story if he had, because if the spray had gone that high he must have hit in a straight nose dive with the engine full on, with the maximum speed of three miles a minute.

We boarded our boat and speeded away to the neighborhood where the plane was alleged to have been last seen. Frantically boats were sent about the harbor of Pensacola in search of the wreck. We got the wrecking barges underway and used their searchlights when night fell. There was always a chance an injured man might be clinging to a wing or broken fusilage.

Meanwhile another complication bobbed up. Lieutenant Hoyt had been flying near the area in which Morgan Draper had crashed. On sighting some wreckage—a wing tip—Hoyt had descended and began diving in hopes of pulling out the missing fliers. Reports now reached us that Hoyt's plane had been sighted empty, drifting. Some one suggested that he and his men had fallen out.

"Or stalled on the water, tried to swim ashore and drowned," was another theory.

The latter was nearer the truth. For when Hoyt and his companion had set about diving, first thing they knew a puff of wind carried their own plane out of reach faster than they could pursue it. They were picked up by a passing boat, nearly drowned.

Meanwhile in the glare of searchlights we hoisted out the pitiful mess of what had been Morgan Draper's machine. Had the plane struck a concrete surface I doubt if it could have been worse shattered. It must have struck, as we had thought, with engine full on, and diving straight without a spiral. Few people realize that water is hard as ice when it is hit going fast. Poor old Morgan had, I felt almost certain, tried the stunt he had long been talking about—changing seats with his co-pilot while flying.

In the center of the wreckage we found the torn body of Draper's friend. Of Morgan himself there was no sign.

With the rest of my rescue party we now set out after Hoyt's plane. The beach was by this time lined with flotsam from Draper's wreck. About 3 A.M. we found the former plane uninjured on the beach. I did not get back to the station until 8 A.M. by which time we were all pretty well done up. Brave young Mrs. Draper would not believe Morgan had been killed. Not until his body was washed up by the tide a fortnight later would she give up hope. Such is the courage of the wives and mothers behind American men.

Exhausted as I was, my day of excitements was not over yet. I managed to keep up through the morning's routine. But after lunch I lay down for a few winks. Scarcely had I dozed off than a friend and shipmate, Lieutenant Alden, waked me up.

"Hey, Dick," he said in some excitement. "Wake up. I've just flown through a hangar!"

I started up, half-dazed. Alden's face was covered with blood; his nose seemed to have been caved in.

He pointed out the window. "There she is now."

Sure enough, there hung his plane affixed to the wall of one of the hangars against which it had crashed when Alden had side-slipped into it. One wing was stuck in the structure, the other rested on the ground. The fusilage hung between the two, half way up.

"I ran out of gas too far inland to make the water," he explained, "and lost my flying speed trying to reach the water." What seemed to make him feel worse than anything else was that he had been taken down out of the plane on a stepladder.

No wonder aviation cost dollars as well as lives in the early days.

An entirely different kind of accident began to crop up during the rush of war training. There were no true general traffic rules in 1917. There weren't enough planes to make many rules necessary. But at places like Pensacola where planes and pilots were being gathered for foreign service there began to be real crowding in the air. As a result the first air collisions came about.

One such accident I remember with peculiar vividness. Several planes were over the station one morning working out the beginnings of air maneuvers, then in their infancy. The planes were flying in formation: that is, close together and turning together on signal. In one was Biern Blair from Richmond, whose family were old friends of the Byrds. He was an only child and the joy of his parents' lives.

The planes were twisting and turning with neatness and accuracy that drew the attention of nearly every one on the station. The rear one seemed to keep its position as if it were joined mechanically to the one in front. Suddenly those of us on the ground saw a breath-taking sight. One of the planes used a hair too much rudder on turn. It side-slipped and skidded into another machine. Instantly the pair locked and fell.

As parachutes were not used then, there was never a chance for the flyers. Nothing can be much worse than a collision in the air.

Another type of accident that always made a great impression on us was that in which the pilot would start out on a flight and never be heard of again. This was not infrequent when navigation methods were so crude and engines so unreliable. I am sure that more than one of our messmates whom we lost in this way flew blindly out over the Gulf of Mexico and, when his gasoline ran out, was carried away to starve or drown on its stormy waters.

I soon began to notice that accidents came in threes; perhaps this is the reason few pilots will light three cigarettes from the same match. Perhaps the cause of this phenomenon was the nervous tension that followed on the first accident.

A group of three especially fine young reserve officers was broken up in one of these bad spells. The lads were sons of rich influential parents. The first of the three went into a tailspin and fell 2000 feet right before the eyes of the other two. The second stalled at a height of only 50 feet and crashed on the beach, dying instantly. I am glad to say I left before the third buddy had his spill.

It may seem as if we got hardened to all this sort of thing. In a way we did. I mean that men could die day after day and we could still go on doing our duty. But there was none of the emotional stimulus of battle. And we were so far from the scene of action that killing young pilots somehow seemed unnecessary. However, as I have said, we felt it was the price that must be paid that man might fly.

It was not pleasant to have to go into the details of a crash. I remember the wreck of an HS boat that crashed on land from banking the plane up on its side too much and so lost flying speed. She side-slipped at an altitude of only about 700 feet and was down before the pilot could control her. (I believe the biggest trouble then was that we didn't have enough power in those days.) A side-slip causes the plane to go through the air sideways and so slows it up, due to the great resistance of the wind.

I was near the plane when it fell. I grabbed a fire extinguisher from the nearest hangar and rushed to the wreckage, knowing that if they were still alive they might be burnt to death before I could reach them. But there was no fire. And both men were killed. The pilot was hopelessly caught in the wreckage. It took ten minutes to cut him loose. He had a terrible gash in his head and the whole left side of his face was mashed in. His leg was badly broken; it stuck out sidewise at a full right angle. Yet he was still moving and trying to talk. He died in a few minutes.

The mechanic was thrown ten feet clear. I could see that bones were broken all over his body. His left leg was doubled up under him and his oil-drenched clothing nearly torn off.

But his face was unscarred. On it was an expression of perfect peace, as if he was glad to know that at last all the danger and toil and anxiety were over.

As time went on I began to analyze my records of crashes. I found that over fifty percent of them were caused by bad judgment and inexperience. Many were caused by disregard of routine orders or carelessness. All of these were in the class of "avoidable crashes."

The balance of the accidents were the result of engine failure, propellers bursting, weak wings, or supports and other smaller details. With the exception of the bursting propellers the great majority of this class belonged to the engine. However, engine failures did not necessarily cause crashes if the pilot kept within gliding distance of the landing field; or if not climbing in a turn too near the water or ground.

No wonder that flying safety has enormously improved in the ten years that have elapsed since then. Our engines must now be a hundred times more dependable and our pilots almost know more before they start to train than our experts did in 1918.

It must always be remembered that to maintain proper speed a plane's engine has also to go at a racking speed. That is why it has been so difficult to develop a reliable engine.

I believe that the high-point in my Pensacola training period came when I rammed another plane going 60 miles an hour. I had just got off the water and was intent on gaining speed so I could zoom upward. The first thing I knew I saw almost directly ahead of me a plane plunging down on the water out of the sky. Its pilot was a beginner. He had been intent, I think, on gauging his distance from the water, so as to make as perfect a landing as possible.

The crash was deafening. We were just enough out of line to make our wings lock. As a result both planes flung around with violent centrifugal force that was the result of the 120 miles per hour aggregate speed we were traveling at the moment.

Both planes were demolished. I fell dazed and bruised into the water. A few minutes later the rescue party hauled us into the speed boat, safe and sound, but very much crestfallen at the damage we had done to our planes.

IV.

Thwarted Hopes

SPRING 1918: And here I was still basking in the Florida sunshine. True, I was no longer a listed cripple. I had my "Wings" to show that I was an accredited Navy pilot, and I could not kick about the lack of excitement at Pensacola, with the unending crashes and deaths that had so marred our training.

But it wasn't war. You have to be young and have your country fighting to know the hideous feeling of incompetence that comes when you can't get into the thick of things.

A kind of intrigue had got me off inactive duty and into flying. For years I had been very keen to fly. I had succeeded. I now began to plan a new conspiracy to get into the war zone. Of course, I use the term "conspiracy" in a relative sense. I was still sane enough to know it would only be hurting the common cause for me to get to Europe without being of any real use there.

Since graduation I had been convinced that the next big feat in flying would be the air crossing of the Atlantic Ocean. Early in 1917 I had written confidentially to my friend, Walter Camp of Yale, asking his advice and help. This plan was reborn in me with new vigor in the spring of 1918.

In January that year the Navy had begun the construction of the largest flying boat ever built. She was named the NC-1. I conceived the idea of delivering the plane to the Commander-in-Chief in Europe by flying her across the ocean, via the Azores. For months there had been loose talk about America's huge "Air effort." Perhaps something concrete, such as direct delivery of one big plane, might have a distinct effect on the morale of the enemy.

The great trouble was that such a flight would require equipment and material beyond the immediate capacity of the Navy Department to furnish.

On the night of May 13, 1918, I sat up until 3 A.M. evolving another letter to Walter Camp. I figured that his large acquaintance among rich and influential men would make him a keystone in importance if only I could win him over. I wrote in part:

My dear Mr. Camp:

I am very anxious to attempt the hydro-aeroplane flight of the Atlantic, and thinking of all of my acquaintances who might be able to help me in putting this through, I have decided that you are about the only one who could fill the bill.

Of course, the next thing is to get you to say you will stand with me and behind me in this undertaking. My plan would be to use one of the big new flying boats built for the Navy. These seaplanes will have three Liberty Motors and will, I think, have sufficient fuel capacity for a trip to the Azores. From the Azores, it is only eight hundred miles to England.

This is quite an undertaking, and will need considerable preparation. I will take a crew of about five men, and we will all train according to plans laid down by you.

A very encouraging telegram reached me from Mr. Camp three days later. And in the following week I learned confidentially that Walter Camp and Admiral Peary, discoverer of the North Pole, had gone to the Navy Department and urged that the flight be undertaken. This touched me in a tender spot also because I had long thought a flight across the North Pole was possible.

I was so encouraged that I took a friend of mine, Lieutenant Walter Hinton, into my confidence. With his help and the permission of the Commandant of the station we installed compasses in some of our planes. After brief instruction we managed to start a series of out-of-sight-of-land flights. We obtained special data on fuel consumption of the Liberty engines and on the cruising radius and seaworthiness of the Navy flying boats. We found also that we had to design a special instrument for making extra rapid calculations, which were necessary owing to the high speed of a plane as compared with a ship. This, I think, was the first practical move to conquer the Atlantic by air.

Hinton was a great help in all this. "If I get my orders," I told him, "you get yours too."

We could almost see ourselves flying the Atlantic that same summer.

Despite red tape and war the situation was soon such that I was in a position to put in my official request for the flight. The big NC-1 was due to be finished in a few weeks and the night flying squadron had been organized for service abroad. On July 9, 1918, I wrote to Washington as follows:

1. It is requested that I be detailed to make a Trans-Atlantic flight in an NC-1 type of flying boat, when this boat is completed.

2. It has long been my ambition to make such a flight and I feel that I am well qualified to be given this detail, in that I have made an intensive study of the subject, have specialized in air navigation and am thoroughly familiar with the large type of flying boat.

3. Should this request be approved, it is further requested that any detail of duty contemplated for me by the department, be not interfered with by such a trip.

As the Commandant of the station had by this time become a convert to my scheme, he put the following endorsement on my request:

1. Forwarded.
2. Approval recommended. Lieutenant Byrd has the spirit and will carry this project forward successfully, and as the Trans-Atlantic flight will be accomplished by some one in the not distant future it would be appropriate and creditable if the United States Navy should furnish the personnel for the first crossing.

Two weeks later I received telegraphic orders to Washington. The gang piled in to congratulate me and I was looked on as the luckiest man at the station. Little did I know that this was only Fate's ironic way of singling me out for the greatest disappointment of my life.

I packed in such a hurry that I left my razor and two of my best uniform shirts behind. Little difference it made, though. "I ought to be on my way across in the NC-1 by October 1 at the very latest," was my thought as the Pullman whirled me northward.

The Navy Department was working under such a terrific pressure that it was difficult to find out on arrival just what were the plans for me and the big seaplane. I could find no one who would actually say she wasn't going to fly to Europe right away with me aboard her. At the same time I could dig up no conclusive proof that she was. As a result I oscillated between bursting optimism and abysmal despondency.

On August 12th I was surprised to receive orders to Halifax, Nova Scotia, for duty as Commanding Officer of our U. S. Naval Air Station to be put there. A supplementary document set forth that I was "in direct command of the U. S. Air Forces in Canada" and that I was "responsible to the Senior British Naval Officer (Admiral W. O. Storye, R. N.) at H.M.S. Dockyard, Halifax, N. S., for prompt response to all demands made upon your forces for co-operation in carrying out the General Mission of the Allied Naval Force in Canada." Further I was told that "your situation as a United States Naval Officer commanding air forces in another country, though the relations with this country be intimate and though the United States and this country be striving toward the defeat of a common enemy, requires the exercise of the utmost tact in every situation which arises."

All very imposing. But what had it to do with my dream of flying the Atlantic Ocean and getting into the War?

I went to an old friend in the Department and despairingly asked him if it were all up with me.

His view was that I was being given an excellent assignment and one full of possibilities. "Don't you know that the German subs have been raising hell in the Northwestern Atlantic?" he asked.

I admitted that I had been paying more attention to what went on in France and the North Sea.

"Your new job is a big step forward," he went on cheerfully. "You will start two stations in Nova Scotia. You will be boss; big responsibility. It will be up to you to keep the enemy subs clear of the coast. Also you will have to convoy seaward the heavy defenceless traffic bound out of North Sydney and Halifax for Europe."

"And then what?"

He lowered his voice as had become the habit in those queer days. "You turn the station over to the Canadians and take your men to France to join the Northern Bombing Group."

Great. But suppose the War ended? Then where would I be?

Later a ray of sunshine came in the shape of still another set of orders supplementing my first ones. (I knew one man who received his fourth set of orders before his second set were delivered! Things moved fast that last year of the war.)

As these latest orders constituted the first official move to bridge the Atlantic Ocean by airplane, and are therefore of historical importance, I am going to give them in full:

NAVY DEPARTMENT,
WASHINGTON, D. C.

From: Chief of Naval Operations
To: Commanding Officer, Naval Air Station, Halifax
Via: Naval Attache, Halifax, Nova Scotia.

Subject: Refueling station in Newfoundland—proposed establishment of.

1. It is desired to locate a suitable rest and refueling station on the east coast of Newfoundland. Such a station should have a beach upon which large seaplanes could be hauled up, but if such a beach is not available, a floating hangar, complete with quarters and small workshop, can probably be supplied by next spring.

2. The general requirements for this rest station are:

    (a) Sufficient area of sheltered water for manoeuvering of large flying boat type seaplane with full load.

    (b) Sufficient depth of water for a destroyer or seagoing tug.

    (c) Telegraph or long distance radio communication is highly desirable, but not absolutely necessary.

3. You are directed to take up this matter with the Newfoundland Government, and obtain permission to make an inspection of their Coast, for the purpose of locating a suitable place. The Department is of the opinion that a suitable place may be found in the immediate vicinity of Cape Broyle, about sixty miles south of St. Johns, and it is particularly desired that this place be thoroughly examined. Upon completion of this inspection, submit a detailed report to the Navy Department. Inasmuch as large seaplanes will probably not be supplied to air stations in Canada before the early part of next spring, the proposed station will not be estab-

lished until that time, but the inspection should be made as soon as practicable without undue interference with your present duties.

(Signed) W. S. BENSON.

It was evident now that the Navy Department was at last underway with final preparations for the great flight. They would have to hurry, though. The season was getting late. The weather, never very good, was growing markedly more and more unsettled. But I knew that if we could only get the NC-1 started up the coast the rest was easy.

I think by this time I was almost in a state of mind that if the enemy learned how easily we could fly our Navy plane across he would give up then and there.

During all these uneasy weeks of the late summer and early fall, 1918, I was nerved by a constant and stimulating busyness. To establish a military station for the basing of aircraft was a walloping job, and the ordinary requirements of men and equipment were complicated a thousand times by the presence of big and delicate flying machines.

Before leaving Washington I was able to put through orders for Walter Hinton to join me. Also I was able to pick up several other good men to help me get started. But most of my crowd I had to take "sight unseen."

A final bit of difficulty came when I tried to start my equipment moving northwards. The railways were taxed to their utmost just to carry routine freight. And though military supplies were supposed to have precedence, the supplies were about three months ahead of the unhappy railroad officials. Usual management had given way to a special wartime control. As a result we had some hot tussles before we were finally able to land our planes, engines, repair equipment and several carloads of other gear at our destination, Halifax.

The site that the Canadians assigned to us for our station was about eight miles across the Bay. This meant that we had to resort to all sorts of expedients to get into commission quickly. I had a natural desire to be efficient in the task. I have always believed in doing things quickly. But what was really driving me was the secret fear that the NC-1 flight, which I still counted on, might be delayed by some dilatoriness on our part.

Though at first we were only two officers and eight men, all told, we worked night and day to go into commission. We floated the wingless bodies of our planes across the water to their new home. We transformed our bare plot of ground on the beach to a hustling camp. As we had no hauling trucks for our heavy flying boats we pried them up on poles and rolled them onto the beach. I have never seen men work harder than that handful of men did. Thanks to them in three days we hoisted the American flag over our station and went into commission as a war unit.

However, we could not start operations against the enemy for the good and simple reason that we had no ammunition. Our airplane bombs had been lost in the shuffle somewhere between Halifax and Washington. Baffled but determined, we borrowed some depth charges from the men-of-war in the vicinity. These charges were used by surface vessels against submarines. They were stowed on carefully built racks on deck and fitted with special depth devices for exploding them below the surface of the water. They were not designed for the rough usage of airplane work; and their exploding mechanisms were altogether unsuited to our use. We were all lucky not to have been blown up during the period we so rashly resorted to so temperamental a form of weapon.

Soon officers and men began arriving by dozens. While we were putting up our tents, Lieutenant Donahue of the Coast Guard was digging in at Sydney. Under my direction he started a station similar to the one at Halifax. Wild rumors soon began to pass between the two groups of men. If a bad rain flooded one crowd out the others felt immensely superior for having made their camp better. No plane of the enemy was ever so carefully scrutinized as was one of either group when met by one from the other station. Condition of machine, tone of engine, apparel of pilot, every detail was taken in and later reported at the home mess for comparison.

A few weeks later our air detachment was added to by several kite balloons. These were elliptical-shaped gas bags with basket hanging underneath. The plan was to keep them aloft all day in order that the neighboring waters might be watched for submarines. The Canadians provided a base ship for them so that they could patrol for submarines at sea.

Part of the balloon routine was parachute jumping by the officers. This was a new practice in those days; and the parachutes were still in an experimental state. I remember the first jump we pulled off. The balloon was floating quietly at the end of its tether about 1000 feet in the air. Beyond it the overcast sky cast a gray gloom over the earth. A little silent group of observers stood on the beach staring at the gently swaying basket just below its gas bag.

Just then a light breeze fanned my cheek. "Better hurry," muttered some one. "Southwest wind picking up." There was a touch of nervousness in the words that made me secretly glad that some one else shared my own anxiety. I knew that in a sense every jump was an experiment; and every experiment a risk greater than average airplane flight. Moreover, each jump was made under my orders, which I think made me unduly apprehensive.

The head that showed above the basket's rim, high above us, suddenly seemed to thicken. By this we knew that the balloonist was clambering overboard. In these days of frequent jumping it is difficult to realize the shudder we all felt when a black form shot downwards dragging with it what looked like a streamer of rag.

"*Good!*" burst out some one involuntarily when the 'chute suddenly spread and billowed, then opened full and checked the jumper into a comfortably slow descent.

We soon were getting all the thrills and excitement we wanted in our own business. The highlands and cliffs of Nova

Scotia made the air rough and the fogs kept it thick. Changes were sudden and violent. I remember going up one morning in bright sunshine. We were about twenty miles out to sea when I noticed a black cloud in the southern sector. Before I could get back to the station I was fighting a half gale that whipped the bay into a running sea. Just before I landed a wall of fog swept over the lower arm of the harbor. I slipped down not two minutes too soon.

One day a submarine was reported thirty miles south-east of the entrance of Halifax Harbor. We immediately got our American squadron underway, consisting of our two planes and a torpedo-boat which had been sent to work with us. Hinton and I were in the pilot seats of our machine with an aviation mechanic forward. We had two bombs aboard, and were full of hope we would see some action.

About the time the land dropped over the horizon behind us we suddenly missed the other plane. We circled back and discovered her floating on the surface of the sea. So we flew back to the torpedo-boat and made signals of distress, following them by short flights in the direction of the disabled plane. When the small vessel found the latter we continued after the enemy.

At about the spot where the sub had been reported we sighted what appeared to be a periscope. Almost cheering for joy that we were going into action we banked and swooped downward. Just as we were about to release a bomb we saw that the periscope was nothing but a vertical floating spar of some sort.

On the way back we passed the torpedo-boat with our other machine in tow. The plane's propeller had burst cutting a big hole in her bottom and severing the king post which supported her tail. She was about to sink when the boat took her crew off. Aboard her were Lieutenant Dietrich and Kerr, a Navy Boatswain, both killed in air accidents soon after the war.

Our personnel was added to one morning when one of my men appeared at my tent with an enormous Great Dane. I think the animal was the largest dog of any sort I have ever seen. "Followed me into the boat," explained the man, "and I thought you might like him, sir."

"Like him well enough," I replied truthfully, "but he must have a master somewhere."

I advertised in the Halifax papers. Two days later the owner appeared. By that time the dog had attached himself to me, and the men had incongruously named him "Violet." If any beast was ever farther from that fragile flower it was this splendid creature. I was much pleased when my crowd, who had learned how attached I had become to Violet, chipped in together and persuaded the owner to sell him to them for me.

When the terrible flu epidemic began sweeping through the surrounding country I made all hands take their food from the central kitchen and eat it in their tents. Once a day I had those who were not on flying duty line up in front of the medical tent and gargle with a disinfectant. Violet used to get in line and gargle along with his shipmates. As a result of this care, I think, we did not have a single death from the dread disease.

I cannot pass over this brief account of those long months without making some mention of the friendship that grew up so easily between us and the Canadians. I had been told that up to the World War the people of Halifax annually celebrated the burning of Washington by the British in 1812, and to look out for anti-American feeling. But never could any people in the world be more tolerant, helpful, cordial and hospitable than were our Canadian neighbors of 1918. It was there I learned the great truth that knowledge makes for understanding and tolerance.

My relations with those under me were also of the most pleasant order. Duty up there on that forbidding coast, far from ordinary comforts and conveniences, continually forced to risk our lives in uncertain flying conditions, was not conducive to domestic peace. Yet during all the months we were there, there was not a single court martial proceeding sent to Washington, and almost without exception the men were later demobilized with spotless records. Indeed, the spirit among the gang was so good that as a rule when one of the number would break the regulations he would be punished by his shipmates, and so save me the trouble.

Meanwhile with fading hopes Hinton and I continued to

work on the Trans-Atlantic Flight problem. We could not understand the silence of Washington on the subject. At every mail, at every dispatch blank that was handed me, I braced myself for the great news that the NC-1 was at last ready to start. But always I was disappointed. Storms were getting more and more frequent. Days were growing shorter. Temperature was slowly falling towards the inevitable zero. But we two deluded young chumps clung to the belief that if the big flying boat would only show up we would be capable of taking her safely to the Azores, and thence to France.

We made some headway with the sextant with which to take an altitude of the sun and stars from an airplane at sea. We thought the problem could be solved by using a bubble level glass to replace the sea horizon which is used in taking sights aboard ship. We actually tired a sextant so fitted by an Englishman, Commander Walker, and achieved some success.

I spent hours plotting our course on the chart. I studied weights and food requirements and clothing. I figured out what would be our course of action if we were forced into the sea before reaching the islands. I worked out a very light first aid kit. Altogether I was in every way prepared to fly the Atlantic: companion pilot, fuel, food, clothing, instruments.

And every minute of the time General Pershing and his Armies were doing their level best to wreck my plan. On November 11, 1918, they succeeded. The Armistice was declared. I was ordered to turn my station over to the Canadians and return to Washington. It was great—wonderful that there would be no more bloodshed. After my first shock of bitter disappointment I realized I must forget my insignificant self and be glad of that.

But personally I had failed. The biggest war we could ever have was over, and I felt that I hadn't done my share. We had danger enough—probably had killed a bigger percentage flying than had been lost in the front line trenches. But my big plan for a trans-Atlantic flight had evaporated: there was no longer need for the NC-1 in Europe; money wouldn't be forthcoming; and I felt that the attendant risk would not be permitted now that peace had come.

I sent my men and planes south. It was not so easy to cut loose from those great shipmates. I took Violet with me and left my dead hopes behind me.

As Peary once said: "Fortunately I did not know that Fate was even then clenching her fist for yet another crushing blow."

Be that as it may I don't believe in waiting for opportunity to knock at the door, and it was and still is my theory that if one sticks at it hard enough and long enough he will at last find the key to the door of success.

V.

First
Trans-Atlantic
Flight

ON MY WAY to Washington I learned to my surprise that the Navy was going to tackle the trans-Atlantic flight after all. The news was enough to play havoc with my reason for the moment. I didn't even stop in Boston to see my people who were ready to welcome me after my "arduous" war experiences.

The minute I hopped off the train at Washington I rushed right up to the Navy Department to get the latest report. I got two reports. The first, very exciting, was:

Captain N. E. Irwin, Director of Aviation, is recommending to Secretary Daniels that Commander J. H. Towers be placed in command of the Trans-Atlantic flight which is to go through at once.

This meant the party was bound to go through. I felt like going out behind the big white building and shouting for joy. Then I got the second and, to me, crushing report:

No officer or man who has had foreign duty will be permitted to be a member of the Trans-Atlantic flight expedition. This includes those who have been on Canadian detail.

I was stunned. I knew that one motive behind this ruling was to give a chance for excitement to some of the poor devils who had fought the war behind their desks in Washington. Yet wretched months at Halifax were to deprive me of realizing my dream. I confess that the wave of bitterness that struck me over this seeming injustice was almost beyond control. It was some time before I could honestly and coolly say that "after all, the important thing is for an American Navy plane to prove that it can first fly the Atlantic Ocean."

I suppose the blow was greater than I realized at the time. Two days later I came down with influenza bordering on pneumonia. The day after I passed my crisis another officer was brought in and placed beside me.

This was Lieutenant Kirkpatrick, Captain Irwin's aide. "Hello, Dick," he greeted me, "I suppose you know the Captain has just directed your transfer from Washington to duty at the Pensacola Station."

I could scarcely believe my ears. "Is the big flight off?" I gasped. It was the only possible thing, I thought, that could account for such orders. Surely the authorities could not be so unjust as to ship me away after I had worked for a year on the idea.

"No, I should say not. But the Commandant down there has asked for you to come as his aide. You are not available for the NC flying boat on account of your war duty. And I gather you have finished most of the navigational plans. Don't you like Pensacola?"

Feeling as if I should faint I staggered to the telephone and called up Towers. "Do you still want me to help out on the flight?" I asked him weakly.

"Decidedly so," was his prompt reply.

As soon as I had enough strength I went to Captain Irwin's office and "went to the mat" with him on my Pensacola detail. The captain is a huge man, over six feet and built like a prize fighter. I suppose I was a pallid-looking object as I wavered before him, putting my cause quietly enough but in words that were loaded with dynamite—for me. I can't say I won. Rather the Captain decided to have a little mercy. My orders were cancelled.

Just before I left the hospital an incident occurred that I had good cause to remember later. Near my bed was Lieutenant-Commander Emory Coil, a classmate and close friend of mine, who had been desperately ill with pneumonia. One morning, when he was so weak that he could still barely lift an arm, I saw him reach for a paper that had been left near him by mistake. He wasn't supposed to read. I heard a groan.

Coil had gone even whiter than before. The paper contained an item describing the death of the poor fellow's wife and mother. This was his first knowledge of the catastrophe that had befallen him.

Twice more was the path of my life to cross that of Emory Coil's, each time under the shadow of disaster.

Josephus Daniels, Secretary of the Navy, gave his final official approval to the trans-Atlantic flight project on February 6, 1919. Eight of us were then formed into what was called the "Trans-Atlantic Flight Section of the Bureau of Aeronautics." We were in accord on the general plans; but I held out on one point. I did not believe it necessary to put warships every fifty miles along the route. I had had enough experience to believe that the pilots could navigate a straight course without depending on station ships.

At the time there was still no proper instrument to measure the amount the course of plane should be changed to allow for drift. A wind blowing forty or fifty miles across the course would soon carry a plane far out of line unless her pilot corrected for the error. This was but one of the problems I had on my hands to solve during the three months left before the planes hopped off.

Red tape was cut at every opportunity. Bureaus of Ordnance, Navigation, Construction and Repair, and Operations were all subordinated at times to help us get ready. Such coordination runs smoothly enough today. But in 1919 the Aviation Office was still looked upon as an ugly stepchild by the balance of the Navy Department. Mr. C. B. Truscott of Aviation turned out the final design of drift indicator. The Chemical Section of the Bureau of Ordnance devised bombs and flares. Mr. G. W. Littlehales of the Hydrographic Office, a mathematical genius, evolved for us a short method of navigation. And so on.

By April 21 the Trans-Atlantic Flight Section was moved to the Naval Air Station at Rockaway, Long Island. Two other NC boats had been built. So now we had a group of three, the NC-1, NC-3 and NC-4. The last named was fated to be the first flying machine to cross any Ocean on Earth.

These NC boats would even today be considered very large craft. In fact, there is no plane in the States today with so great a wing spread. Wing spread of the upper wing was 126 feet. If laid on top of one of our largest Pullman coaches it would extend several feet beyond it. The overall length of the boat was 63 feet. Each was equipped with four Liberty engines, making a total of 1600 horsepower, over thirty times the aggregate of the average automobile. I know of no other plane today, nine years later, that is more highly powered.

The total weight of an NC boat was 15,100 lbs. including radio. Its weight with full load was about 28,000 lbs., or over five times heavier than the Bellanca monoplane which recently broke the world's endurance record. Our economical cruising speed was about 75 land miles per hour. We estimated the cruising radius, with full equipment and emergency gear and crew of six men, to be 1475 miles.

The NC type of flying boat was not a step forward in aeronautical design. It was a whole jump. Such sudden departure in the design of aircraft is rarely wise. But in these ships the Navy had access to the best design brains in the world at the time. Among them were such men as Glenn Curtis and Naval Constructors Richardson, Westervelt and Hunsaker.

One day fifty-one men, including the pilots, were crowded into the NC-1 and it was successfully taken into the air!

On May 3, 1919, the three NC flying boats were regularly placed into commission. To the best of my knowledge this was the first time in history a plane had been given official individuality like a ship.

Each plane carried a commanding officer who also navigated, two pilots, a radio operator, an engineer and a reserve pilot engineer. Commander Towers took command of the NC-3, using it as his flagship. Lieutenant-Commander P. N. L. Bellinger took the NC-1. Lieutenant-Commander A. C. Read had the NC-4. Three better men could not have been selected. Towers was a student, quiet and reserved and methodical; Bellinger a rugged seafaring type with sanguine temperament and a likable nature; Read was slender, and uncommunicative, though nothing missed his sharp eyes and quick brain.

As the weeks flew by a thousand new details of preparation seemed to crop up every day. There were complications with the State Department in getting permission to land on foreign soil. Navigational instruments and methods we had evolved had to be given special tests. We made flights for measurement of fuel consumption. Careful plans were laid for communication with the ships that would cover our course. Fuel depots and repair stations were prepared up the coast. Radio tests were made a matter of routine.

On May 8, 1919, we were ready for the first ocean crossing by air in history.

I was to have a taste of the early flight after all. Through the efforts of Towers I was permitted to go with him in the NC-3 to assist in the navigation and look after the navigational instruments in the first two legs of the flight.

Just before we left several distressing events tended to mar the joy of getting away. On a trial flight with the NC-4 we got back to the beach just as the wires to the up-and-down rudder carried away. Had this happened in the air we should all have been killed. The day before our departure I heard a scream from a lady visitor to the station. Following her eyes I saw an HS-2 flying boat tail-spinning towards a big gas tank nearby. It crashed squarely into the structure and killed both occupants. A few hours later Chief Special Mechanic E. H. Howard, Engineer of the NC-4, while working around the plane accidentally stuck his arm into the propeller and had his hand cut off at the wrist. He calmly grabbed his arm and walked to Sick Bay.

This series of accidents were said by local pessimists to be a sure sign of the fatal outcome of our flight.

At 10 A.M. on May 8, 1919, we left the water in the NC-3,

with the NC-1 and NC-4 taking position on either side of us. For the first time a division of seaplanes, regularly commissioned, was underway with orders to fly across the Atlantic Ocean. For the first time in history airplanes were to navigate out of sight of land just as a transoceanic steamer must do without land marks to go on. Could we do it? We were flying into the unknown.

The roar of our four engines was terrific. Of course, we were used to it. And we were stimulated by the excitement of being off at last. But I think our attention was riveted more on the thunder of our engines than on any other single factor. Reliable power plants were not so common then as now. And if ours failed we must fail with it.

Towers wrote of this part of the flight:

Byrd spent the afternoon vibrating between the forward and after cockpits, trying smoke bombs, sextants, etc. My cockpit was not very large, and with all the charts, chart desk, sextants, drift indicator, binoculars, chronometers, etc., stacked in there, very little room was left. As I wore a telephone all the time, wires were trailing all about me, and Byrd and I were continually getting all mixed up like a couple of puppies on leashes. Occasionally one of the pilots would come forward for a cup of coffee and a sandwich, or to take a look at the chart to find out how we were progressing. All these little festivities were rudely broken up about the middle of the afternoon when a squall hit us.

That squall Towers spoke of did not bother us. We headed down through it. Just before it struck us we received a radio from Read saying that the NC-4 was having engine trouble, was running on three engines and would probably have to land. When Read began to drop astern and descend and Towers thought that the NC-4 was landing close to the destroyer that had been stationed on our route, we proceeded on our course with the NC-1. The destroyer at the time was still visible to us. However, it turned out later that Read missed it.

As we passed the coast of Newfoundland I was not surprised when Towers wrote me a note saying, "This is fearfully rough air." I already had been flying around that rocky coast and I had learned there are no rougher air conditions anywhere else in the world.

We reached Halifax Harbor at 7:00 P.M. Rockaway time, which was 8:30 Halifax time. The first leg of the great hop of 621 statute miles was successfully completed. It had taken us just nine hours to do it. It was very pleasant to me to be landing near the naval air station I had erected in the previous autumn. I was more pleased the next day when that station was able to be of some benefit to our expedition. We had made an early morning inspection of the NC-3 and found several cracked propellers. The base ship, the U. S. S. *Baltimore*, which had been sent ahead, had some spare propellers on board but no hub plates. I remembered that I had turned over some of these hubs to the Canadians. Jumping into a speed boat I found them still on hand.

Between Cape Cod and Nova Scotia we had for the first time in history done some real out-of-sight-of-land navigating in a seaplane and had been successful. Another test lay ahead of us when we left Halifax with the NC-1 for Trepasse, Newfoundland, the following day at 12:40 P.M. Soon after we got out of sight of Nova Scotia the wind drift indicator showed that we had a sudden and big change of wind direction. If this were correct, it would necessitate a change of course of a number of degrees. Here was a real test of this instrument. When I asked Towers to take a sight on the water with the indicator he got the same result that I did. Luckily we had the courage of our convictions and changed our compass course accordingly. When we hit land exactly where we hoped to, we knew that the first drift indicator had proved its worth. And, I knew then that at last an airplane could be navigated without land marks. I was delighted.

As we flew along Newfoundland at about 5000 feet it was bitterly cold. A lot of white objects began to appear below which I at first took to be a fishing fleet under sail. When I looked down with my binoculars, I saw that the objects were icebergs, hundreds of them. They made a beautiful sight. I was getting thrills enough at the moment; but I wonder what they would have been had I known then that almost exactly eight years later I should be flying over the same area with thick fog covering everything, having flown all the way from New York without a pause, having still ahead of me a non-stop flight of 2600 miles and with the lives of three shipmates and friends in my care.

I was numb from cold. The icebergs a mile beneath us did not add to my feeling of warmth. I was thinking how pleasant it would be to warm myself before one of our Virginian log fires, when suddenly I saw smoke coming towards me from aft. It looked for a moment as if I were going to get more heat than I wanted. I hurriedly wrote a note to Towers saying the plane might be on fire. I then crawled aft to try to get at the flame. To my great relief I saw that the smoke was coming from a cigarette McCullough was smoking.

Suddenly my head struck the top of the navigator's compartment and several articles flew upward out of the cockpit. I felt as if gravity were acting away from the earth instead of towards it. We had struck a terrific down current of air which caused us to fall faster than gravity would have taken us. I was afraid that Towers was going to fall out of the cockpit. When we got settled again he handed me a note which read "roughest air I have ever felt."

Soon we were gliding down into Trepassey Harbor. In a few minutes we could see our mother ship, the U. S. S. *Aroostock*, anchored beneath us and the NC-1, which had landed ahead of us, tied up alongside of her.

Up there on the dismal coast of Newfoundland, the Director of Aviation, with his rules and regulations, seemed a very long distance away. Feeling that Towers and Bellinger wanted me to go on the flight, I had hopes that I might still be one of the lucky ones. But soon after our arrival Towers handed me a radio from Captain Irwin which specifically directed that I should not accompany the expedition. My Nemesis was still on duty.

My gloom was broken by a strange diversion. Sudden telegraphic orders came for me to report for duty in connection with the dark horse of the trans-Atlantic flight: the tiny Navy dirigible, the C-5. My duties would be primarily concerned with navigational methods and instruments of the C-5. I was further directed to do all I could for the C-5 in regard to navigation.

The C-5 was a fragile non-rigid gas bag of only about 200,000 cubic feet capacity, or only about one-tenth the size of a modern airship. While we had been flying north in the big planes she had been in the air on a non-stop flight from Long Island to St. John's, Newfoundland, a world's record for a dirigible of this type.

I was reading the dispatch over for about the sixth time and trying to collect my thoughts when one of my friends who knew of my long series of disappointments over the NC flight said: "There's your chance, Dick."

"You think the C-5 will make it?" I asked him.

"Sure of it. As long as she has gas in her bag she'll stay in the air. You can drift over if you don't do anything else."

I didn't have the heart to bring up the point that if there were any adverse winds they would take us away from land. I grasped at this straw. Perhaps I would fly the Atlantic after all!

Further, Emory Coil, the one who had been in the hospital with me and read about the death of his wife and mother, had recovered and was now in command of the C-5. I had already turned over to him before I left New York all our navigational data and one each of the instruments we had developed for the big flight.

Now began a brief but exciting period for me while I nursed my last thin hope that I might still be in one of the aircraft to cross the ocean. There would be a fine chance to get some real scientific data with the C-5. Two of the NC boats were ready to start, those of Towers and Bellinger. The weather was right. But Read on his way to Trepassey, where we were, had been forced to land off Cape Cod. Now he was waiting there weatherbound. The C-5 was just around the corner from us at St. John's. If I got away and aboard her, and she flew, there was still a chance that the miracle for which I hoped might happen.

At sea fifty warships patrolled the course the NC boats were to take. The press of the country was beginning to growl at the expense of keeping so many vessels at sea, now that war was over.

On May 15th, the NC-1 and NC-3 were about to take off when a speck appeared in the sky far to the south of us. It turned out to be the NC-4. Had Read been an hour later he would have been left behind. I grabbed a boat and rushed over to congratulate him. He had had a hard trip. When he had fallen behind us one engine had gone out of commission, then another. As the two engines left were not enough to keep the heavily-laden plane up he had to come down at sea. A sextant observation told him he was 100 miles off Chatham, Mass. With his good engines he taxied westward reaching Chatham next morning at daybreak. At least he had proved the seaworthiness of the new planes.

One of Read's sentences stuck in my mind: "Not far from Trepassey I saw an airship headed out to sea," he said.

Could it be that Coil had gone?

The mystery was solved a few minutes later when a radio was passed around: "The C-5 has broken loose from her moorings in a storm and blown away with no personnel aboard her."

My last chance gone!

But I could not forget that this was the third blow Emory Coil had suffered this spring. However, fate was not yet through with my gallant and unfortunate friend.

Towers sportingly decided to wait until Read was ready. The situation was pretty critical due to the presence of the foreign contestants for first trans-Atlantic air honors. British Captains John Alcock and Arthur Brown, R.A.F., were there with their little plane all ready to start. Lieutenant Commander Grieve R. N. and H. B. Hawker were also grooming to hop off for Ireland or England. As both had single-engined planes we felt they were taking big chances. Engines were not so reliable those days as now.

Of course Trepassey was now infested with journalists and photographers. I think that, despite their usual bland indifference to sensation, they were every bit as excited as we were over the prospect of making air history.

On May 16th the weather was reported still to be good. Read was ready. Our English rivals were not quite in shape. The great moment had come.

Weary I climbed the hill behind the rough field and sat down to see the take-off. To be here on the spot and see three planes hop off for Europe for the first time in history and, after all my hopes and work, not be in one of them, was a cataclysmic actuality that no amount of philosophy could efface. My depression was tempered only by the fact that our navy was doing the great job.

After three trials all the planes got into the air, led by the NC-3. A sharp wind cut down from the arctic regions not far above us and the blue sea ahead was dotted with huge white icebergs. But the three planes bravely roared their way out into the unknown and were soon lost to view in a cloudless sky.

I hurried down to St. John's. I was very anxious about my friends. After a slow trip I put up at a little hotel. Just as I was signing the register I heard newsboys shrilly calling "Extra!" I ran out and seized a paper. In a glance I read the black headlines:

SKYWARD

AMERICAN PLANES NC-1, NC-3 LOST;
NC-4 REACHES HORTA.

For hours I went through great distress worrying about Towers and Bellinger and their shipmates. Of course the story of the adventures of my shipmates is an old one now. Towers' time of take-off had been 7.30 P.M. Until dark the other two planes followed him in column. Towers climbed above the clouds to take advantage of the moon. About 9.30 P.M. the NC-4, whose running lights had gone out, came dangerously close to the NC-3 without being seen. At this time the NC-4 began to speed up, Read deciding that his plane did not do so well at the slower speed.

The NC-1 and NC-3 kept in touch until dawn, when clouds hid them from one another. From that time on none of the planes sighted each other. Star shells from the destroyers were visible throughout the night. However, at times the visibility was so bad that the flyers could not see the tips of their wings. Passing through rain-squalls made the men sleepy. Towers used strychnine to offset this.

During the following morning Towers' rougher calculation put the NC-3 near the Island of Flores. He was afraid to get too close lest he strike the high mountains in the fog that prevailed. As he had only about two hours of fuel left he decided to go down, attempt to locate his position exactly, and take off again for his goal.

Unfortunately the sea proved rougher than he thought.

The NC-3 hit the top of a wave, porpoised to the top of another, and then slid down into the deep trough beyond until she struck a third heavy head-on blow that split the bow in several places, and she began to leak. Luckily the plane's life was not ended then and there. As the radio ground wire had broken messages could not go out, though reports were received. A severe storm warning was the first news that came in.

The first thing the party did was to rig two canvas buckets out as a sea anchor. These were secured to the bow, and by dragging in the water kept the damaged craft head-on. After a bad night the storm broke with full fury on May 18th. The wind began to blow sixty miles an hour. The fusilage then began to leak so badly that it took the full energy of the crew to keep her bailed out. Towers, being a good mariner, had oil put over the side but they drifted so rapidly it didn't do much good.

At nine o'clock a heavy sea carried away the left wing pontoon. With this gone it looked as if the NC-3 could last but an hour or two longer. The men took turns strapping themselves out on the end of the opposite wing in order to keep the plane from capsizing.

The second night came on with hope for rescue very faint. The plane was leaking worse than ever and had drifted off her original course but they found that by manipulating the controls they could drift at an angle to the waves and wind. To add to their misery the radio operator intercepted a message that search was being made for them many miles to the west-ward. Toward morning they had hardly strength enough to bail. All were weak from exposure and lack of food, their sand-wiches having in the beginning fallen into the bilge and be-come soaked with salt water.

Just as they reached the limit of their endurance land was sighted astern. It was the Island of San Miguel. Gradually they worked in close. Towers' report reads:

A destroyer came roaring out of the harbor, and when she got close I saw it was the *Harding,* Commander H. E. Cook commanding. We sent a signal by blinker light for her to merely stand by, as we intended making port without aid if possible.

Just after this another wave took off our remaining wing pontoon and we very nearly capsized, but by this time we were off the entrance to the harbor, so we started the three serviceable engines, and with Moore on one wing, Richard-son on the other, Lavender working signals, McCullough at the controls, and myself in the bow we came slowly into Ponta Delgada, amid a perfect bedlam of whistles, sirens, twenty-one gun salutes, waving of flags and wild dashing about of dozens of motor boats.

The NC-1 had an almost identical experience up to nearly the end of her vicissitudes. I am sure that during this past summer most of the ill-fated planes that have been lost had the same experience upon landing. They hit the top of a high wave and porpoised to the top of another and then struck the oncoming wave with a bang, and of course being land planes they had no chance. Caught in fog, Bellinger decided to come down to avoid the mountains that might loom up at any moment. Like Towers he also found the sea rougher than he expected and banged his boat up badly. He, too, used a sea anchor. He nearly capsized several times. After six hours of misery he was picked up by the S. S. *Ionia* of the Hellenic Transport Company from Athens, Greece, and taken into Ponta Delgada.

The NC-4, with Read and five others aboard, made better speed than the other two and missed the worst of the fog though the next morning she ran into fog at 1200 feet and the pilot nearly lost control of her. After 13½ hours of flying, her navigator sighted the southern tip of the island of Flores through a rift in the fog. She was flying at 3400 feet, but now spiralled down to 200 feet above the water hoping to pick up a destroyer and check her position.

At this moment the weather began to thicken and things looked bad. Then Read, with excellent judgment, decided to make Horta. Here he landed at 1.23 P.M. Greenwich time, May 18, 1919, after 15 hours 18 minutes of flying. He joined the others at Ponta Delgada on the 20th.

I recall that Lt. J. S. Breese, Engineer Officer of the NC-4, had put less gasoline in his plane than the others had and that I think was why the NC-4 was able to make better speed than the others.

At this point the Navy Department ruled that Read would go on alone, though it had been taken for granted that if Towers' plane should be damaged, he, the commander, would board another plane. Read was weatherbound at Ponta Delgada until May 27th. He left for Lisbon at 8.01 A.M. Greenwich Civil time and arrived at the Portuguese city after 9 hours and 43 minutes in the air.

The Atlantic had been crossed by air for the first time in history.

Once more I turned south, sure my big chance had come and gone. But the American navy—bless her—had once more won the admiration of the world; and the Stars and Stripes had been the first across the Atlantic through the air.

VI.

Political Interlude

WITH THE WAR OVER and the Atlantic Ocean crossed by air a lot of people thought aviation had passed its peak.

"Why not get out of flying?" my brother, Captain Tom Byrd of Virginia, asked me. "You've done your bit, Dick. Try something less dangerous for a change."

Another, a friend more given to violent speech, said:

"It's all a delusion, Byrd. Flying will never be any safer than it is now. It's only a question of time before you break your neck."

"Got to die anyway," I laughed at him.

"Surely. But why hasten the great day? The man in the street is never going to fly. Commerce doesn't want to risk valuable articles to the air. There's still plenty of room on the earth—"

"But not for long," I broke in. "City traffic has got out of hand. Already the big suburban transits are jammed in rush hours."

"Their own fault. Besides, why push flying and kill a lot of people until humanity really needs it?"

"Don't we need it now?"

"Only the fighters, the Army and Navy. The war is over; why keep on building weapons?"

And so on indefinitely. Reaction against the war included a wide reaction against flying; at least among a certain kind of people. The Navy was not thoroughly organized as far as aviation was concerned, which was only natural, due to its youth, so we were having our internal troubles. General William Mitchell began at that time harassing the Navy and its aviation, and he had plenty to talk about due to our poor internal organization.

Many in our military forces, and a proportion of the press, blamed troubles of Army and Navy flyers on Congress. It was said widely that Congress wouldn't make the proper laws or appropriate enough money. This was not so. Both Senate and House were keen about the new means of transportation that would mean so much to many of their outlying districts.

Before I knew it I was drawn into the maelstrom of doubt, rumor, threat and conspiracy that surrounded American aviation.

When I reached Washington after the trans-Atlantic Flight

aviation held a more unenviable position in the Navy Department than I had realized. Many Admirals and others in power were dead set against it. There was no Bureau to handle it. Captain Irwin, "Director of Naval Aviation," with little authority as compared with heads of other branches of the service, was opposed to creating a special Bureau of Aeronautics in the Department. Members of the General Board were growing irritable over what they called "absurd fancies of young flying radicals."

And in the midst of it all General William Mitchell was quietly going ahead with his plans for a United Air Service that would take the aviation out of the hands of both the Army and the Navy. Those of us who had come into intimate contact with England's troubles with her Royal Air Force believed that, in principle, such a plan was wrong.

So we—a group of young flyers—began to organize. What an assemblage it was: full of enthusiasm and enormous belief in the future of aviation. I suppose we had all seen so much violence and death in one form or another that we didn't quail as much as formerly at charging a few elderly admirals.

In a moment of expansion I volunteered to write a bill to present to Congress for the creation of a Bureau of Aeronautics in the Navy Department. If this could be done aviation would at once be put on an equal footing with other naval activities. My fellow conspirators took me at my word and I was chosen to do the job.

When the bill was ready a picked handful of shock troops, three other pilots and I, took the masterpiece to our superiors. It didn't occur to us to go directly to Congress the way Billy Mitchell had done. I have always felt very keenly that whatever differences naval officers have should be fought out in the navy. Younger officers are never intimidated for expressing their honest opinions. I don't believe there has ever existed a purer or more high-minded organization than our navy.

The start was not auspicious. Captain Irwin and the majority of the admirals were against us.

Then, abruptly, the enemy's works began to crumble. Captain T. T. Craven relieved Captain Irwin and though not with us at first soon became convinced that he was "Director of Aviation" in name only and shifted to our side. Admiral Taylor, Chief of the Bureau of Construction, joined us, a brilliant ally. In fact, he had been for the Bureau from the first. Admiral Benson, keen as a whip, began by consigning us to the devil, then became one of our strongest advocates. Franklin Roosevelt, Assistant Secretary of the Navy, came in strongly from the first. When we went to Secretary Daniels and presented our list of credentials he didn't even make a fight.

"Now what are you going to do?" asked Mr. Daniels.

"Get Congress to pass the bill," we said, little knowing the size of task we were setting.

The Secretary smiled and dictated for me a strong letter of endorsement for the plan.

My first call "on the hill," as the Capitol is called, was at the office of Senator Page of Vermont, Chairman of the Naval Affairs Committee of the Senate. He listened quietly while I told my story. Somewhat to my astonishment he asked some intelligent questions. Men who were not fanatical aviation enthusiasts did not know much about flying then.

"Well, what do you want me to do?" he said at last.

After a quick breath I plunged in. "Call a special meeting of the Naval Affairs Committee and let me make an appeal for a Senator to champion and father the Bureau of Aeronautics Bill," I told him.

Had the roof fallen in at that moment I should not have been a bit surprised.

The Senator rose, resting his capable hands solidly on his desk as if he had at last come to a weighty conclusion. He looked at me with unblinking eyes. Was I to be committed to an insane asylum for daring to interfere with the routine of so august a body as a senate committee? Or was I only going to be sent to sea at short notice for being an impertinent young upstart?

"Mister Byrd,—" The Senator paused a moment that seemed an hour. "Will Friday do?"

For sending me to a sanitarium or to sea? That was my thought. But I said, in a voice that sounded flat and foolish: "For a meeting of the Committee, sir?"

"Yes."

"Yes—yes, sir. Of course, sir."

I got out before I embraced the gentleman from Vermont.

Before the Committee I did better. By that time I began to find out that a senator was a human being like the rest of us, only often a little more human and always more harassed. Also I had "spoken my piece" so many times now that I knew it by heart and could put my sole energy into its delivery. I didn't exactly win the Committee, but I made a start.

Senator Keyes of Vermont consented to father the bill in the Senate. Then Congressman Hicks got Thomas Butler, Chairman of the House Naval Affairs Committee and the next ranking member, Fred Britten, on our side. Before I knew it, the Committee approved the bill.

The next task was to get it voted on. There are always hundreds of meritorious bills floating around Congress. But like seeds of the lavish cottonwood, few fall on fallow ground and take root. By some ingenuity our bill's friends managed to get the floor leader, Frank Mondell, and Martin Madden on the Appropriations Committee, to tack the bill to the Naval Appropriation bill as an amendment. That made a vote sure.

So far I had spent all my time holding myself at the beck and call of the men in whose hands the fate of the bill would lie. I had rushed about the city like a detective looking for clues. I had preyed on my friends and acquaintances until I was about as popular as a case of smallpox. I had nearly worn out my office telephone and one operator had left in disgust at overwork.

Now, I heard at the last minute that one silver-tongued

congressman was going to speak against the amendment. People knew so little about aviation in general and naval aviation in particular that any sort of eloquence against the bill had a good chance to kill it.

At the bad news I dashed about in desperation wondering how to head the enemy off. I was not an experienced lobbyist; I knew that I shouldn't lobby anyhow, but the situation was desperate. At that moment I could think only of the effect of failure on aviation. I didn't even know who would be a good man to take up the cudgels for the bill on the floor of the house.

I decided to call up Captain Craven to see if he could suggest any one. At the moment I was standing outside the office of Congressman P. P. Campbell, Chairman of the Rules Committee. I went into his outer office and got permission to call Captain Craven. The call was a failure. The Captain couldn't suggest any one.

Five minutes more and it would be too late. The bill would be up and defeated if some thing couldn't be done in a hurry. Just then Mr. Campbell came into his office. I didn't know him. I had no right to accost him. But in desperation I got him to give ear to my story and to the need of the Navy for a Bureau of Aeronautics so that aviation could get a fair chance in our military service.

Even while I was talking the Congressman opposed to the bill began to hold forth on the floor.

Suddenly, to my intense joy, Mr. Campbell held out his hand, with, "You're absolutely right, young man! Certainly I'll answer him."

Whereupon he hastened to the floor of the House and, without preparation other than my jumbled words, launched himself upon a speech so eloquent that it not only carried the day of naval aviation but aroused his colleagues to loud applause.

In the Senate we struck another snag. Senator LaFollette, the elder, had been persuaded by General Mitchell to offer an amendment that would kill the whole thing. It is very easy for one senator to kill such a bill. He was ready to propose that the Chief of the Bureau of Aeronautics must be an air pilot. On the face of it this was a fine idea. It certainly looked as if the man who would run naval aviation ought to be able to fly. But none of the admirals, such as we should have to head the new bureau, had taken up airplane work yet. They all looked upon flying as a young man's game. The bureau chief could however be an airplane observer and I suggested that substitute.

I went directly to Senator LaFollette. I found him to be exactly the strong character I had pictured him. He sat silent as I talked.

"What would you like the bill to say?" he suddenly snapped out at me.

Though taken aback at this unexpected show of consideration I replied: "Strike out the part that requires captains of aircraft carriers and tenders to be flyers, sir, and require the

Chief of Bureau of Aeronautics only to be an aviation observer."

He asked me a few questions to clear up my reasons. Then he thanked me without telling me what he was going to do. I left in some doubt as to whether I had succeeded or not. But I took my troubles to Senator LaFollette's son, young Bob, who is now senator in his father's place; he promptly intervened with his father and won the day for us.

The bill passed the Senate without opposition. The Navy at last had a formal Bureau, a complete organization, and one authorized to take care of its aeronautical activities.

Rear Admiral William A. Moffett was made the first Chief of the Bureau. By law his pay was increased 75% for flying. As a result he was the most affluent officer in the Navy, even counting the Vice and full Admirals.

Flying stock went up in the Navy Department. With an Admiral to fight our battles we began to get things done. We soon had more money, safer planes, bigger fields, better experimental laboratory and other lesser things that we so vitally needed. Best of all, we had a well informed group of properly accredited officers to present our case to Congress when aviation matters came up.

The fight was won in the nick of time. General Mitchell had been getting stronger every day. Tirelessly he was working for his one pet idea, that would put army and navy aviation under the control of another department of the government.

Some day, when flying is very far advanced over what it is

today, such a service may be justified. But, despite the wonders of aviation, airplane units are just as closely wrapped up with the Navy today as are units of battleships or destroyers or submarines. To be fully competent, officers of each must be intimate with the problems and tasks of officers of all the others. To create a separate air force just now would be to set up a force of officers and men that would tend to lose touch with what constitutes a well-handled naval action on the high seas. As a result there would be lost that fine naval co-ordination which from the days of Nelson has stood for victory.

Mitchell got busy on his plan right after the war. All the time we were struggling for a Bureau of Air he was winning one supporter after another in Congress. Most regular Navy officers paid very little attention to what he was doing. They were not interested enough in aviation then to care much whether it was taken away from the Navy or not.

As early as 1919 Mitchell got a hearing for his bill before the Military Affairs Committee of the House of Representatives. The few naval officers who intelligently testified against the bill were impugned as having been swayed against it by insidious propaganda or outright intimidation.

I remember once testifying in a hot session that nearly broke up in a fist fight. Commander Callan of the Reserves followed me on the stand. An ex–army aviator happened to be chairman of the sub-committee before which we stood. Callan fiercely opposed Mitchell's plan. In refutation of a point that had previously been made by Major Foulois about an army aviator he made a startling statement.

"That aviator, I happen to know," declared Callan bluntly, "was removed from his post in Europe for incompetency."

"That aviator" happened to be the chairman before whom we testified.

Instantly the fireworks began. The impugned Congressman shook his finger in Callan's face. "You're a liar!" he shouted. "And a coward! You haven't the guts to do what you ought to do the minute this meeting is over."

Having been a boxing enthusiast at Annapolis I concluded that I would soon have the fun of participating as second in an old-fashioned fight. But I soon discovered that this sort of thing was just part of the political game. After a bit the rumpus calmed down, "ill-chosen" remarks were expunged from the record and the hearing went on as if nothing had happened.

From that time until 1925, when General Mitchell was suspended from the Army, hearing after hearing was held in Congress to determine the justice of his claims. As early as 1920 he declared that the Army would take over all the Navy's coastal air patrol stations. He even managed to get a clause to this effect inserted in the Army Appropriation bill. The lethargic conservatives in the Navy Department only half waked up.

I was given the job of getting this clause out of the bill. Senator Wadsworth of New York, Chairman of the Military

Affairs Committee, agreed to handle the thing for the Navy. Then I took to my bed with another bad attack of influenza. One day as I lay in bed I telephoned Wadsworth to check up.

"Sorry, Byrd," he said, "but the energetic General Mitchell has already been around to see all the other members of my committee and they now side with him."

Without bothering to ask the doctor I hopped out of bed, hurried to the Navy Department where I got a letter from the Secretary of the Navy to the senate and orders to represent him. Then I made the round of the Naval committee members just as Mitchell had done with the Committee on Naval Affairs. It was only a matter of giving the facts involved.

When the clause came up on the floor for debate and vote two days later the Navy won, giving me a chance to go back to bed and get well.

All this sounds very simple and easy; just a lot of running around and talking to people. But it was a thankless and nearly always misunderstood job. By some of my shipmates I was looked on as "politician," a term of mild contempt in the Navy. Many thought I was grinding my own ax. Not a few came to the conclusion that we naval aviators were after the same thing as General Mitchell, a separate air force, only we wanted to run it ourselves.

I remember one morning finding a Congressman in his office about to blow up. "A great lot of naval officers you've got down there," he answered. "Damn it, they ought to be all sent to sea! That's where they should be anyway!"

As this man had just spent a week fighting the Navy's battles in debate on the floor, I was much concerned. When he calmed down I found he had telephoned the Department for some information about a naval officer from his district. With scant courtesy he was referred from one officer to another, and finally cut off altogether.

I got him to let me man the telephone and in a few minutes had the desired information. Finally I soothed his injured feelings.

When I got back to the Department I reported the incident to the Admiral who headed the particular bureau that had failed the Congressman.

"Bosh!" exploded the Admiral. "Don't you know that Congress is only a damned nuisance?"

Of course this was an extreme case. But it shows the difficulties and lack of understanding that often exist between the executive and law-making branches of our government. Also it shows some of the barrier of friction that so often slowed the work many were trying to do on behalf of aviation.

Here again knowledge finally made for understanding.

Mitchell did not cease for one moment to try to sink the battleships and bring about a United Air Service. But the violence of his attacks and the extent of his activities finally stirred up the high ranking officers of the Navy whom we young aviators had not been able to influence. Presently we had large reinforcements in rank as well as in numbers.

The finish fight on the United Air Service plan came in

1925. I find in a Congressional Report part of my testimony before the joint committee of Congress which shows my own views. I quote it here as relevant, although it must be remembered that I was only one of many and my part relatively small.

For 40 centuries—ever since the world has known towns and ships—there have been two objectives in warfare: The towns and the ships. This great division of the armed forces of nations is natural since cities are usually attacked and defended by armies, and ships are attacked by sea craft.

Cities and ships can now be approached through the air but the air does not and can not provide a third objective. Therefore no reason exists for a third division of the armed forces of a country. A city can be bombed but can not be captured by aircraft. The Army must be there to take it. Ships can be bombed, but the ships and their personnel can not be taken prisoner by aircraft. The Navy must do that.

There is nothing in the air to attack unless it is put there—then it is only temporarily there. The same is true of the submarine. There can be no objective that exists under the surface of the water to attack except submarines. It does not supply an enemy with a third objective.

Until there is a third objective no reason for a third military department exists.

Our conclusion is clear. Experience has shown beyond peradventure that if the Navy is to reach its maximum war efficiency, it must entirely control its air arm in peace as well as in war.

The forming of a united air service is seen to be so costly that it would place a tremendous financial burden on the country. It would be plain folly, then, to form a department of aeronautics that would not only endanger the effectiveness of our national defense but increase enormously our national yearly expenditure.

With the whole Navy and half the Army against him General Mitchell was finally squashed. In the end he was court-martialed for insubordination and suspended from the Army. I believe he was sincere; but his sincerity was the ruthless pertinacity of a zealot. He did a great deal for aviation, if only by making it a sharp issue before Congress and the country. The valuable appointment of three air secretaries for the Departments of the Army, Navy and Commerce were the direct result of his fight for a separate air service. The trouble was he was ten to twenty years ahead of aviation.

One result of the fight on Capitol Hill was to increase my loyalty and devotion to the Navy. In spite of the general squareness of Congressmen the Navy was at that time often at the mercy of some member from some state that knew nothing of the sea, while the Navy itself had no defense.

VII.

The ZR-2 Disaster

STRANGE HOW SEEDS OF DRAMA lurk in trivial things. In times when I was alone I used sometimes to count my disappointments, failed to get into aviation sooner because of my crippled leg; failed to join the NC-Trans-Atlantic planes because of my war duty; failed to cross the Atlantic in the C-5 because she was blown away; surely if hard work should again bring things to the point of success, fate would not persist in dealing me the joker.

But now another failure was brewing, although I didn't know it.

In retrospect I realize the seed of it was revealed to me in 1921 on a day between battles "on the Hill" when a man in naval ordnance observed:

"Emory Coil is a lucky skate."

"Glad to hear it," said I. "He certainly has had enough tough breaks so far. What's happened?"

"Detailed to the ZR-2 as executive officer."

The ZR-2 was the British dirigible R-38 being built in England for the American Navy. She was to make a non-stop flight from Howden where she lay, with a mixed complement of American and British personnel aboard. She was a splendid airship. Her length of 700 feet, diameter 85 feet and cubic capacity 2,720,000 feet made her far and away the biggest airship in the world.

I was glad that Coil at last was in line for achievement befitting his proficiency as an officer, and which would offset all that the poor fellow had been through, between the tragedy in his family and the loss of his ship, the C-5.

But I did not confide in my friend that I myself was still secretly nursing a determination to cross the Atlantic by air. Indeed, I was not telling any one. I knew that I would be looked on as mildly insane at this moment if I pushed my scheme to fly the ocean alone. Our NC detachment had missed tragic failure by a hair. Alcock and Brown had barely got to Ireland. Hawker and his companion had escaped death as by a miracle. It didn't look as if either the Navy Department, Congress or the country would stand for another attempt until aviation had advanced a good deal.

However, I felt deeply that a successful long flight in a small plane would do much toward winning people over to flying. Further, it might help stem the disagreeable reaction against aviation that had definitely set in right after the war.

The biggest step would of course be a non-stop flight from the United States to Europe. This was my goal. But before that I wanted to see developed a big three-engined plane that would fly with one engine dead, thus having a factor of safety large enough to be the trans-Atlantic plane of the future. I was still continuing my studies of air navigation over the ocean and was determined to see the full Atlantic conquered by an American.

News of the ZR-2 plans impelled me to hasten my own. Perhaps with an air liaison already established between us and England I might find my plan more easily carried out. I tackled Rear Admiral Moffett, who had just been made Chief of the new Bureau of Aeronautics in the Navy, for permission to fly the Atlantic alone. By going alone I could take gasoline instead of a passenger and so fly farther. Then I wanted to prove for the benefit of the single seater combat planes that a flyer could navigate at the same time he was piloting. My request read:—

> NAVY DEPARTMENT,
> OFFICE OF NAVAL OPERATIONS,
> WASHINGTON,
> July 30, 1921.

FROM: Lieut. Commander R. E. Byrd, Jr., (U.S.N. Ret.)
TO: Chief of Naval Operations.

The ZR-2 Disaster

VIA: Chief of Bureau of Aeronautics.

SUBJECT: Trans-Atlantic Flight.

1. It is requested that I be permitted to make a non-stop flight alone across the Atlantic Ocean from St. John's, Newfoundland, to England, in a JL type airplane. This is the only type we now have which is capable of a non-stop flight.

2. The distance from St. John's, Newfoundland, to Clogher Head Island is 1909 miles, and by a very conservative estimation the Naval JL airplane is capable of making 1850 miles by leaving out the extra passenger.

3. The prevailing winds during August and September are westerly and would increase the speed of an airplane traveling east by at least fifteen miles an hour. This also is a conservative estimation. As the wind-speeds at five or six thousand feet are generally from twenty to thirty miles per hour, the speed of the wind then would increase the radius of the plane 330 miles, which would enable the plane to make 2180 miles leaving a margin of safety of 270 miles.

4. The above calculations were made taking into consideration the extra weight which would be added to that of the machine by placing the air bags in the wings and fuselage, the hydrovane under the fuselage and navigational equipment.

5. The hydrovane would enable the pilot to land in very rough water without crashing the machine and the airbags would keep the plane afloat for at least sixty hours. Small combination light and smoke bombs could be carried in

order to attract attention of passing steamers in case of a forced landing.

6. The JL is the only type of airplane now owned either by the Army or Navy which is capable of making a non-stop flight from America to Europe.

7. It is thought that this flight will demonstrate that the pilot can both navigate and pilot his machine at the same time. The greater distance and maneuvreability obtained by one seater reconnaissance or combat aircraft, by leaving out the extra personnel and seats, would make possible long distance reconnaissance flights from battleships. Also it is thought that much data could be obtained from such a flight which would be of considerable use in solving many problems which now face the sea-going aviator.

8. No destroyers or other such aids to navigation would be needed or desired on this trip.

9. Attention is invited to the enclosures. I have made a deep study of Trans-Atlantic flying since I first received my orders to Aviation in 1917.

10. It is requested that this matter be kept strictly confidential on account of the publicity which would ensue should the project get into the hands of the newspapers.

R. E. BYRD, JR.

To this request Admiral Moffett attached the following endorsement before forwarding it to the Secretary of the Navy:

July 30, 1921.

1st Endorsement.

From: Director of Naval Aviation.
To: Chief of Naval Operations.
Subject: Trans-Atlantic Flight.

1. Lieut. Commander Byrd has made a deep study of long distance flying and he is strongly of the opinion that an aviator alone can not only pilot and observe but can navigate by utilizing short methods of navigation. This does away with extra personnel and gives a greater range of action which is of such vital importance in scouting at sea. Commander Byrd designed the drift indicator and the aircraft bubble sextant both of which are now used in the service, and it is believed that his experience with these instruments will make it possible for him to navigate and pilot at the same time.

2. Byrd also believes that an all-metal plane, such as the JL, can be made watertight so that the fuselage and the boat can be put into one thus making a seaplane that will have nearly the maneuverability, speed and endurance of a land plane. In this particular flight, however, as the JL airplane was not designed for water tightness, Byrd will have to depend partly upon airbags and empty fuel tanks to keep him afloat (the method which the Navy contemplates using in case of land planes flown from battleships). He will get some

protection, however, from some watertight bulkheads in the fuselage.

3. The United States has never attempted a non-stop flight of the Atlantic in heavier-than-aircraft and it is believed that a successful flight of this kind would add to the prestige of the Navy. It is strongly recommended that Byrd be detailed to make this flight and that he be ordered for temporary duty at the Naval Aircraft Factory in order to oversee the making of the necessary alterations in the JL airplane.

4. As it will take twenty days approximately to get this plane in condition for flight, and as the best winds are encountered in August, it is suggested that immediate action be taken.

5. Byrd held up this request for three months on account of important work which had been assigned to him.

W. A. MOFFETT.

Having got my document started on its way I went around and won over the Chief of Operations and Navigation. I can't say they were any too kindly disposed toward the flight I wanted to make. But they gave me every consideration—were willing to listen, and in the end said they would not put any obstacles in my way.

There remained only the Secretary of the Navy. It so happened that his assistant, Theodore Roosevelt, was acting Secretary at the time. So to him fell the job of seeing what could be done by "that lunatic Byrd" as some thought of me.

The Colonel sent for me and, characteristically, came at once to the point:

"I will approve this project if you insist, Byrd," he said. "But we do not want to lose you. We need your services in the Navy for a while yet. Why don't you wait until the Navy develops an airplane that can make a non-stop flight clear from New York to Europe? When we have such a plane you will have my unreserved approval."

His attitude gave me a chance to go into detail. I explained that the success of such a flight might do something towards bringing Europe and America closer together; that it would enlist wide popular support of aviation; and that it would clear up much of our ignorance of flying conditions in the North Atlantic.

But he would not budge from his position that the end did not warrant the risk. I think he ultimately won me to his views through our discussion of the airplane engine, which was certainly still unreliable in long flights. But I don't believe I would have given in if I had not a card up my sleeve.

I went straight to Admiral Moffett's office.

"Why can't I join the ZR-2?" I asked him. "I might help with her navigation and in the test of her piloting instruments."

The Admiral smiled. "Why didn't you ask that in the first place? It's just the job for you."

I decided then to postpone the solo flight until engines were more reliable.

Again as had happened before, I left the Navy Department with the bouyant feeling that I was going to have my adventure after all.

I felt that an airship voyage could give me much first hand knowledge I could later use on an airplane crossing. As our trip from England to America in the ZR-2 would take about two days and nights we should have more chance to study air conditions. I would get an intimate view of how the British handled flying. Altogether, as I packed my bag for the voyage, I felt thoroughly satisfied with the turn things had taken.

The big airship was at Howden, England, in command of General Edward M. Maitland, senior officer in the airship service of Great Britain. This world flyer was already a brilliant and romantic figure, with a long record of heroic achievement behind him.

In command of the American group sent to take over the ship, which we were buying at a price of $15,000,000, was Commander Louis Maxfield, a splendid officer and old friend. Lieutenant Ralph Pennoyer was navigator. Also my good friends Lieutenant-Commanders Emory Coil and Valentine Bieg were assigned to duty with the ship.

I reached London on August 20, 1921. When I called at the office of the U. S. Naval Attaché I was told that the ZR-2 was going to make a trial flight on the following day in charge of the British. A number of Americans would be taken along. At once I telephoned Commander Maxfield and asked him to put me down on the list of those to go on the trial flight. He replied that billets were very scarce but that if I came right down the British would put me on the list.

As luck would have it, I missed the morning train for Howden, finally not arriving until the night of the 22nd. This accident saved my life. The flight was to begin the following morning. As I had not shown up Maxfield had decided I was not coming and the British took me off the list.

I reached Howden armed with a letter of introduction to General Maitland from the British Air Attaché in Washington, Colonel Charlton. The minute I learned that I was still off the list of those to go up on the morrow I asked Maxfield if there was any way to change the plan. He told me the British had left me off because I had not put in an appearance and said that so many were very anxious to go that they were very touchy about changing the list. I decided that in spite of my great desire to go it would not be courteous to ask them to change the list again. I then suggested that I might request them to leave one of our enlisted men behind and take me because it was important that I have as much experience as possible before we set off for America. Since it was late we left the matter until the following morning.

I sat up until long after midnight talking things over with Coil. He had remarried, this time an attractive English girl. I found him very worried about the forthcoming flight. He felt there was something wrong with the ship, though he confessed he was not sure what it was. Before I left his wife took me off in a corner and confided that he had had a premonition that the ship would never get across the Atlantic. Afterwards she told me Coil had sat up nearly all that night worrying.

Strange to say this same spirit of apprehension pervaded the entire camp. Maxfield's face was drawn with strain, as were those of the other officers. The men were unusually quiet. There was little or no talk about the airship herself. Medical officer Taylor told me that one of the men had come to him the day before with a tale of a dream that the ship had exploded over the Humber River.

However, the officers realized that this state of mind was not uncommon when men were about to face a test of acknowledged hazard.

I was called early with word that the ship was being taken out of her hangar. I dressed hurriedly and went to the field. The big airship was much like our present *Los Angeles*. But the novelty of her mammoth size and bright silvery body inspired me more than ever with an intense desire to make the trip on her.

I went aboard with Coil to arrange to take the place of one of our enlisted men. I found that the only one of the mechanics that actually could be spared was a mate named W. J. Steele. When I suggested that I replace him his disappointment was so great that I did not have the heart to force the issue.

"I've sent my whole family and baggage ahead to Pulham, sir, where we're going to tie up to the mooring mast," he said.

"Really, sir, it would make a mess of things for me if I don't go up in her."

How futile our plans when fate wills otherwise. The mess poor Steele pictured was microscopic as compared with that of which he was a gruesome part but a few hours later.

The only thing left for me to do was to catch the train to Pulham and rejoin the ship there. I was so grouchy that when I got off the airship just before she took the air I did not go over to say hello to my beautiful cousin Mrs. Maxfield.

An hour later the ZR-2 took the air. How magnificent she looked, the rosy light of sunrise tinting her bright sides a series of soft violet and lavender tints. Officers and observers aboard, lines cast off, she rose slowly and with dignity befitting so huge a craft, sailed away into the cloudless sky.

Feeling that my fate was always to see my friends hop off on air voyages that I should have been the one to take, I boarded the train back to London. From there I could go on to Pulham. As I traveled the sky gradually became overcast, draping a gloom over the landscape that was in keeping with my depression. At the Attaché's office we received messages that the ZR-2 would cruise all night.

About 6 P.M. the next day, en route to catch the train for Pulham, I went into a barber shop. After what seemed an endless half an hour I emerged to go on to the station. Suddenly I stood stock still. A cry from the street had reached my ears:

"Extry! Extry! Read all about the big airship accident!"

SKYWARD

I literally tore a paper out of the nearest boy's hand. The headlines told the story:

R-38 EXPLODES IN AIR
OVER HUMBER RIVER.

I hailed a taxi and drove top speed to the Embassy. Yes, the story was true. The big ZR-2 had broken in half, caught fire and fallen into the river near Hull. She had had fifty officers and men aboard. A handful seemed to have survived. The reports were so vague we couldn't be sure. Cream of the British and American lighter-than-air aviators were lost. Despite the long list of deaths in the past no such tragedy had ever befallen aviation.

The Attaché ordered me to proceed at once to the scene of the disaster with Commander Newt White and take charge of the American end of things. Not until I was settled on the train did I realize the full extent of the shock I had received. Only by looking at other people, hearing them talk, listening to the noise of the train and then reading over again in the paper on my lap the broken report of the wreck could I bring myself to believe that this all was not a nightmare.

Inside of me was a queer involuntary feeling of thankfulness. It was instinct telling me how narrow the margin was by which I had escaped death. Had I caught the train to Howden in the first place, had any one been ill, had the enlisted man given way to my importuning, had any one of a dozen contingencies been different, I, too, would now be lying dead in the chill waters of the Humber River. Yet I felt unworthy to give myself a thought at that time. The question kept on recurring again and again in my mind. Had any of my old friends and shipmates been saved and if so, which one?

I reached Hull at 5.30 the next morning. Day dawned as crisp and clear as had the morning of the fateful taking off. For what does the spoiled plans of man matter to the profundity of nature? To brace myself I took some black coffee at the station, then hurried to the dock. There I found a small huddled group of men. One pointed seaward as I came up. With my eyes I followed the direction of his arm towards the middle of the river.

At once I saw the wreckage, just a small tent-like projection of the shattered airship's body that lay below the surface. The 20-foot tide had well nigh covered what was left of her.

At this moment Charley Broom, Chief Aviation Mechanic, came up to me.

"How many left?" I asked him.

"Five."

"Any ours?" I could scarcely get out the words.

"One." He swallowed. "Young Walker; enlisted man."

That told the story—my friends, all of them, had gone "west."

Broom had been watching the ship when she broke. He

said an explosion came almost at once. One parachute came hurtling down with two men attached to it. Parachutes were considered too cumbersome.

The forward end of the ship fell straight down and disappeared under the water. The after end floated for a while. Broom and others pursued it in a boat, rescuing three uninjured out of four aboard this fragment. My friend Little was still alive when picked up, but died on the way to the hospital.

I asked about poor Coil. He had been seen by one of the survivors just at the point at which the ship broke in half. Coil knew the ship was weak at this point and was there to watch it. His body was later found at frame ten, the critical section he had told me about the night before he died.

Survivors declared there was a ghastly tearing noise when the break came. Though the ZR-2 had been flying at 5.38 P.M., at the time of the accident at an altitude of about 1200 feet above the river, the noise was clearly heard over the countryside. She had finished her speed test of 60 knots. Her rudder tests at 50 knots were being carried out when she crumpled just abaft the rear engine cars. Fire breaking out immediately was thought to account for the large loss of life. As almost extreme helm was being used at the moment this no doubt put an excess stress on longitudinals, causing them to fail. Yet the British, always great sports, had previously given the ship very severe tests so that if anything were to happen it would do so before they would turn the ship over to us.

Flight-Lieutenant Wann, injured for life, was the only one rescued alive from the forward section.

I determined not to leave Hull until I had recovered the bodies of my shipmates.

We had a lot of trouble with the treacherous tide. Each day large silent crowds gathered on the banks as we toiled away with barges and cranes. One girl who waited was the daughter of an English Lord. She had been engaged to Lieutenant J. E. Pritchard, attached to the ZR-2. Like Mrs. Draper at Pensacola, she would not believe her man had been killed.

We found General Maitland in the wreckage of the control car, his hand grasping the water ballast lever in an heroic effort to save his ship. He had died at his post. I thought of the undelivered letter of introduction to him I still had in my pocket. Little had I dreamed that our first meeting would be so tragic. Machinist Steele we found wedged in the girder at which he had been stationed. As his limp body came up I thought of the little twist of fate that prevented my being in his place and he in mine.

One by one we found them all. Meanwhile the British organized an impressive funeral service in Westminster Abbey. As we had but a handful left of our detachment English officers and men filled in the gaps by the gun carriages when the day came to take our shipmates to the station. I marched with the last unit by the side of my friends Coil, Bieg and Maxfield.

Hundreds of thousands of people turned out along the

line of march of the funeral cortège to do respect to our dead. I lived many years during that march to the station.

More of our small detachment lay on the gun carriages than were left to walk beside their shipmates on their last parade.

The English did homage that day to the American flag that covered the biers. England won me then and there. I cannot describe what that crowd did to me. Not a sound was heard but the rumble of the cortège. Not one of the women had dry eyes. Not one of the men or boys had his head covered. The spirit of them got to me and I realized then and there that my dream of international good fellowship was not senseless or useless; that aviation in tragedy as well as in success held within it an unpalpable something that could bring peoples to a better understanding.

In Westminster Abbey the Chaplain-in-Chief of the Royal Air Force spoke impressively. In part he said:

> The blow has fallen with awful suddenness on two kindred Forces of two great Nations. Nations united through a common descent, enjoying a common speech, animated by common aspirations, who yesterday—as it were—were fighting shoulder to shoulder against a common foe for ideals which have ever appealed to our race, and the younger nations sprung from it.
>
> The Rigid Air Detachment of the United States Navy and the Royal Air Force have been associated in developing

a once formidable engine of destruction into a pioneer of closer commercial relations, and, consequently, of a better understanding between the two nations they represent. A triumph, so we fondly thought, embodying the lessons and experience of the past, the Airship R-38 lies submerged in a river-bed, and beneath it many of its splendid crews. So tragic! Long months of training and then to be almost home! The goal well-nigh in sight! The trials all but completed! Only the eagerly-awaited voyage remaining! Then the sudden and awful collapse.

The price of progress, the toil of science, a bitter enough price in lives, and yet—thank God—never a lack of splendid men ready so to do and so to dare. 'Tis best so. To be in the forefront of the fight, to conquer what half a generation ago was an untried field, will ever appeal to our splendid manhood.

H. M. S. *Dauntless* of the British Northern Squadron brought home the Americans' bodies.

It was all a very grievous thing. And yet there was this great bit of solace: I knew that a common grief, this loss we shared, had helped bring these two of the greatest nations on the globe a little closer together in peace and understanding. So, in still another sense, those old friends of mine who had sacrificed to this great new science had not died in vain.

VIII.

I Turn Explorer

I RETURNED TO THE STATES on the battleship *Olympia*, which carried the remains of the Unknown Soldier. When I reached the Navy Department my position seemed to me to be untenable.

I was about to be demoted along with the rest of my class from Lt. Commander to Lieutenant (which ranks with Captain in the Army). The promotion we had gotten during the war was only temporary.

My class would soon get a permanent promotion but I would remain a Lieutenant, since a retired officer even if he has had as much active duty as his classmates cannot be promoted in peace time without an act of Congress, and that has been done only a few times in the history of our Navy.

On top of that I felt that I could continue with air expeditions with less handicap if I were not subject to military orders. So I wrote an official letter requesting that I be placed on inactive duty. Admiral Moffett did not approve it and the Personnel Bureau returned the letter to me without comment (as by law my request would have to be granted), stating that there was some more liaison work with Congress necessary and asked me to hold up my request for retirement until that work was done.

Of course I withdrew my request for inactive duty and I went to the bat again on the Hill.

Everywhere I met with uniform courtesy. Those fellows up there in Congress are likeable and human and don't deserve the mud that is slung at them. Many times I saw party lines break where the good of aviation and the navy was concerned.

During this last battle on Capitol Hill I had been urging the Bureau of Aeronautics to establish some aviation reserve stations throughout the country so we could keep on tap some of the fine aviators whom we had developed during the war and so that we could have an inflow of young blood.

"But there isn't any money for such stations," I was told again and again by the Chief.

"Build them without money," said I on the spur of the moment one day soon after Congress had adjourned.

"All right, you do it," came the prompt retort.

It was a challenge I could not resist, so I again delayed asking for inactive duty. Twenty-four hours later I had orders to establish a reserve air station at Squantum, Massachusetts, the function of which would be to train a certain number of carefully selected young men each year and keep in training the war aviators of New England.

I was given nothing but orders; no money, no men, no instructions. I think the Admiral had a quiet laugh to himself over my predicament when I left Washington.

In Boston I went to Rear Admiral Louis R. de Steiger, the Commandant of the New England Naval District, and told him what I wanted to do. He felt the principle was sound and gave his enthusiastic backing, as did the Assistant Commandant Commander Fred Poteet. Next I got in touch will all the war aviators I could locate, who helped as I thought they would. They were enthusiastic beyond my highest expectations.

This was early spring. By summer we were able to put the station into commission, thanks to the reserves. It was a hand-to-mouth proposition in a good many ways. I borrowed working parties of sailors from battleship friends to build runways; lumber from the Navy Yard's junk pile, and tools from whomever I could beg, borrow or steal. But when we were finished and had fixed up an old plane, we had an "honest-to-goodness" air station, preserving the skill of those who had learned to fly in the war, and the whole outfit had cost Uncle Sam almost nothing.

Well, that was convincing enough proof for the Navy Department. As a result I soon received orders to go to the Great Lakes Training Station at Chicago and erect another air station and organize the reserves in thirteen of the middle western states. I got the enthusiastic support of the Commandant Captain Evans and the Assistant Commandant Commander Jonas Ingram.

From this start there have grown up reserve stations at Rockaway, L. I., and Sand Point, Washington, besides the two mentioned above. After courses at these places students are sent for advanced work to the regular big stations at Hampton Roads, Va., and San Diego, Calif.

Then when Congress met again I went before the Naval Affairs Committee and asked for enough money properly to operate the stations, which was readily granted.

In the meantime, soon after New Year's Day, 1924, just when I was finishing my job at the Great Lakes Station, I received telegraphic orders from Washington to report to the Navy Department in connection with a proposed flight of the dirigible *Shenandoah,* across the Arctic Ocean from Point Barrow, Alaska, to Spitzbergen. This route would take the big airship directly across the North Pole. My job was to assist Admiral Moffett in preparation for the expedition. A committee appointed by President Coolidge and composed of Captain Bob Bartlett, Peary's old skipper, Commander Fitzhugh Green, who had been out on the Polar Sea and who is one of the greatest authorities in the country on the Arctic, Admiral Moffett, and Commander Furlong, had already gone into some details of the geographical and technical end of the flight.

The newspapers were full of the expedition. As Amundsen had not yet flown to the Pole it was considered that it might be a great feat for Americans to fly there first. But just as we had the party well under way the President, without explanation, called the whole project to a halt.

Once more I found myself in my usual position, out on the end of a limb. There was not yet a proper plane for the transatlantic flight.

But the momentum I had gained in the way of Arctic interest, and the idea that ultimately America might first reach the Pole by air, stimulated me to continue on my own hook. I had never gotten out of my head my lifelong ambition to fly to the Pole.

Then came along the Navy and Congress and did that most gracious thing for me which I had always thought of as being so remote a possibility that I didn't dare even hope for it.

They promoted me by special act of Congress to Lieutenant-Commander—not for any spectacular feat but on my general record. It was simply a recognition of the fact that I had plugged strenuously for the service I am so devoted to.

I could accomplish more as a Lieutenant-Commander than as a Lieutenant. I acted at once. My eyes were on the North Pole.

I joined forces with Captain Bartlett and at once began to plan a private Arctic air expedition. The fact that there still remained about 1,000,000 square miles of unknown area north of the Arctic Circle seemed to justify a serious effort at arctic exploration by air.

I succeeded in securing the promise of $15,000 from Edsel Ford, and a like amount from John D. Rockefeller, Jr., while Captain Bartlett scraped up $10,000 from another source.

We found that Donald B. MacMillan had asked the Navy for a plane. His letter to the Navy Department said that he planned to do some flying around the south and western part of Greenland. As our idea was to use the northwestern corner, Etah, as a base and seek for land out in the Polar Sea I believed there would be no conflict of interests. Also I deemed it would be a sporting thing to do to tell the other man of my project, adding that we had asked for two amphibian planes and I didn't see how he could get along with only one. I knew that only one suitable plane was available in the Navy but felt that we might get two of the amphibian planes from the Army.

At once MacMillan asked for two planes instead of one. But since there were only three available the Navy Department insisted that we join forces. MacMillan was to direct his expedition, with me commander of the naval unit which was to do the flying. He had the schooner *Bowdoin,* the naval unit was on the steamer *Peary,* which ship was under the command of Eugene McDonald, a business man and a very close friend of MacMillan's. Our mission was to locate land supposed to exist in the Arctic Ocean in the Polar Sea northwest from Etah. The combined party organized under the auspices of the National Geographic Society of Washington, D. C.

I was allowed two pilots in addition to myself, Lt. Schur and Chief Warrant Officer Reber, very fine pilots, and had the pick of the whole Navy for mechanics. The mechanics who do all the gruelling work on the planes are generally forgotten or unnoticed, don't let us forget them here. Their cheerful industry under the most trying conditions of wind, cold, rain and sleepless days and nights, made them all potential medal wearers.

It was in this group that I discovered Floyd Bennett who afterwards flew to the North Pole with me. Up to the time of the Greenland expedition he had been an obscure aviation mechanic aboard a man-of-war, not even specially well known on his ship. Once he had his chance, he showed that he was a good pilot and one of the finest practical men in the Navy for handling an airplane's temperamental mechanisms, and above that a real man, fearless and true—one in a million.

We left Wiscasset, Maine, on June 20, 1925. After an uneventful voyage of three thousand miles we reached on August 1st, Etah, North Greenland, the home of the northernmost Eskimo tribe in the world—a fascinating primitive people who live as they have for thousands of years because they dwell north of the ice that fills the dreaded Melville Bay and so are little touched by civilization. Ice and heavy weather had de-layed us at times, but never seriously menaced our plans.

At 5.30 A.M., August 2, the morning after the *Peary* reached Etah, the eight officers and men comprising the Naval Aviation Unit started to work. With the enthusiastic assistance of the Eskimos and all hands, they built with our wing crates a runway for the planes on the ridiculously inadequate, very rocky beach—the best beach anywhere near Etah and one of the worst ones I had ever seen.

Working in the open on the delicate parts with bare hands, and at times exposed to snow squalls, my men got the wings and disassembled planes to the beach, erected them and we flew them by August 4. The rapidity with which these fellows did this is still a matter of wonder to me. When I gave the test flight to our machine the NA-1, I got a great satisfaction from the realization that aviation could function so far north at the very outpost of life. With any other planes than the Loening Amphibians, with their combination wheels and boats, I do not see how the flying ships could have been put in water and then dragged up on land.

As the beach proved entirely too small and rough, we moored the planes out to buoys which were dropped several hundred feet offshore. We thereafter operated entirely from the water.

We selected Etah to fly from because it is the nearest accessible harbor to the area in the Polar Seas we wanted to reach. For some reason the harbor is free enough of ice to be able with care to take off the plane without striking a hunk of it. Many harbors even hundreds of miles south of it we found to be filled with jagged cakes of ice.

Some of the gales which the planes had to ride out in the harbor were so severe that our anchors, which ordinarily would have held planes twice the size of our amphibians, dragged badly and it finally became necessary to keep the planes most of the time tied up astern of the *Bowdoin* and the *Peary.* Almost invariably our hours of sleep were interrupted by the deck watch with a report that one of the buoyed planes was dragging anchor, that the wings of another were about to strike the ship's side, or that a miniature iceberg was bearing down upon a third.

On August 4 we took our ten specially picked carrier pigeons ashore in the pigeon house, to get them oriented to the locality. On the 10th we turned them loose, but only four of them returned. Chief Aerographer Francis, who acted as Navy phototrapher, meteorologist and pigeon man, reported to me that they had been killed by Arctic falcons. It would seem, then, that pigeons are not practicable for communication purposes in that part of the Arctic. We had thought that they might be used for communicating with Etah in case of a crash, if our radio were put out of commission.

We spent August 5 making radio and full-load tests. As we found that, with the load of food, rifles, ammunition, boat, etc., stowed in the tail, the plane was thrown out of balance, we spent the 6th taking a 33-gallon emergency gasoline tank out of the bow to make room for stowing the gear. At 7.00 P.M. August 6, fog descended, visibility became very poor, and it began to rain. The downpour continued for 24 hours, after which a southwest gale sprang up. This blow turned into a snowstorm the following day at 2.00 P.M.

From general conditions and information supplied by the Eskimos, it was realized from the first that we were having scarcely any summer at all, so the Naval unit put forth its greatest effort in accomplishing its work in the shortest possible time. In fact, it turned out that after the planes were ready for flight there were but fifteen days of "summer" in which to accomplish our mission.

It is an astonishing fact that of those fifteen days only three and three-quarters were good for flying; two were fair flying days and one indifferent. More than half the time was either dangerous or very dangerous for flying. Yet due to the great work of the mechanics the three planes flew more than 5000 miles counting all flights without any forced landing. While in the air we saw 30,000 square miles, some of which, being inaccessible to foot travelers, had never before been seen by human eye.

Our first reconnaissance flight was to Cape Sabine, which lay on our proposed course toward the Polar Sea, 30 miles from Etah. We found that the ice began several miles north of

Etah, and covered all the water to the northward as far as we could see. We flew low, hoping to find the ice smooth enough to land on but it was rough and corrugated, and generally in such condition that landing upon it would have been as disastrous as landing among large rocks—a plane would have been completely demolished and, of course, the flyers probably would not have been able to walk away from the wreck.

We realized that the ice-landing skis which we had brought to use in place of wheels would be of no use to us under such conditions. There were pools of water on the ice and here and there open leads filled, more or less, with detached pieces of ice. It was easy to see why Ellesmere Island is inaccessible in the summer to the dog-sledge travelers.

In all the hundreds of square miles of ice over which we flew later on, both land and sea, we did not see a single place on the ice where a landing could be made without disaster!

As the engine on the NA-1 developed a knock on the 5th we decided to put in a new motor. We felt that we must do everything humanly possible to prevent a forced landing on the ice. So my mechanics set about shifting a 900-pound motor with our jerky ship's boom, while the plane bobbed up and down in the water alongside the ship. Though I watched the men work, it is still a mystery to me how they did it.

Bennett and Sorensen, also a perfect shipmate, worked all day and all night connecting up the intricate mechanism of the motor, out in the cold and the wet, and reported the plane ready on the morning of the 7th. The work had been accomplished in about one-fourth the time I expected it to take. When the motor started and hit on all twelve cylinders it was a very pleasant surprise. Then Bennett and Sorensen reported themselves ready to fly! Rest seemed to mean nothing to them. But as the weather was nasty I made them turn in.

That is the kind of spirit all but one of the men with me displayed. No handicaps—and there were plenty—were too great for them to overcome. It is a pleasure to record the great courage, indomitable spirit, and unusual ability of those fellows.

At 4.00 A.M. on the 8th, during a gale, the NA-3, which was tied up to an anchored buoy, barely missed destruction from a drifting iceberg. As later she began to drag anchor we finally had to tie her up astern of the *Bowdoin*. The bad weather persisted until 7.00 P.M. when it abated. I immediately gave orders to prepare for our first long flight into Ellesmere Island to attempt to put down an advance base, as the distance we should have to go was such that we should have to advance by bases.

We left Etah Harbor at 9.10 P.M. with Schur, pilot, and Rocheville, mechanic, and MacMillan, passenger, in the NA-2; and Reber, pilot, and myself, relief pilot and navigator, in the NA-3. Just before we took off, a herd of a dozen walrus came up a few feet from our plane. They apparently became enraged at it and dived toward us, but we gave the motor the gun and could not see them when they rose to the surface again because of the spray kicked up by the propeller.

As the midnight sun did not set for some days yet we had normal daylight for 24 hours.

We set a course for Cannon Fiord, which lies on a line from Etah through Cape Thomas Hubbard on the Polar Sea, from which Peary in 1906 thought he saw the high peaks of a great land to the northwest.

At last we were to find out whether or not we could navigate a plane where the north magnetic pole is on one side, off to the southward, and the North Pole is on the other side, and where the force of the earth's magnetism acting on the compass needle is very weak. I noted immediately that the steering compass did not move at all, but pointed east all the time. Fortunately we had provided a more sensitive instrument which we called the navigator's compass. It began to oscillate slowly at first; but after we had steered a steady course for a while it finally settled down.

In clear weather the sun compass enabled us to do accurate navigation. I was delighted with it. Mr. Albert H. Bumstead, of the National Geographic Society, devised it for our trip and I consider it a great contribution to science.

When we reached Cape Sabine we took a bearing on two points 30 miles apart, the direction of which Peary had established, and found that in addition to the 103 degrees of error caused by our being north of the magnetic pole, there was an additional and unexpected error of 30 degrees, an unheard-of deviation. (Deviation is that error caused by local disturbance, such as metal in the plane.)

When we wanted to fly north by compass the compass needle pointed nearer south than north. A curious sensation indeed!

As we flew over Smith Sound, we could see to the north at a glance the ice-packed area Peary and Bartlett had such a difficult time getting through with the *Roosevelt* in 1908. The thought occurred to me: How we could have helped Peary by indicating to him the direction of the very few open leads of water so easily visible to us, but so difficult to locate even from the crow's nest of a ship! I was impressed, too, with the fact that we were traversing in a few minutes areas that it had taken him days to cross. In fact we crossed in thirty minutes a stretch that took Hayes thirty days about fifty years ago.

We reached Cape Sabine at 9.40 P.M., and passed directly over the spot where 18 of General Greely's men died from cold and hunger. I have never seen a bleaker spot. Over to the northward we could make out Bache Peninsula, which Peary traversed in 1898 and where his hunters killed musk oxen for a fresh meat supply.

Beyond Cape Sabine, the view that opened was superb. We were stirred with the spirit of great adventure—with the feeling that we were getting a comprehensive idea, never before possible, of the Arctic's ruggedness and ruthlessness.

I believe that we have a new story to tell of the grandeur of Ellesmere Island. It was evident that the greater part of the land we saw had been inaccessible to the foot traveler, who, keeping largely to the water routes, with the view cut off by the fiords' great perpendicular cliffs, could not have realized the colossal and multifold character of the glacier-cut mountains.

But there was no time to enjoy the view. Since any slight engine trouble might require a landing, I naturally looked about for some suitable place in which to put a plane down if necessary. With our load the landing would have to be made flying at 50 or 60 miles an hour.

I searched carefully and did not see a single place on the land or on the water where a landing would not have meant disaster. The land was everywhere too irregular and the water was too filled with ice either broken up into drifting pieces or in large, unbroken areas. At that moment I realized we were confronted with an even more difficult and hazardous undertaking than we had anticipated. I knew, too, that no matter what judgment we exercised we should have to have a little luck to comply with Secretary Wilbur's last admonition to me to bring the personnel back safely.

We had confidently believed that the fiords would be free of ice. That they were not was due probably to the fact that we were having scarcely any summer. We could not use the sun compass because the sun was obscured. So we continued steering east by the magnetic compass. By sighting astern on known points I was delighted to find that we were almost exactly on our course. A little later, however, the wind-drift meter indicated a strong wind from the north and we had to change course about 10 degrees to allow for it.

No idea of the extremely irregular and rugged character of Ellesmere Island can be gathered from the maps and charts. In fact many of the mountains we saw were uncharted. The higher mountains were largely snow-covered and their glaciers extended down to the sea.

We continued on to Knud Peninsula (the tongue of land lying between Hayes and Flagler Fiords), flying at an altitude of 4000 feet. Low-lying clouds hung over the peninsula, with many rugged peaks appearing above them.

Ahead we saw very high snow and cloud-covered mountains which appeared to be impassable. We kept on, hoping to find some way through. However, we soon realized that the clouds were so high that no aircraft loaded as ours was could possibly get over them. The weather astern had begun to thicken and the clouds covered most of the landmarks.

Weather conditions change very rapidly in the Arctic, a fact which is of great concern to the aviator who cannot fly through fog and clouds over the land as he can over the sea. There is too great danger of running into a mountain or cliff. Neither can he land and wait for the weather to clear, if he has no landing place. Nor can he keep on flying around for the good reason that his gas eventually gives out.

We decided to turn back, fly over the clouds and take a chance on finding Etah. Without a landmark it was necessary to steer a compass course. Luckily, we found a rift in the clouds over Smith Sound, with fog only in places here and there on the water. After a hazardous trip we were finally able to make the ships' base, although a 30-mile wind from the north made rough landing.

Upon our return, Aerographer Francis handed me a report that a gale of great intensity was rushing toward Etah from the south. All flying equipment was, therefore, "secured." A driving snowstorm soon set in, bearing out Francis' prediction. The next morning at 3 o'clock a piece of iceberg weighing perhaps 500 tons was driven by the gale between the *Peary* and the planes, barely missing the latter, and giving us some anxious moments.

A few hours later I called the Naval unit together and told them *that I would never again order any of them to fly over Ellesmere Island.* It was too risky a business. Engines were not so reliable as now. Yet when the time came my men were ready and eager to volunteer for any flying that was to be done.

That afternoon it was decided that we should try to get beyond the high, snow-covered mountains by going through a gap to the south of our course, even though this was a roundabout way to reach our proposed Polar Sea base on Axel Heiberg Island.

When the gale subsided at 5.30 P.M. we made a reconnaissance and radio test flight to Cape Sabine. We ran into snow over the Cape and found Ellesmere Island completely smothered by fog and snow.

The weather cleared toward Ellesmere Island the next morning, August 11, so all three planes prepared to leave immediately for Bay Fiord to attempt to put down a base of fuel, food and ammunition on its shore.

We got away at 10.40 A.M. in all three planes. Schur piloted the NA-2, Reber the NA-3 and Bennett and I the NA-1. Our mission was to locate a landing place suitable for a base between Etah and the Polar Sea; a non-stop flight would be too far to go with the cruising radius of our planes. Also, we felt a base to be absolutely necessary because food and fuel had to be deposited on the shore of the Polar Sea before we should dare to make a flight over it. Otherwise we faced starvation in case we had to walk back.

At 11.15 A.M. we passed over the north end of Cape Sabine. We reached the eastern end of Flagler Fiord at 11.45, flying at an altitude of 4000 to 7000 feet. At the latter altitude temperature was several degrees below zero, which felt bitterly cold in the sharp wind.

Hundreds of mountain peaks, dazzling white with snow, ranged along our northern horizon. As clouds rested on their summits we could not see beyond in the direction of Greely Fiord. Below us was a chaotic landscape of glacier, fiord and showy highlands, the latter cut by sharp black ravines.

At 12.45 we were across the land, reaching the eastern end of Bay Fiord. The crossing of the glacier had taken us a few minutes. This was a curious contrast to the crossing Fitzhugh Green made in 1914 when he struggled up over the steep ice slopes and crevasses for days in temperatures down to 60 degrees below zero. Surely the plane has altered polar work.

Here the clouds increased and visibility northward was ruined by a heavy mist that hung over Eureka Sound. Below us the fiord was covered with ice. Soon the NA-2 disappeared entirely in the clouds. As the NA-3 was having trouble getting altitude she turned back toward Etah. I took the NA-1 on down toward Eureka Sound and finally found one suitable landing place on the north shore of Bay Fiord. But this spot was only a temporary opening where the wind had blown the drifting ice to one side.

I was greatly worried about the other planes. I had had an extremely difficult time keeping track of them against the dazzling snow background. A forced landing would have been bad indeed. It was important that if one came down we should know where to search for her, but we could find no trace of them. My joy was unbounded when we got back to base and found them safely anchored in the harbor. The NA-2 and NA-3 having arrived at 2.30 P.M. and we about an hour and a half later. We were pretty well chilled when we clambered stiffly out of our seats.

On account of the good weather I decided I must waste no time. On our return that afternoon I noted that Beistadt Fiord was comparatively free of ice and clouds. This meant I could leave a cache in it, even though it was slightly south of the line we hoped ultimately to travel towards the Polar Sea.

Though tired from the day's flight, my men did not demur at preparing at once for another. We hopped off at 9.30 P.M.

with all three planes and the same pilots. But when we reached Beistadt Fiord a heavy crosswind prevented us from landing. Probably its high cliffs, 2000 vertical feet I judge, create a suction from the glacier above just as New York skyscrapers do.

We turned back and recrossed the inland ice-cap. At the western end of Hayes Sound we found enough open water for a landing. We came down and taxied toward shore. But the high wind made it impossible for us to reach the beach without wrecking the plane. So cold and wet from the spray of the high sea we took off again and reached the ship about midnight. On the way we saw still another spot where a landing would be possible; the inner end of Flagler Fiord.

At last we had been able to land in the interior of Ellesmere Island, but the water had been dangerously rough. We noted on this occasion a very interesting thing. The wind rushed down the glacier, but changed its direction several miles from its foot. We afterward found that no matter what the direction of the wind elsewhere it generally flowed down the glacier and then subsided or changed its direction some miles beyond the foot.

Another interesting phenomenon experienced in the Far North was the difficulty of judging distances—something at which the aviator must be expert. This difficulty was occasioned by the great size of the cliffs, and the clearness of the atmosphere—when it is not misty. When we landed in Hayes

Fiord we thought we were landing a few hundred feet from the ice fringe on the shore line at the foot of the 2000-foot cliffs, whereas to our great surprise we found ourselves more than a half mile away.

Now came a period of very cold winds. After being buffeted by a gale on the morning of the 13th, the NA-2 began to sink. When the engine was half covered with water, the members of the expedition, by prompt and heroic effort, saved the plane. We later hoisted it on the deck of the *Peary* to change the water-soaked motor; but it was never able to fly again.

Having seen open water at the mouth of Flagler Fiord, we decided to attempt to put down a base there. At 11.45 on the morning of the 14th of August the NA-3 and NA-1 left Etah for this spot. After an hour and a half we came down at our destination and got the planes to within 50 feet of the shore. We waded in the icy water to the beach, carrying 200 pounds of food and 100 gallons of gas. In addition we left 5 gallons of oil, primus stove, camping outfit, smoke bombs, rifle and ammunition, and matches. An iceberg drifted into our plane and we had a great tussle keeping it from being smashed. We were much relieved when we got the NA-1 off for Etah.

In order to take advantage of the fair weather that had blessed us momentarily we again took off at about 5 A.M. the following morning. Surely it was a strenuous campaign. When we reached Flagler Fiord we found that during the few hours we had been away the ice had closed in and completely covered our landing place. We then cruised about for some 60 miles attempting to locate a landing place in one of the other fiords, but were unsuccessful.

About a half hour before midnight there was the effect of twilight among the fiords. I wondered if any human being had ever before witnessed such a weird, mysterious, desolate scene. There was a sense of great loneliness and the plane seemed very small indeed. Once when we flew down into one of the black chasms in the dimness we lost track of Nold alone in the NA-3. He evidently had missed us also for finally we located him, just a speck in the distance and apparently headed for the North Pole! We gave our motor all the power she had and after a good race overhauled him. What Nold's compass was doing, or what he was about, I never have found out. Nold told me he had felt very lonely indeed when he got lost.

I had on polar bear trousers, Eskimo boots lined with sheepskin, and a reindeer-skin jacket—the warmest clothes known—but while leaning out of the cockpit to navigate I got very cold.

The next day we started out again. For a week Bennett had had very few hours' rest, but he insisted on going with me. He did most of the flying while I navigated and flew from time to time when I was sure of our location, and could let the navigating go for a while.

We now headed into the northwest. The season was getting late and I wanted a look at the regions above the well-traveled route down Hayes and Flagler inlets. At midnight fog came on and we were forced to land in Sawyer Bay, a magnificent place with its high cañon-like cliffs. We ate a midnight lunch of pemmican and tea and lay down in our skin clothes to rest to wait for the clouds to clear ahead.

Finally on taking off the NA-3 developed such a knock that Schur preferred not to try a flight over the mountains to the north. About 5 A.M. Bennett and I in the NA-1 crossed the high snow covered peaks and got a look beyond.

There followed for Bennett and me one of the greatest battles of our lives. We looked down on an unexplored part of Grinnell Land into areas cut jagged by ages of ice into pinnacles and precipitous cliffs. The view was awful in its magnificence, and the air was the roughest I had ever experienced. We were tossed about like a leaf in a storm and often it looked as if we would certainly be dashed down on the irregular ice of the glaciers beneath us. Bennett showed there the stuff he is made of. Ahead of us were higher snow covered mountain peaks that disappeared into the clouds. We made a desperate effort to get through but there was no opening in the clouds. Most reluctantly we turned back fighting every inch of the way.

We returned to Sawyer Bay and joined the NA-3. We left a cache of gasoline, oil and food and hopped off for Etah at 7.05 A.M.; when we rejoined the ship at Etah a gale was blowing.

On the 17th the gale finally subsided. At 8 P.M. some gasoline on the water around the *Peary* caught fire and for a few moments it looked as if the NA-3, which was tied up astern, and the whole ship would go. Sorensen used splendid head work in casting the NA-3 adrift immediately and some one procured a fire extinguisher and threw it to Nold, who was on the flaming plane.

My diary for the 17th has the following entry:

The saving of the NA-3 from destruction by fire today was just another example of the fine spirit of the personnel the Navy has assigned to me for this duty. Whether we succeed or fail, they deserve the highest success. They have overcome almost insuperable odds that the elements and poor facilities have brought about. They have been indefatigable and courageous, and whenever there has been a job to do they have needed no commanding officer to tell them to do it, to spur them to greater effort.

What they have accomplished on this trip has been almost superhuman, and even if we succeed in the highest measure it cannot increase my pride in them. Their attitude seems to have been to live up to the best traditions of the Navy. They never hesitated to spend hours flying over areas where their lives depended entirely on the reliability of the engines.

There was one forced landing during our Arctic work, but it did not come until we were ready to leave Etah, where there was open water.

By the 20th the burned wings on the NA-3 had been replaced by new wings, and a new engine installed. But due to Bennett the NC-1 seemed to be in better shape than any of the other planes so he and I loaded up to use our sub-base and fly to the limit of our cruising radius or bust. We were ready to go again. But MacMillan gave us orders not to go and we couldn't change him. That night the head of Etah Fiord froze over. This meant, MacMillan declared, that a forced landing in Cannon Fiord or Eureka Sound would certainly result in a freezing-in of at least one of the ships that could not desert us.

Bennett and I were greatly depressed that we could not go on with our work, for we were learning the location of the few water landing places and we never gave up the hope of discovering an island in the Arctic.

However, there was another great adventure ahead of us—the flight over the Greenland ice-cap. We spent several days making photographic flights, and on the 22nd the NA-1 and NA-3 left Etah for Igloodahouny, 50 miles south of us. Reber piloted the NA-3, with Gayer as photographer and Nold as mechanic; Bennett, Francis and I were in the NA-1.

Half a mile from Etah the engine of the NA-3 threw her connecting rod and stopped dead. Reber was forced to land and had to be towed back. The NA-3 was then put on the *Peary* alongside the NA-2. I was sorry to see Reber have that hard luck, for, due to serious illness, he had been able to make only two flights over Ellesmere Island.

After landing to see that the NA-3 had gotten down without of injury, we continued in the NA-1 to Igloodahouny, an Eskimo village south of Etah, where we found a fine beach. We landed and made camp.

At 3.15 I took the NA-1 for a flight over the Greenland ice-cap. The visibility was wonderful. We climbed to an altitude of 1000 feet and could see 100 miles in every direction. As we got farther in over the ice-cap it grew very cold, although at 7000 feet we encountered a warmer stratum of air.

We were flying in a direction a little south of east over a part of the ice-cap never before explored. Soon we saw in the direction we were going that the ice reached an altitude which appeared to be equal to that of the plane—over 10,000 feet.

I especially enjoyed this flight. The Greenland ice-cap is one of the great natural wonders of the world—1500 miles long, about 500 miles wide, with an area of 700,000 square miles of solid ice and averaging over a mile in height—the world's great iceberg factory. The glaciers near the foot are greatly crevassed, but farther up, where they join the ice-cap, they are fairly smooth and firm. The shape of the ice-cap seems to be that of the crystal of a watch, so that it would be difficult to land an airplane near its edge without dashing into a crevasse; but 50 to 60 miles inland, though a bit rolling, there seem to be flat places where a plane with skis could land.

We returned to Igloodahouny almost literally frozen stiff. But we were proud of the NA-1, for thanks to Bennett she had flown more than 2500 miles in the Arctic in every kind of weather, and she appeared to be in just as good condition as when we started.

I was stirred with the conclusion that aviation could conquer the Arctic. Contrary to the expectation of the world we were returning without disaster.

We had a cold and stormy passage back to New York, but reached there safely about October 1. Once more I had been close to something very big. However, I came back with secret confidence that I was perhaps very close to the biggest thing in my life. With Bennett I quietly talked over the possibility of reaching the North Pole by air. Our Greenland experience convinced me this feat was possible.

So as had often happened before I tried to use hard knocks as a step for the next sortie against fate and the beckoning future.

IX.

The
North Pole

THERE WERE TWO fairly good reasons for our wanting to fly to the North Pole: first, by traveling at high altitude over unexplored regions we might discover some new land or unexpected scientific phenomena; second, a successful flight would, like the first crossing of the Atlantic, be sure to accelerate public interest in aviation.

We could have used any one of three places for our attack upon the Pole: Point Barrow, Etah and Spitzbergen. Of course there were an infinite number of potential bases on or near the shores of the Polar Sea; but all had the characteristics of at least one of the three named.

Point Barrow, Alaska, is not accessible on account of the ice until late summer, except by a long flight over the mountains. By that time clear weather over the Polar Sea is replaced by fog. Also Point Barrow though it is the northernmost point of Alaska is nearly 400 miles farther from the Pole than Etah or Spitzbergen. Etah is reasonably accessible by August 1, but presents no good take-off for a land plane. Moreover, it is foggy and the local winds are sudden and strong. In contrast, the ice surrounding Spitzbergen is subject to the warming influence of the Gulf Stream. On that account, Kings Bay which is only 750 miles from the Pole, can be reached as early as April. Unquestionably it is best suited for an attack on the earth's north polar axis.

My plan was to fly westward at first and explore that part of the north end of Greenland known as Peary Land. I hoped to come down on some large snowdrift, using skis, and leave supplies in case we were forced to walk back from near the Pole.

Many explorers claimed that we could never get back should we have a forced landing on the ice. Others thought that there might be a possibility of getting back in two years by working our way down to Etah.

Neither Bennett nor I could begin serious work of preparation on our return from Greenland in the fall of 1925. Official duties engaged us both until the middle of January 1926. Then Secretary of the Navy Wilbur and my Chief Admiral Moffett allowed Bennett and me leave. We were going this time on our own hook. We didn't even ask the Navy to send us as we felt the hazardous nature of the undertaking made it unfair. From then on came a crescendo of toil which culminated when we sailed from the Brooklyn Navy Yard on April 5th.

After carefully weighing our own experience, as well as the opinion of aeronautical experts, we selected for our flight a Fokker three-engine monoplane.

One was available that had already flown 20,000 miles. It had 200 horse-power Wright air-cooled motors, any two of which would keep it up for a certain reduced distance. That, of course, added to our chances of success.

The plane was 42 feet 9 inches long in body, with a wing spread of 63 feet 3 inches. Two 100 gallon gasoline tanks were set in the center of each wing; and two others, each holding 110 gallons, were carried in the fuselage. The additional gasoline we might need we decided to carry in 5-gallon cans.

We named the plane *Josephine Ford* in honor of Edsel Ford's three-year-old daughter, as Edsel had taken a greater interest in our expedition than anyone else. Careful tests of the plane were made before we sailed. Its fuel consumption at cruising speed was 27 or 28 gallons per hour—lower than was anticipated, and therefore most encouraging. It was capable of a speed as high as 120 miles an hour.

Through the generosity of the Shipping Board I was able to secure the steamer *Chantier*. She was of about 3500 tons displacement and had ample deck space for our flying gear, while her hold took the plane's wings and body.

There were half a hundred members of the expedition, nearly all volunteers, all young and full of the zest of great adventure. I selected them primarily by writing to nearly all of the men who had had 16 and 20 years in the Navy and were then in the reserves. We obtained the others by culling out the best of the thousands who had volunteered from all over the country. This was a difficult job. I think I could have successfully manned a dozen expeditions with what I had at my disposal.

The Commandant of the Marine Corps gave two of his best men leave, Charles Kessler and R. McKee, a private and a corporal. My two radio operators were ex-marines who had just resigned from their service, Lloyd K. Greenlie and George H. James. Another marine, Touchett, had just been paid off. Aviation Machinist's Mate Leo M. Peterson was given leave from the Navy. The Marine Reserves granted Lieutenant A. N. Parker permission to leave the country.

Through the help of the Shipping Board I secured Captain M. J. Brennan, an ex–naval reserve man; F. deLucca, ex-bluejacket; J. A. Slaughter, a second mate, and E. J. Nolan, a third mate. The Weather Bureau in Washington loaned me W. C. Haines, one of their most valuable physicists. My boatswain, Jim Madison, was an old navy shipmate of mine. A. C. Geisler, who went as a seaman, had become a friend in a Washington gymnasium I frequented, where he was known as the "strong man." Johns Hopkins University loaned us the services of Daniel O'Brien to go as expedition surgeon.

It was Geisler who took an oath not to shave until we had flown across the North Pole. He grew a huge bush during the weeks of preparation. When the time came for his great shave he found himself in the hands of the whole crew who took delight in doing the job for him.

Joe Deganahl came aboard with bag and baggage the day we left New York and said he had to go. I looked him over, sized him up as a good man and took him. He turned out to be a perfect wonder. Winston Ehrgott and Paul Todaro also came aboard with baggage on the last day and announced that they had to go. Mind you, I had never even heard of them before. They were ex–West Pointers. I had a hunch and took them. They, too, lived up to expectations. In the interests of truth I must record that Ehrgott was put to work at washing dishes. But when he broke twenty dishes in the first five minutes I had to shift him to a detail that could better withstand his energy.

Roy Bryant, a captain in the Army Reserves during the war, and John Reed, a lieutenant in the army reserve, both heroes, went as ordinary seamen. Utterly without sea experience, they knuckled down and stood hardship and toil like old mariners. The eight seamen had a terrific job and it is remarkable that they could stand what they did.

It was Bryant who amused the real sailors when we got up anchor. Madison told him to "shake a leg" and "get the fire hose started," routine procedure in washing mud off the anchor chain and anchor as they come off the bottom. Bryant, thinking the ship was on fire, sprang aft, seized a patent fire extinguisher and dashed to the forecastle. The boatswain nearly collapsed when he was handed the extinguisher.

Of course there were feminine applicants for jobs on the expedition but not many of them. Just before we left New York harbor a very pretty young lady came out in a launch with her complete baggage and declared that she was going along. She wanted to write the history of the expedition. It took a good deal of tact to persuade her that our quota was already full.

I think the most heartbreaking job I had before we left was that of raising funds. I hated to be a beggar. A few men were so generous that I disliked asking them for more. But several times I was on the verge of bankruptcy before we sailed. And if the expedition had failed, which it might well have done with all hope centered in just one plane, I should still be trying to pay back my obligations.

In spite of many supplies and much equipment that were either donated free or given at cost by patriotic business concerns, we had to raise over $100,000. As it was, I left with a deficit of more than $20,000. Being personally responsible for this amount and since it would grow during my absence, life was not the only thing I was risking.

After months of toil on the part of all hands, we left New York on April 5, 1926, with half a hundred men and six months' food supply aboard. I suspect to this day that Captain Brennan and his three mates from the Merchant Marine had many misgivings in starting out on a 10,000 mile cruise with a ship's company made up mostly of rank landlubbers. I knew he and De Luca would have a great time getting sea legs on to them, but they did it. As for Chief Engineer Mulroy, I look on his achievement of steaming north and back without a single breakdown as something close to a miracle. He claimed afterwards that his assistants were to blame for his "luck" as he called it. But I happen to know he did his share.

At first our green helmsmen took us on a course as tortuous as a snake's crawl. One night one of the landlubber lookouts insisted that the evening star was a light from a ship ahead.

We had coal for 15,000 miles of steaming stowed away in the bunkers in the hold. It was a stiff job shifting this coal from the hold to the bunkers, a very dirty job that had to be done every single day. Most of the landlubbers were staggering with seasickness while they worked. In time the following ditty grew up amongst the shovelers:

> *Sweet little coal bunker, don't you cry;*
> *You'll be empty by and by.*
> *When our Commander is crossing the Pole,*
> *We'll be in the bunker shoveling coal.*

The second night out from port a fellow tried to slouch past me on deck. When I shot my flashlight into his face to my astonishment I recognized my old friend, Malcolm P. Hanson, civilian employee of the Naval Research Laboratory in Washington. "I confess to stowing away, Commander," he said. He had not quite finished his work on our radio before we left. It was too late for him to get leave. So he took the bull by its horns and stowed away. He did not want to give me the responsibility of taking him so he took the responsibility himself though he was due for a promotion. I've been thrown with many hard-working men but never anyone who could stand as much or who did as much work as Hanson. He was a corker. That was a big thing he did for us. When we returned the Navy had in mind adequate punishment since Hanson's desertion was a serious offence. But the end of it all was that he got his promotion and his absence was booked as leave.

We arrived at Kings Bay, Spitzbergen, at 4 P.M. April 29th and found the Amundsen-Ellsworth-Nobile Expedition members well underway in their preparation to receive the great Italian dirigible *Norge*. This revelation of the energy of another air expedition had a tonic effect on the eager young American spirit of our crew.

Fate lost no time in placing serious obstacles in our path. The little harbor of Kings Bay was choked with ice, but skillful work by Captain Brennan brought the *Chantier* to anchor within 900 yards of the shore.

To my dismay I found that there were no facilities for landing my heavy plane. I had counted on the dock at the coaling station. Previous inquiry told me the water there was deep enough for our ship; and permission was only a matter of asking the local manager.

Now we found tied up to this sole landing a small Norwegian gunboat, the *Heimdahl,* taking coal. Of course I went ashore immediately and asked if we could have the dock for a few hours, at least.

"Sorry but our ship was nearly lost a few days ago," I was informed. "Drifting ice caught her and carried her helplessly toward the land." I knew the danger from the drifting ice.

I could see it was no use to argue. Reports indicated that the *Norge* was on its way north. While I was not actually racing to be the first man to fly across the Pole, I knew the public construed our relative expeditions this way. If I beat Amundsen and Ellsworth at the expense of losing one of the Norwegian gunboats, had I in any way been able to force the *Heimdahl* to clear the landing, I should be thought guilty of poor sportsmanship, though Amundsen and Ellsworth also did not consider themselves racing.

The only thing for us to do was to anchor as close as possible to the shore and send our plane through the drift ice by means of some sort of raft. When the Norwegians heard what we planned to do they sent word urging us to desist. "You know nothing about ice," was the gist of their message, "or you would not attempt such a thing. The ice is almost certain to start moving before you can get ashore."

I do not mean to imply that the people there were in any way discourteous. Their warning was solely for our own good; and a very sound warning it was, too. I shudder now to think of the risk we took. But it was the only answer to our problem.

By laying heavy planks across the gunwhales of our four whaleboats the crew constructed a big raft. Of course that left the *Chantier* without boats, which I did not like on account of the dangers from the ice. It began to snow; and the air was cold and raw as all hands worked at top speed to meet the emergency of a landing that was far from safe. I was secretly bursting with pride in my shipmates for the job they did that day.

The First Mate, de Lucca, a great fellow, hoisted the body of the *Josephine Ford* from the ship's hold in a swirl of flakes. A change in tide began to close the lane we had opened among the heavy cakes of ice that blocked our course ashore. Yet by tireless work and unswerving determination our men managed to prop the awkward body of the plane on its frail support.

We were taking a tremendous chance in doing this, for had a wind sprung up the pontoon would have been crushed or blown out to sea. It was either get our personnel and equipment ashore this way or come back to the States ignominious failures. My men were anxious to take this risk with their lives. They wouldn't have had me do otherwise. This great struggle and great hazard set our expedition apart from the other spectacular flights I had taken part in, where hangars and fields were nearby. Here we had great risks even getting the

equipment ashore and we knew greater risks were ahead before we could get into the air for the final flight.

No wage or ordinary urge could have evoked such enthusiastic industry and courage as the men displayed during
those first nerve-racking days.

We had plenty of narrow escapes, especially for the plane
and equipment. For example, just as we were about to hoist
the wings out and bolt them on the body now waiting on its
raft, the wind rose and threatened the safety of the whole
structure. We had to secure the great wing firmly to the deck
of the ship to prevent it being blown away. As we had only one
plane for our polar flight even a slight accident at this juncture
would have been fatal to the whole project; the reputation I
had spent my life making in the Navy would be gone and I
would be a bankrupt as I would not be able to pay my debts
from newspaper stories.

Just as we finished the raft the very thing we dreaded happened. The ice started moving with great force and we had
quite a struggle saving the raft and even the steamer itself. A
big iceberg came galloping in with the tide. On account of
drifting snow we did not see it until it was almost upon us. It
seriously threatened the ship's rudder and we had to rush dynamite to the corner of the oncoming monster and split it into
pieces that could be handled or were swept clear by the current.

We had an amusing, though semi-tragic time battling our

way shoreward through the ice. Most of the men had never had an oar in their hands before. When I would order "give way port" half of the lubbers would begin to row with starboard oars. Engineer Grey, who had never rowed before, insisted on using his oar backwards all the way to land.

During this crazy maneuver, in spite of the seriousness of the moment, I could not help thinking of the time George Washington crossed the Delaware.

It was anxiety for my shipmates that made that trip a most anxious one for me. I felt entirely responsible for their safety.

My relief was great when we at last reached the ice foot protruding from the beach. Great luck was with us—we must admit that.

The Norwegians gallantly lined up and gave us a ringing cheer.

When the plane was pulled over planking from the ice foot the wheels sank deep down in the snow. We replaced them immediately with skis. Little did I realize then how soon those great looking skis which I had had made with a tremendous factor of safety would be broken like paper in the rough snow.

No one knew what a big plane like the *Josephine Ford* would do taking off the snow with skis. We had much to learn. We were truly pioneering.

The start of the landing field was about a mile from the ice foot. If it was a very big undertaking for my men to get the plane ashore it surely was a muscle-tearing job for them to get the plane and equipment up to the top of the long incline through the deep snow in a temperature 15 degrees below zero.

A field-kitchen was put up in the vicinity of the plane and meals were served in the open in the cold as we worked. No one even thought of sitting down for a meal. Fuel drums were hauled up by hand and sled, heavy parts brought alongside, equipment and instruments for the flight assembled near by under cover, and all was made ready for a hop-off the minute we felt it safe to hazard a full flight.

We found that we had to dig down through the snow and build a fire and put the cans of oil in the fire before we could pour it into the engines which had already been heated by a big fireproof canvas bag covering them leading by a funnel down to a pressure gasoline stove below.

As there was no level stretch available that was smooth enough to take off from with a heavy load we were forced to try another new stunt—to take off going down hill. To get the snow on our take-off field smooth was the biggest job of all. The boys had to work 18 hours a day but never did I hear a single complaint from any of them.

The plane's first attempt to take off for a trial flight ended in a snowdrift and nearly upset—which not only would have hurt us, but would have upset the expedition as well! A ski was broken to bits and the landing gear bent and broken.

Things then looked black, but the men refused to lose heart. Then twice again we broke our ski in pretty much the same way. We were having difficulties—that would never be experienced in the States—in getting off the snow with the lightest possible load. What would happen when we tried our total load of about 10,000 pounds?

Noville, Mulroy and "Chips" Gould the carpenter worked two days and two nights making new skis, whose strength was doubled by using some of our oars. There was no other hard wood available in all Kings Bay. Profiting by our first experience, we treated the bottom of the skis with a mixture of rosin and tar. The runway was fairly smooth for the second attempt and the plane was lightly loaded. We held our breath.

This time our airplane moved forward rapidly, then rose gracefully into the air. With Lieutenant Noville and Lieutenant Parker aboard, in addition to Bennett, she made a trial flight of more than two hours and showed a remarkably low gas consumption. The cold-weather cowling on the engines came up to our highest expectations. Our worst fears were at an end.

At this point came a complete and sudden reversal of our plans. The trial flight and the low gasoline consumption showed that we could probably take off the snow with sufficient fuel to visit Cape Morris Jesup and the Pole in one nonstop flight. It had been our intention to land at Cape Morris Jesup. But since we could explore the whole distance without landing, the question naturally arose, "Why not go direct to the Pole and return via Cape Morris Jesup?" Especially since we had learned that landing with skis in strange areas meant taking big risks. So it was decided.

Final preparations were completed on May 8. W. C. Haines, a meteorologist loaned us by the U. S. Weather Bureau, told us that the weather was right. Haines was a splendid weather man and a great shipmate.

We warmed the motors; heated our fuel oil; put the last bit of fuel and food aboard; examined our instruments with care. Bennett and I climbed in and we were off. Off, but alas, not up. Our load proved too great, the snow too "bumpy," the friction of the skis too strong a drag. The plane simply would not get into the air. It was an extremely anxious moment. We went a little too far and got off the end of the runway at a terrific speed, jolted roughly over snow hummocks and landed in a snowdrift, coming within an ace of upsetting, which, of course, would have smashed the plane.

A dozen of our men ran up to us weary, heartsick and speechless. They had worked almost to the limit of their endurance to give us our chance. I waded through the deep snow to the port landing gear. Great! Both it and the ski were O.K. Then I stumbled to the other side and found that they also had stood the terrible pounding.

My apprehension turned to joy, for I knew that if the landing apparatus would stand that strain we would eventually take off for the Pole with enough fuel to get there.

We took off hundreds of pounds of fuel to lighten the load; dug out of the snowdrift and taxied the *Josephine Ford* up the hill to try again. We held another council, and concluded to work through the night lengthening and smoothing the runway. At the same time we would take out of the plane as much equipment as we could spare, and attempt a take-off with a little less fuel.

One little discovery I made was interesting, also characteristic of the truly boyish spirit that prevailed throughout. In searching the plane for gear with which we might dispense and so lighten her, I found that nearly every man on the expedition had hidden some souvenir aboard. No doubt this weight was a factor in keeping us from taking off. However, I never did find a ukelele secreted aboard by the notorious "Ukelele Ike" Konter. He produced it out of the plane after we returned from the Pole and now has it back home as a wonderful souvenir of the trip.

It went against the grain to be severe about such trifles. But we were on the ragged edge of failure and couldn't spare an ounce of weight. As it was, we had cracked up three times in the snow already. One more smash and it would be all off. We had no more material out of which to makes skis. The last pair had been put together by enormously painstaking efforts of my artisans.

The weather was still perfect. We decided to try to get off as near midnight as possible, when the night cold would make the snow harder and therefore easier to take off from. Finally, at a half hour past midnight Greenwich time, all was in readiness to go. Bennett and I had had almost no sleep for 36 hours, but that did not bother us. Dr. O'Brien and Captain

Brennan begged us to get a good sleep before making another attempt. But our opportunity was at hand.

We carefully iced the runway in front of the skis (so that we could make a quick start), while Bennett and Kinkaid made their motor preparations. The crew put the finishing touches on the runway.

Bennett came up for a last talk and we decided to stake all on getting away—to give the *Josephine Ford* full power and full speed—and get off or crash at the end of the runway in the jagged ice.

A few handclasps from our comrades and we set our faces toward our goal and the midnight sun, which at that moment lay almost due north.

X.

Success
at Last!

WITH A TOTAL LOAD of nearly 10,000 pounds we raced down the runway. The rough snow ahead loomed dangerously near but we never reached it. We were off for our great adventure!

Beneath us were our shipmates—every one anxious to go along, but unselfishly wild with delight that we were at last off—running in our wake, waving their arms, and throwing their hats in the air. As long as I live I can never forget that sight, or those splendid fellows. They had given us our great chance.

For months previous to this hour, utmost attention had been paid to every detail that would assure our margin of safety in case of accident, and to the perfection of our scientific results in the case of success.

Success at Last!

We had a short-wave radio set operated by a hand dynamo, should we be forced down on the ice. A handmade sledge presented to us by Amundsen was stowed in the fuselage, on which to carry our food and clothing should we be compelled to walk to Greenland. We had food for ten weeks. Our main staple, pemmican, consisting of chopped-up dried meat, fat, sugar and raisins, was supplemented by chocolate, pilot-bread, tea, malted milk, powdered chocolate, butter, sugar and cream cheese, all of which form a highly concentrated diet.

Other articles of equipment were a rubber boat for crossing open leads if forced down, reindeer-skin, polar-bear and seal fur clothes, boots and gloves, primus stove, rifle, pistol, shotgun and ammunition; tent, knives, ax, medical kit and smoke bombs—all as compact as humanly possible.

If we should come down on the ice the reason it would take us so long to get back, if we got back at all, was that we could not return Spitzbergen way on account of the strong tides. We would have to march Etah way and would have to kill enough seal, polar-bear and musk-ox to last through the Arctic nights.

The first stage of our navigation was the simple one of dead reckoning, or following the well-known landmarks in the vicinity of Kings Bay, which we had just left. We climbed to 2000 feet to get a good view of the coast and the magnificent snow-covered mountains inland. Within an hour of taking the air we passed the rugged and glacier-laden land and crossed the edge of the polar ice pack. It was much nearer to the land than we had expected. Over to the east was a point where the ice field was very near the land.

We looked ahead at the sea ice gleaming in the rays of the midnight sun—a fascinating scene whose lure had drawn famous men into its clutches, never to return. It was with a feeling of exhilaration that we felt that for the first time in history two mites of men could gaze upon its charms, and discover its secrets, out of reach of those sharp claws.

Perhaps! There was still that "perhaps," for if we should have a forced landing disaster might easily follow.

It was only natural for Bennett and me to wonder whether or not we would ever get back to this small island we were leaving, for all the airmen explorers who had preceded us in attempts to reach the Pole by aviation had met with disaster or near disaster.

Though it was important to hit the Pole from the standpoint of achievement, it was more important to do so from that of our lives, so that we could get back to Spitzbergen, a target none too big. We could not fly back to land from an unknown position. We must put every possible second of time and our best concentration on the job of navigating and of flying a straight course—our very lives depended on it.

As there are no landmarks on the ice, Polar Sea navigation by aircraft is similar to that on the ocean, where there is nothing but sun and stars and moon from which to determine one's position. The altitude above the sea horizon of one of these celestial bodies is taken with the sextant. Then, by mathematical calculations, requiring an hour or so to work out, the ship is located somewhere on an imaginary line. The Polar Sea horizon, however, cannot always be depended upon, due to roughness of the ice. Therefore we had a specially designed instrument that would enable us to take the altitude without the horizon. I used the same instrument that we had developed for the 1919 trans-Atlantic flight.

Again, should the navigator of a fast airplane take an hour to get his line of position, by the time he plotted it on his chart he would be a hundred miles or so away from the point at which he took the sight. He must therefore have quick means of making his astronomical calculations.

We were familiar with one means of calculation which takes advantage of some interesting astronomical conditions existing at the North Pole. It is a graphical method that does away largely with mathematical calculations, so that the entire operation of taking the altitude of the sun and laying down the line of position could be done in a very few minutes.

This method was taught me by G. W. Littlebales of the Navy Hydrographic Office and was first discovered by Arthur Hinks of the Royal Geographic Society.

So much for the locating of position in the Polar Sea by astronomy, which must be done by the navigator to check up and correct the course steered by the pilot. The compass is generally off the true course a greater or less degree, on account of faulty steering, currents, wind, etc.

Our chief concern was to steer as nearly due north as possible. This could not be done with the ordinarily dependable magnetic compass, which points only in the general direction of the North Magnetic Pole, lying on Boothia Peninsula, Canada, more than a thousand miles south of the North Geographical Pole.

If the compass pointed exactly toward the Magnetic Pole the magnetic bearing of the North Geographical Pole could be calculated mathematically for any place on the Polar Sea. But as there is generally some local condition affecting the needle, the variation of the compass from true north can be found only by actual trial.

Since this trial could not have been made over unknown regions, the true directions the compass needle would point along our route were not known. Also, since the directive force of the earth's magnetism is small in the Far North, there is a tendency of the needle toward sluggishness in indicating a change in direction of the plane, and toward undue swinging after it has once started to move.

Nor would the famous gyroscopic compass work up there, as when nearing the Pole its axis would have a tendency to point straight up in the air.

There was only one thing to do—to depend upon the sun. For this we used a sun compass. The same type instrument that had been invented and constructed for our 1925 expedition by Albert H. Bumstead, chief cartographer of the National Geographic Society. I do not hesitate to say that without it we could not have reached the Pole; it is even doubtful if we could have hit Spitzbergen on our return flight.

Of course, the sun was necessary for the use of this compass. Its principle is a kind of a reversal of that of the sundial. In the latter, the direction of north is known and the shadow of the sun gives the time of day. With the sun compass, the time of day is known, and the shadow of the sun, when it bisects the hand of the 24-hour clock, indicates the direction after the instrument has been set.

Then there was the influence of the wind that had to be allowed for. An airplane, in effect, is a part of the wind, just as a ship in a current floats with the speed of the current. If, for example, a thirty-mile-an-hour wind is blowing at right angles to the course, the plane will be taken 30 miles an hour to one side of its course. This is called "drift" and can be compensated for by an instrument called the drift-indicator, which we had also developed for the first trans-Atlantic flight.

We used the drift-indicator through the trapdoor in the plane, and had so arranged the cabin that there was plenty of room for navigating. There was also a fair-sized chartboard.

As exact Greenwich time was necessary, we carried two chronometers that I had kept in my room for weeks. I knew their error to within a second. There seems to be a tendency for chronometers to slow up when exposed to the cold. With this in mind we had taken their cold-weather error.

As we sped along over the white field below I spent the busiest and most concentrated moments of my life. Though we had confidence in our instruments and methods, we were trying them for the first time over the Polar Sea. First, we obtained north and south bearings on a mountain range on Spitzbergen which we could see for a long distance out over the ice. These checked fairly well with the sun compass. But I had absolute confidence in the sun compass.

We could see mountains astern gleaming in the sun at least a hundred miles behind us. That was our last link with civilization. The unknown lay ahead.

Bennett and I took turns piloting. At first Bennett was steering, and for some unaccountable reason the plane veered from the course time and time again, to the right. He could glance back where I was working, through a door leading to the two pilots' seats. Every minute or two he would look at me, to be checked if necessary, on the course by the sun compass. If he happened to be off the course I would wave him to the right or left until he got on it again. Once every three minutes while I was navigating I checked the wind drift and ground speed, so that in case of a change in wind I could detect it immediately and allow for it.

We had three sets of gloves which I constantly changed to fit the job in hand, and sometimes removed entirely for short

First Command. Byrd, at 16, in the uniform of the Virginia Military Institute.

Tom, Dick and Harry Byrd. And Admiral Byrd's fox terrier Judy. For 18 years, these two were devoted and inseparable friends. The three famous Byrd brothers, seen here in an early portrait, served their state and country to a remarkable degree. By the time this photo appeared in the first edition of *Skyward* (1928), Tom (left) had won his captaincy on the Hindenburg Line; Harry (center) was Governor of Virginia; and Dick (right) had completed 20 years of distinguished service in the United States Navy.

Pals—Commander
Byrd and Violet.

Summer 1918. Halifax air station—officer personnel. Violet, the great dane,
is lying directly in front of Byrd in the center of the bottom row.

Filming at Spitzbergen by Pathé News as the Fokker was being prepared for its flight. Soon to become the first plane to fly over the North Pole, the *Josephine Ford* was named in honor of Edsel Ford's three-year-old daughter.

(Ohio State University Archives)

Camp at King's Bay. The spot was chosen because it was 750 miles from the Pole and the ice surrounding it was subject to the warming of the Gulf Stream, allowing for an April landing by ship.

(Ohio State University Archives)

ABOVE: Lieutenant A. N. Parker (left), Byrd (center) and Floyd Bennett (right) in front of the *Josephine Ford*. While Parker accompanied Byrd and Bennett on a trial flight, it was the latter two who reached the North Pole on May 9, 1926.

(Ohio State University Archives)

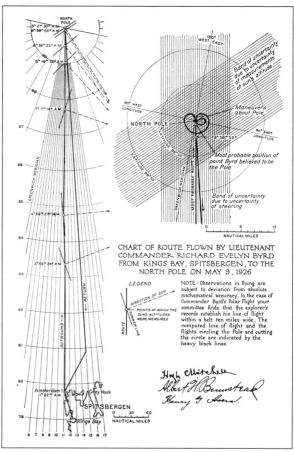

CHART OF ROUTE FLOWN BY LIEUTENANT COMMANDER RICHARD EVELYN BYRD FROM KINGS BAY, SPITSBERGEN, TO THE NORTH POLE ON MAY 9, 1926

LEGEND

NOTE: Observations in flying are subject to deviation from absolute mathematical accuracy. In the case of Commander Byrd's Polar Flight your committee finds that the explorer's records establish his line of flight within a belt ten miles wide. The computed line of flight and the flights circling the Pole and cutting the circle are indicated by the heavy black lines.

ABOVE: Home Again! Byrd and Bennett landing at Battery, New York, on the return from their North Pole flight. Later the duo marched up Broadway amid a paper snowstorm. *(AP/Wide World Photos)*

LEFT: Official mail carrier Richard E. Byrd being sworn in by the U. S. Post Office Department. *(Ohio State University Archives)*

Byrd with an injured Floyd Bennett, out of the hospital after the crash of the *America*. Bennett would not be able to make the trans-Atlantic flight. *(Ohio State University Archives)*

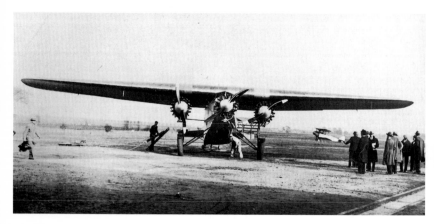

Paris bound. The *America* at Roosevelt Field in New York before its historic trans-Atlantic flight. Byrd and his crew left a month after Lindbergh began his journey from the same spot of land.

(Ohio State University Archives)

Byrd was welcomed as a hero in France. When the crew of the *America* reached Paris, the crowds were so great that many people were hurt and the car in which Byrd rode suffered broken fenders and windows.

(Ohio State University Archives)

Home Again—1927. Back to New York after his trans-Atlantic flight, Byrd was the first man in history to have two such triumphal homecomings. This would not be the last—he was already making plans to conquer Antarctica.

(AP/Wide World Photos)

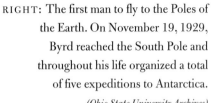

RIGHT: The first man to fly to the Poles of the Earth. On November 19, 1929, Byrd reached the South Pole and throughout his life organized a total of five expeditions to Antarctica.
(Ohio State University Archives)

BELOW: Skyward.
(Ohio State University Archives)

periods to write or figure on the chart. I froze my face and one of my hands in taking sights with the instruments from the trapdoors. But I noticed these frostbites at once and was more careful thereafter in the future. Ordinarily a frostbite need not be dangerous if detected in time and if the blood is rubbed back immediately into the affected parts. We also carried leather helmets that would cover the whole face when necessary to use them.

We carried two sun compasses. One was fixed to a trapdoor in the top of the navigator's cabin; the other was movable, so that when the great wing obscured the sun from the compass on the trapdoor, the second could be used inside the cabin, through the open windows.

Every now and then I took sextant sights of the sun to see where the lines of position would cross our line of flight. I was very thankful at those moments that the Navy requires such thorough navigation training, and that I had made air navigation my hobby.

Finally, when I felt certain we were on our course, I turned my attention to the great ice pack, which I had wondered about ever since I was a youngster at school. We were flying at about 2000 feet, and I could see at least 50 miles in every direction. There was no sign of land. If there had been any within 100 miles' radius we would have seen its mountain peaks, so good was the visibility.

The ice pack beneath was criss-crossed with pressure

ridges, but here and there were stretches that appeared long and smooth enough to land on. However, from 2000 feet pack ice is extraordinarily deceptive.

The pressure ridges that looked so insignificant from the plane varied from a few feet to 50 or 60 feet in height, while the average thickness of the ice was about 40 feet. A flash of sympathy came over me for the brave men who had in years past struggled northward over that cruel mass.

We passed leads of water recently opened by the movement of the ice, and so dangerous to the foot traveler, who never knows when the ice will open up beneath and swallow him into the black depths of the Polar Sea.

I now turned my mind to wind conditions, for I knew they were a matter of interest to all those contemplating the feasibility of a polar airway. We found them good. There were no bumps in the air. This was as we had anticipated, for the flatness of the ice and the Arctic temperature was not conducive to air currents, such as are sometimes found over land. Had we struck an Arctic gale, I cannot say what the result would have been as far as air roughness is concerned. Of course we still had the advantage of spring and 24-hour daylight.

It was time now to relieve Bennett again at the wheel, not only that he might stretch his legs, but so that he could pour gasoline into the tanks from the five-gallon tins stowed all over the cabin. Empty cans were thrown overboard to get rid of the weight, small though it was.

Frequently I was able to check myself on the course by holding the sun compass in one hand and steering with the other.

I had time now leisurely to examine the ice pack and eagerly sought signs of life, a polar-bear, a seal, or birds flying, but could see none.

On one occasion, as I turned to look over the side, my arm struck some object in my left breast pocket. It was filled with good-luck pieces!

I am not superstitious, I believe. No explorer, however, can go off without such articles. Among my trinkets was a religious medal put there by a friend. It belonged to his fiancée and he firmly believed it would get me through. There was also a tiny horseshoe made by a famous blacksmith. Attached to the pocket was a little coin taken by Peary, pinned to his shirt, on his trip to the North Pole.

When Bennett had finished pouring and figuring the gasoline consumption, he took the wheel again. I went back to the incessant navigating. So much did I sight down on the dazzling snow that I had a slight attack of snow blindness. But I need not have suffered, as I had brought along the proper kind of amber goggles.

Twice during the next two hours I relieved Bennett at the wheel. When I took it the fourth time, he smiled as he went aft. "I would rather have Floyd with me," I thought, "than any other man in the world."

We were now getting into areas never before viewed by mortal eye. The feelings of an explorer superseded the aviator's. I became conscious of that extraordinary exhilaration which comes from looking into virgin territory. At that moment I felt repaid for all our toil.

At the end of this unknown area lay our goal, somewhere beyond the shimmering horizon. We were opening unexplored regions at the rate of nearly 10,000 square miles an hour, and were experiencing the incomparable satisfaction of searching for new land. Once, for a moment, I mistook a distant, vague, low-lying cloud formation for the white peaks of a far-away land.

I had a momentary sensation of great triumph. If I could explain the feeling I had at this time, the much-asked question would be answered: "What is this Arctic craze so many men get?"

The sun was still shining brightly. Surely fate was good to us, for without the sun our quest of the Pole would have been hopeless.

To the right, somewhere, the rays of the midnight sun shone down on the scenes of Nansen's heroic struggles to reach the goal that we were approaching with the ease of an eagle at the rate of nearly 100 miles an hour. To our left lay Peary's oft-traveled trail.

When I went back to my navigating, I compared the magnetic compass with the sun compass and found that the westerly error in the former had nearly doubled since reaching the edge of the ice pack, where it had been eleven degrees westerly.

When our calculations showed us to be about an hour from the Pole, I noticed through the cabin window a bad leak in the oil tank of the starboard motor. Bennett confirmed my fears. He wrote: "That motor will stop."

Bennett then suggested that we try a landing to fix the leak. But I had seen too many expeditions fail by landing. We decided to keep on for the Pole. We would be in no worse fix should we come down near the Pole than we would be if we had a forced landing where we were.

When I took to the wheel again I kept my eyes glued on that oil leak and the oil-pressure indicator. Should the pressure drop, we would lose the motor immediately. It fascinated me. There was no doubt in my mind that the oil pressure would drop any moment. But the prize was actually in sight. We could not turn back.

At 9.02 A.M., May 9, 1926, Greenwich civil time, our calculations showed us to be at the Pole! The dream of a lifetime had at last been realized.

We headed to the right to take two confirming sights of the sun, then turned and took two more.

After that we made some moving and still pictures, then went on for several miles in the direction we had come, and made another larger circle to be sure to take in the Pole. We thus made a non-stop flight around the world in a very few minutes. In doing that we lost a whole day in time and of course when we completed the circle we gained that day back again.

Time and direction became topsy-turvy at the Pole. When crossing it on the same straight line we were going north one instant and south the next! No matter how the wind strikes you at the North Pole it must be traveling north and however you turn your head you must be looking south and our job was to get back to the small island of Spitzbergen which lay somewhere south of us!

There were two great questions that confronted us now: Were we exactly where we thought we were? If not—and could we be absolutely certain?—we would miss Spitzbergen. And even if we were on a straight course, would that engine stop? It seemed certain that it would.

As we flew there at the top of the world, we saluted the gallant, indomitable spirit of Peary and verified his report in every detail.

Below us was a great eternally frozen, snow-covered ocean, broken into ice fields or cakes of various sizes and shapes, the boundaries of which were the ridges formed by the great pressure of one cake upon another. This showed a constant ice movement and indicated the non-proximity of land. Here and there, instead of a pressing together of the ice fields, there was a separation, leaving a water-lead which had been recently frozen over and showing green and greenish-blue against the white of the snow. On some of the cakes were ice hummocks and rough masses of jumbled snow and ice.

At 9:15 A.M. we headed for Spitzbergen, having abandoned the plan to return via Cape Morris Jesup on account of the oil leak.

But, to our astonishment, a miracle was happening. That motor was still running. It is a hundred to one shot that a leaky engine such as ours means a motor stoppage. It is generally an oil lead that breaks. We afterward found out the leak was caused by a rivet jarring out of its hole, and when the oil got down to the level of the hole it stopped leaking. Flight Engineer Noville had put an extra amount of oil in an extra tank.

The reaction of having accomplished our mission, together with the narcotic effect of the motors, made us drowsy when we were steering. I dozed off once at the wheel and had to relieve Bennett several times because of his sleepiness.

I quote from my impressions cabled to the United States on our return to Kings Bay:

"The wind began to freshen and change direction soon after we left the Pole, and soon we were making over 100 miles an hour.

"The elements were surely smiling that day on us, two insignificant specks of mortality flying there over that great, vast, white area in a small plane with only one companion, speechless and deaf from the motors, just a dot in the center of 10,000 square miles of visible desolation.

"We felt no larger than a pinpoint and as lonely as the tomb; as remote and detached as a star.

"Here, in another world, far from the herds of people, the smallnesses of life fell from our shoulders. What wonder that we felt no great emotion of achievement or fear of death that lay stretched beneath us, but instead, impersonal, disembodied. On, on we went. It seemed forever onward.

"Our great speed had the effect of quickening our mental processes, so that a minute appeared as many minutes, and I realized fully then that time is only a relative thing. An instant can be an age, an age an instant."

We were aiming for Grey Point, Spitzbergen, and finally when we saw it dead ahead, we knew that we had been able to keep on our course! That we were exactly where we had thought we were!

It was a wonderful relief not to have to navigate any more. We came into Kings Bay flying at about 4000 feet. The tiny village was a welcome sight, but not so much so as the good old *Chantier* that looked so small beneath. I could see the steam from her welcoming and, I knew, joyous whistle.

It seemed but a few moments until we were in the arms of our comrades, who carried us with wild joy down the snow runway they had worked so hard to make.

Among the first to meet us had been Captain Amundsen and Lincoln Ellsworth, two good sports.

In a sentimental sense this ended the polar flight. But I was schooled too well in the troubles of other Arctic explorers to permit myself to believe that my job was done until I had the scientific approval of proper authorities.

Success at Last!

On my return to New York I sent a radio asking that an officer messenger come for my charts and records. The Navy Department complied. Through the Secretary of the Navy I submitted everything to the National Geographic Society. The papers were referred to a special committee of the Society, consisting of its President, Dr. Gilbert Grosvenor, the Chairman of its Research Committee, Dr. Frederick Coville, and Col. E. Lester Jones, a member of the Board of Trustees, who is also Director of the United States Coast and Geodetic Survey.

This committee appointed a sub-committee of expert mathematicians and calculators. The final report was submitted to the Secretary of the Navy and read in part as follows:

We have the honor of submitting the following report of our examination of Lieutenant Commander Richard Evelyn Byrd's "Navigation Report of Flight to Pole." We have carefully examined Commander Byrd's original records of his observations en route to and from the North Pole. These records are contained on two charts on which Commander Byrd wrote his observations, made his calculations, and plotted his positions. We have verified all his computations. We have also made a satisfactory examination of the sextant and sun-compass used by Commander Byrd.

At 8 hours 58 minutes 55 seconds May 9, 1926, an observation of the altitude of the sun gave a latitude of 80° 55.3′ on the meridian of flight. This point is 4.7 miles from the Pole. Continuing his flight on the same course and at the speed of 74 miles per hour, which he had averaged since 8 hours 18 minutes, would bring Commander Byrd close to the Pole in 3 minutes 49 seconds, making the probable time of his arrival at the Pole 9 hours 3 minutes, Greenwich civil time.

At the time Commander Byrd was close to the Pole he estimated the moment of his arrival there at 9 hours 2 minutes. Our calculations differ from his estimate less than one minute, during which time he would have flown about one mile. From this it appears that he chose the right place to maneuver.

Flying his plane to the right long enough to take two sextant observations, he turned around and took two more observations. These four observations confirmed his dead-reckoning position of the Pole. He then attempted to fly his plane in a circle several miles in diameter, with his Pole position as a center.

Flying at and about the Pole at an altitude of 3,000 feet, Commander Byrd's field of view was a circle more than 120 miles in diameter. The exact point of the North Pole was close to the center of this circle, and in his near foreground and during more than two hours of his flight was within his ken.

Soon after leaving the Pole, the sextant which Commander Byrd was using slid off the chart table, breaking the horizon glass. This made it necessary to navigate the return trip wholly by dead reckoning.

In accomplishing this, two incidents should be specially noted. At the moment when the sun would be crossing the 15th meridian, along which he had laid his course, he had the plane steadied, pointing directly toward the sun, and observed at the same instant that the shadow on the sun-compass was down the middle of the hand, thus verifying his position as being on that meridian. This had an even more satisfactory verification when, at about 14 hours 30 minutes, G.C.T., he sighted land dead ahead and soon identified Grey Point (Grey Hook), Spitzbergen, just west of the 15th meridian.

It is unfortunate that no sextant observations could be made on the return trip; but the successful landfall at Grey Hook demonstrates Commander Byrd's skill in navigating along a predetermined course, and in our opinion is one of the strongest evidences that he was equally successful in his flight northward.

The feat of flying a plane 600 miles from land and returning directly to the point aimed for is a remarkable exhibition of skillful navigation and shows beyond a reasonable doubt that he knew where he was at all times during the flight.

It is the opinion of your committee that at very close to 9 hours 3 minutes, Greenwich civil time, May 9, 1926, Lieutenant Commander Richard Evelyn Byrd was at the North Pole, insofar as an observer in an airplane, using the most accurate instruments and methods available for determining his position, could ascertain.

PUBLISHER'S NOTE

We have secured the author's permission to introduce at this point what we consider an essential part of the record: viz., report of presentation of the Hubbard Medal in Washington, and the President's speech on this occasion. Later the thanks of Congress were given Byrd and he was promoted to the rank of Commander, U. S. Navy, and the Congressional Medal of Honor presented.

In the presence of 6000 members and friends of the National Geographic Society, including the President of the United States, members of the Cabinet, distinguished Army and Navy officers, members of Congress, ambassadors and ministers of foreign countries, and other representatives of official life in the National Capital, Commander Richard Evelyn Byrd, Jr., received the Society's Hubbard Gold Medal in the Washington Auditorium on the evening of his return to America, June 23, after his flight to the North Pole.

On the same occasion the explorer's associate, Aviation Pilot Floyd Bennett, also received a gold medal. Only six other men have ever received the Hubbard Medal. They were Admiral (then Commander) Robert E. Peary, Captain Roald Amundsen, Vilhjalmur Stefansson, Captain Ernest H. Shackleton, Grove Karl Gilbert, and Capt. Robert A. Bartlett.

President Coolidge in presenting the medals said:

Word that the North Pole had been reached by airplane for the first time was flashed around the globe on May 9. An American naval officer had flown over the top of the world. He had attained in a flight of fifteen hours and thirty minutes what Admiral Peary, also a representative of our Navy, achieved, seventeen years before, only after weary months of travel over the frozen Arctic wastes.

The thrill following the receipt of this news was shared by everyone everywhere. It was the spontaneous tribute to a brave man for a daring feat. We, his countrymen, were particularly proud. This man, with a record of distinguished service in the development of aeronautics, had by his crowning act added luster to the brilliant history of the American Navy.

In no way could we have had a more striking illustration of the scientific and mechanical progress since the year 1909. Then Peary's trip to the Pole on dog sleds took about two-thirds of a year. He reached his goal on April 6. It was September 6 before news of the achievement reached the outside world.

The naval officer of 1926, using an American invention, the airplane, winged his way from his base, at Kings Bay,

Spitzbergen, and back again in less than two-thirds of a day; and a few hours later the radio had announced the triumph to the four quarters of the earth. Scientific instruments perfected by this navigator and one by a representative of this organization were in no small degree responsible for success.

We cannot but admire the superb courage of the man willing to set forth on such a great adventure in the unexplored realms of the air; but we must not forget, nor fail to appreciate, the vision and persistence which led him ultimately to achieve the dream of his Naval Academy days. He never ceased the effort to prepare himself mentally, scientifically, and physically to meet the supreme test. His deed will be but the beginning of scientific exploration considered difficult of achievement before he proved the possibilities of the airplane.

Lieutenant Commander Richard Evelyn Byrd, your record as an officer and as a man is illustrious. You have brought things to pass. It is particularly gratifying to me to have this privilege of welcoming you home and of congratulating you on behalf of an admiring country, and to have the honor of presenting to you the Hubbard Medal of the National Geographic Society.

And I take further pleasure in presenting to you, Mr. Floyd Bennett, aviation pilot, U. S. N., this medal, awarded to you by the National Geographic Society for your distinguished service in assisting and in flying to the North Pole with Mr. Byrd.

XI.

This
Hero Business

BEFORE THE *CHANTIER* had steamed many miles toward home, I began to realize that we had stirred up something by flying to the Pole. First there were radios of congratulation and good wishes. Then radios of inquiry. And finally, radios that literally ordered me to do things I had never even dreamed of doing, couldn't do even if I wanted—such as make a speech at three different banquets, to be held in three different cities on one and the same night. I felt rather stunned about it; but, of course, greatly appreciative.

It was all more of a surprise than people could realize. To go back for a moment: When I broke my leg at Annapolis I was only trying to best the other fellow. When I crowded into aviation during the war I was only satisfying my great desire to fly and at the same time doing what any patriotic American would do to help his country. When I took charge of the navigational preparations of the Navy's trans-Atlantic flight in 1919, I believed I was contributing to my service and to the art of flying. I felt pretty much the same about my Greenland work and during my preparations to fly to the North Pole.

Now I discovered that success of our flight from Spitzbergen touched some responsive public chord which loosed a torrent of attention upon me and my expedition. I was much pleased, of course. But I was also astonished, and secretly worried. My fear was that personal notoriety might overlay the good I had hoped to do for aviation.

I wondered exactly what it all meant. What I ultimately found out about "being a hero" gave me almost as much of a "kick" as did the sensation of circling the Pole.

We arrived at New York on the morning of June 22, 1926. We were met by the mayor's official tug, the *Macom,* on board of which were several official welcoming committees, a delegation of senators and representatives from Congress, a regiment of newspaper reporters, and enough photographers to man a battleship.

For half an hour I was tossed about like a leaf in a storm. Then a friend cornered me. I could see he was laboring under high tension. He spoke feverishly:

"We arrive at the Battery at noon. You will be presented with a medal and the keys to the city at twelve-fifteen. You will make two speeches in reply. At lunch you will make another speech. At four-thirty-two we leave for Washington. On arrival you will be met by a committee of welcome. Twenty minutes later President Coolidge will present you with a gold medal. You will make a speech—"

"But I'm not a speech maker," I protested.

My friend seemed to grind his teeth. "Makes not the slightest difference," he snapped. "You are now a national hero. You—"

I felt myself whirled bodily about. "Look up, Commander. Stick an eye on that airplane up there," yelled someone.

Involuntarily I glanced skyward. Twenty cameras clicked.

A heavy man jostled against me. "I want you to meet the president of the—" He didn't finish. I found myself grasping the hand of an important-looking individual.

"You are a national hero," he declared. "I am pleased—"

"Be sure you speak of leaving this port in the mayor's speech," broke a hoarse whisper in one ear. My feverish friend again.

Before I could answer, the broad-shouldered chairman of the reception committee elbowed his way in.

"Excuse me, Commander, but these fellows want a picture of you and your mother." Ten more cameras infiltrated through the crowd. I began to feel like a promising halfback who has to carry the ball at every down. Things began to be going more rapidly. Between the erupting fireboats, the airplanes and the yacht escorts I felt a stiff neck coming on. The whistles were deafening.

All of this was entirely unexpected. I felt bewildered. But

most grateful that the nation should do all this for us. Of course, I didn't take it all to myself. Far from it. There was Bennett by my side who deserved equally with me and perhaps more. Then there were our half hundred shipmates who had unselfishly put every ounce of their strength and energy into the job. Then my thought dwelt on the dozen or so other men who had formed necessary links in our success.

The scene at the Battery resembled a riot. A parade was formed. As we passed up Broadway the air grew thick with a blizzard of paper streamers and confetti. The sidewalks were packed with people. Traffic stopped.

The City Hall was surrounded by a dense mass of humanity. A cordon of mounted police kept open just enough space to let our party pass. We wound up into the ceremonial chambers. The auditorium was jammed to its doors. The oratory began. . . .

And so on all that day, ending with President Coolidge's presentation in Washington that night. And all the next day. And the next, and the next. The high point came in Richmond, Virginia, my native state. Thousands turned out the night we arrived. There were glare-lights, speeches and brass bands; a swirling friendly multitude.

What did it mean? I asked myself the question; but could find no answer. I asked my friends. But all they would reply was the same refrain in one form or another, "Don't you know you are a national hero now?"

Of course I realized that an adventure like our polar flight aroused great public interest. I knew before I left that there would be a certain amount of risk in crossing the polar ice, just as there is in any flight over an unknown terrain. I had a notion that such a stunt is great stuff for the publicity people.

But my idea of a national hero was somebody like George Washington or John J. Pershing. They had held the safety of our country in their hands. They had suffered the agony of long campaigns. They had led armies to victory against a public enemy.

We hadn't done anything so valiant.

"But what is a national hero, and why?" I asked a newspaper friend of mine.

"Oh, someone who's worth two columns and a front-page streamer, fireboats and a basket of medals," came the cynical reply.

But I wasn't satisfied; not when I thought of the thousands of American citizens who had grasped my hand since my return; and of the tens of thousands of jubilant letters and telegrams that had reached me.

No, there was something more, something deeper.

The first inkling of the great discovery came in Washington just before I faced the President and a large audience of distinguished diplomats. I had never spoken before so august an assemblage. To rehearse some of the thoughts that crowded my mind, I managed to sneak away for a few moments in the stage wings of the giant auditorium where the ceremony was being held. I stood in a little bare alcove glancing over my notes. Suddenly a door behind me opened, then softly closed. I turned. Facing me stood a little white-haired lady in black bonnet and gown. Despite the age in her face, her eyes were brown and bright. They looked into mine unblinking.

"You are Commander Byrd?" she asked.

"Yes, madam."

She came a step forward in a sudden wistful eagerness. "And you reached the North Pole?"

"There seems to be no doubt of it."

Her lips parted as if to speak again. But before she could utter a word an abrupt change came over her. She gave a quick sigh. Her mouth trembled. She thrust out one hand as if to touch me. Her eyes dimmed and filled. Then she cried out:

"Oh, I'm so glad!" Before I could stop her she was gone.

I heard a step behind me. "All right, Byrd." The same irritating whiplash of necessity that notoriety brings. "The President is arriving. You will have to go on the stage at once."

I went on the stage. But the mystery of the little lady in black clung to me. I espied her in the audience. I managed to inquire about her during a lull in the ponderous proceedings of the evening.

"Poor thing," whispered my informant. "She's had a tough break in life. Lost her husband twenty years ago. Brought up two fine boys on what she could make herself. Lost both of them in the World War. Now she's all alone."

In a flash of understanding I knew something of the answer to my question: What is a national hero?

I was a hero to that sad little mother, but not in a way the word is usually used. No doubt she admired us for having succeeded. Probably the story of it all gave her daily newspaper a fresh flavor. Possibly she speculated over what it felt like to fly. But those weren't the things that made her seek me out and face me first-hand with her gladness.

What that mother saw in me was the living memory of her husband and sons. They had been splendid men. I later learned that they had been adventurous and so were the kind who would have liked to have flown to the North Pole. They were fine, keen, courageous men. And if they were all that to the passing acquaintance who retailed their virtues to me, what demigods must they have been to that little white-haired lady.

To her I was the living flesh she so longed to touch. I, she knew, was son and husband. Now she would sit out there among a great throng and listen while the President of the United States extolled Bennett and me, even as she might have sat and listened had Fate been equally generous to her.

It may sound incredible, but in that moment I got the philosophy of the thing. I had been human in my home-coming. The grand public welcome had moved me, though I had felt humble and more or less undeserving of such recognition. I had had to pinch myself every now and then to see if it were all true. I had felt like a man who had unexpectedly reached a mountain top and finds a gorgeous panorama spread before his eyes. I had wanted to throw my hat in the air and shout, "Gosh, but this is great!"

Now, in a trice, another man's mother had wiped away my smug acceptance of unexpected fame.

My memory sprang back to Annapolis days. I recalled the first time I marched down the town street as color bearer. The band was playing. As I passed, men uncovered, ladies applauded, children waved their hands. I was stirred by this show of admiration. Pride filled me. I seemed walking on the air. I felt brave, superior, triumphant. Then with a thump, came the truth. People weren't saluting and cheering me. They were saluting the Stars and Stripes which I carried.

Exactly that was happening now. The cheers and the handclasps, the waving hats and flags, the music and the speeches, weren't really meant for me any more now than that boyhood morning in Annapolis when I marched at the head of the procession holding aloft the flag of my country. The banner I carried now wasn't so visible, nor easily painted. It didn't in its symbolism depict the stormy history of a people. It never would stir a nation to righteous indignation against an invader. It couldn't be nailed to the mast of a sinking ship.

No, my banner was none of these. In our success people saw success that might have been their own. In Bennett and me mothers saw their sons, wives their husbands, sisters their brothers. In us men saw what they too might have done had they had the chance. In us youth saw ambition realized.

In us America for the moment dramatized that superb world-conquering fire which is American spirit. For the moment we seemed to have caught up the banner of American progress. For the moment we appeared to typify to them the spirit of America.

It was great to think that, even for these precious moments, we were destined to carry the banner.

Was I proud? Of course. But humble, grateful. There were a half hundred members of our expedition who deserved equally with me to carry that banner.

Now that my eyes were opened I began to look about for more manifestations of this discovery of mine. I went to the Middle West to lecture. In a small town off the beaten track I stopped for a one-night stay. A leading citizen drove me about just before sunset.

"We are very proud of our parkways," he said. "They are all built by personal contribution. Those who can't give money contribute their services. By the way, the engineer of our steam roller told me the other day he hoped I'd introduce him to you when you came here."

"Why not see him now?" I suggested. The thought of the people building their home town's boulevards by pure community spirit appealed to my imagination.

We drove to a frame bungalow near the edge of the town. Two urchins hung on the gates of an untidy yard. A tired-looking woman with a kindly smile met us at the door. Two more urchins clung to her skirt.

"Come right in. Jim's just back from the factory. He'll be out soon's he's changed his shirt."

Jim came in wiping his hands. He was tall and lean. His whole face lit up when his townsman introduced me.

"Commander Byrd speaks at eight," said my escort. "Don't forget." Jim nodded, his eyes fixed on my face. His wife must have felt the strain of the situation; her husband's sudden inarticulate silence.

She made a few irrelevant remarks, then suddenly turned to him: "Jim, tell Commander Byrd about your invention."

Jim flushed. He began to talk, haltingly at first, about a scheme for vertical flight, a sort of helicopter. He had a small workshop out in the woodshed. He was building a model of his device.

"You ought to get someone to back you," I told him. "If the idea is practicable the right sort of engineering assistance will put it through in no time."

"But that isn't it." Jim put up his hands as if to shape the thought he could not accurately convey in words.

His wife broke in with, "I told him that very thing."

Jim's fingers groped. He said:

"It isn't a question of money. It's somebody to look ahead and see what we're coming to." The words were tumbling out now. "All they think of is profits. One man turned me down because he said it wouldn't pay dividends this year.

"Another said he'd pay me a big lump sum if I'd give him what I'd worked out so far. They're both wrong.

"I want to move slowly. The Wrights did when they started. They could have sold out early to an amusement company. We wouldn't have been flying today if they had."

The wife was angry now. "Don't go on like that," she said.

But Jim could not be stopped. I didn't want to stop him. He poured out his whole story, a lifetime of struggle and hard work. Yet he could not sacrifice his idea for quick gain.

We had to break away before he finished. As we drove back my friend the leading citizen said: "I have known him for years. That is the first time he has ever loosened up. You see what it is, of course. He thinks you would do the same as he is doing if you were in his boots. I believe your visit helped him."

That gave me my second cue to appreciation of my discovery, and again I felt humble and grateful. Listening became one of the best things I did. What a paradox it was too! I had always looked on the returned explorer as a sort of traveling oracle. True, people seemed to like my films of the flight and politely followed my yarn of how we reached the Pole and returned. There were speeches of introduction beforehand, and handshaking afterward. But these were routine. The interesting moments I looked forward to were where someone got me off in a corner and told his story.

These stories were superior to mine. Mine was hemmed in by realities like time and distance, whereas the others were usually bounded only by the elastic horizon of human imagination.

It would take a dozen thick volumes to record all my experiences that confirm that discovery I had made in Washington. My mail alone in the months since my return contains a thousand stories of human happiness, hope and heartbreak.

"Why don't you get out a form letter thanking these people who write you?" suggested an efficient friend of mine.

Coincidence played into my hands. I handed him two letters I had just opened. "Read these and you will understand."

He read aloud:

Dear Captain Byrd: You never heard of me, and will probably never see me. I keep house for my two brothers. Our mother and father are dead. It may sound silly to tell you such things, but all last winter we have had a hard time. One of my brothers lost his job. The other had an abscess on his back and couldn't work for several months. Then we began reading about your plans and later about your fine trip to the North Pole. I have to work so much there is no chance to get about. We have lived your adventures with you. It has been fun and I want to thank you and wish you luck on your next flight.

Then he read the other letter which was typical of thousands I had received from boys and girls:

My dear Commander: I like you. I like your trip to the North Pole. I have made a model of the *Josephine Ford.* Will you please put your name on a piece of paper so that I can paste it on my little airplane. I hope you get across the Atlantic all right. I know you will. I will be reading about you.

My friend tossed the letters back. "Sounds like testimonials for a patent medicine," he said skeptically.

"It might," said I, "if there were only these two. But there are hundreds. Many talk like that when I meet them. The adventures have a real meaning to many people and to all the great youngsters."

"Well you're a national hero, aren't you? Isn't that what does it?"

I looked him in the eye. "I'm really only carrying the banner for a little while," said I.

He looked at me as if I had suddenly lost my mind. "The what?"

A tumult in the street below our window put an end to our talk. We looked out. I knew what was happening.

In the sunshine flags twinkled. Black ribbons of humanity lined the avenue. At upper windows were crowding faces. Extra traffic men pranced to and fro. Long gay streamers of confetti floated down from the skyscrapers. A band flashed into view. The quick march it played was the music of victory. Uniformed ranks swung rhythmically behind the band. Then came a column of automobiles.

In the leading car, framed with flowers, stood a sturdy youthful figure, arms outstretched to the cheering multitude. It was Gertrude Ederle.

I leaned far out. I wanted to shout a message, to deliver something I had been holding.

I wanted to shout: "Here is the banner!" and cast that invisible something into the outstretched hands of the girl in the leading car.

But I did not need to. The lusty throats of ten thousand Americans were shouting my message. And the banner was already in the hands of its next fortunate bearer.

That's what this hero business means.

XII.

Trans-Atlantic Flight

FOR TWELVE YEARS I had been dreaming of a flight across the Atlantic Ocean. The NC boats had done the trick in stages. The R-34, the airship which had flown from England to New York and return, was not an airplane. No one had as yet crystallized my dream into a single successful nonstop flight from New York to Europe.

When we hoisted anchor at Spitzbergen after the North Pole flight I turned to Bennett and said:

"Now we can fly the Atlantic."

To which he replied: "I hope you take me with you."

"We go together," I retorted, not knowing that cruel circumstances would prevent my ever carrying out this promise.

I have decided to go into details for the first time about the trans-Atlantic flight of the *America*.

Thirty valuable lives were lost in trans-oceanic flights last summer. Aviation lost some of its best flyers. But it was not aviation's fault that so many brave men were lost. They were pioneering. Enough sacrifice has been made. My purpose in facing facts is to show reasons why disaster is preventable and so prevent a recurrence of many similar deaths in the future of trans-oceanic flying.

I want to say with emphasis that commercial aviation should not suffer on account of these pioneer flights.

I am going to speak out in plain words which I so often wished I could use in the summer of 1927:

"I have spent years planning and thinking about this trans-Atlantic flight problem," was my constant feeling about the poor fellows who were going to their deaths. "I know some of you are going to kill yourselves for you haven't prepared properly."

Yet shouting this in the newspapers after our successful flight in the *America* would only have unsaid it. I would have been accused of poor sportsmanship and egotism. I tried every other way to stop them but they were fixed with some spirit that would not be quenched.

WHILE CROSSING THE ATLANTIC returning from Spitzbergen Bennett and I discussed types of planes at great length. We wanted to be scientific, to point the way for the trans-Atlantic plane of the future, to the practical way of crossing the Atlantic commercially. I knew from past conversations on the subject, that many good aeronautical men at home would favor our using a single-engined plane. We had a number of single-engined planes that could cross the Atlantic; and engines were already reliable enough for the flyer to put considerable trust in them. But we did not want our flight to be a matter of chance. We felt that if we could fly to Europe in a machine that would be a precursor of the practical trans-Atlantic plane of the future we would be contributing more to the progress of ocean flying.

I knew that it had long been the desire of Rodman Wanamaker to send an airplane to Paris. He felt deeply the value of such a flight to international goodwill. He was a lifelong friend of France and had for years lived in Paris. Hence the destination he chose for his project was the French capital. I had always felt the same way about the goodwill aspects of such a flight. The disaster to the ZR-2 showed what aviation, even in tragedy, could do for international good fellowship. I knew that in success it could do still more.

For years as I contemplated this project it had given me much pleasure to formulate in my mind messages of friendship to drop over England. My relations with Englishmen during the war had been extremely pleasant. Even before that I had cause to be grateful to England. While on a cruise once during sea duty I had been carried from one of our battleships, on a stretcher in a most desperate condition, to the

Royal Naval Hospital at Plymouth. I pulled out by the skin of my teeth and I owed my recovery to the extraordinary and friendly care the English gave me.

I had no difficulty in gaining Mr. Wanamaker's approval and backing for our plan for a New York to Paris flight. It was his wish that we build an entirely new plane at his expense. But I foresaw the chance of hitting on a design that would not be practicable on first production. There are always many kinks to get out of an entirely new design. So I stuck to the type which had successfully carried Bennett and me over the Pole, only we planned a bigger plane.

As we had thought, there rose much criticism against taking a multi-engined plane. A machine with a single engine, it was pointed out, would have a longer cruising radius; would be cheaper to run; would have less resistance in the air; and its one engine would be a great deal less care before we started—nothing like so complicated as the great three-engined plane. This was all true, I had to admit. It seems extraordinary that a small one-engined plane has a bigger cruising radius than a big three-engined plane. Unfortunately, the airplane is not like a steamer, where the bigger the ship, the longer the ship can cruise.

We had just a single powerful demurrer to make to all these points; if anything went wrong with a single engine the expedition would end then and there, and the prestige of aviation, we felt, would be damaged in the public mind.

How many times we have been glad that we clung to this

theory. For it was want of just the lack of this extra engining that I think had much to do with the long list of tragedies in the fatal ocean flights which followed ours.

Mr. Wanamaker, whom I have found to be a very patriotic man, decided to name the plane the *America* after a trans-Atlantic plane he had built in 1914.

It gives me much pleasure to mention the quality of the backing we got from Mr. Wanamaker. He denied us nothing we needed and the experimental nature of the expedition made it a very expensive proposition indeed. He assigned Mr. Grover Whalen of New York City as his representative and Whalen did everything that was humanly possible for the expedition.

From a scientific standpoint there were a lot of things we wanted to prove by the flight of the *America* that would help point the way for the regular trans-Atlantic flyer. It would take a whole book to cover that aspect of our flight. But I will discuss here some of our experiments that we hoped would bring us very near the trans-Atlantic plane of the future.

In the winter of 1926 the Atlantic Aircraft Corporation set about building the *America*. It was to be a big three-engined plane similar to our North Pole machine, except that it had an increase in the wing spread from 63 to 71 feet. With this extra surface we expected to be able to get off the ground with at least 3000 pounds more than we had taken on the North Pole flight.

This extra capacity would permit us to take fuel for our

very long flight and 800 pounds of equipment over and above that which was absolutely necessary. We wanted to show that some pay load could be carried across the Atlantic. We took a special radio set, as well as a water-proof installation in case of a forced landing; two rubber boats for the crew; and emergency food and equipment of all sorts; Very's pistols for night signalling, etc., etc. Also we wanted to take three or four people to demonstrate that passengers could even now be taken across the Atlantic.

We even went in for a kite with which our wireless antennæ would be kept in the air if we settled on the ocean; and which would act as a sail to pull the plane along at the same time. We put in an extra sextant and hand compasses for navigating. Our food was a scientifically worked out ration that would permit us to subsist for at least three weeks. We had a special apparatus that would make water so that we would not thirst to death.

I was sworn in by the Post Office Department as the first trans-Atlantic air mail pilot and we carried the first bag of U. S. air mail from the States to France.

In addition to the preparation mentioned above, we had built a big 1200-gallon gasoline tank. The building of that great gas tank designed to carry over 7000 pounds of gasoline was an interesting experiment. We put a dump valve in it. This was the first time such a device was used in aviation. Its purpose was to empty our fuel in a few seconds in case we saw we were going to crash. There is a vast difference between a forced landing on rough ground with a light load, and such a landing with a very heavy load. Also the empty tank would give flotation in case we landed in the ocean. Then it gave another great advantage; if an engine should stop we could dump gasoline down to the point where we could fly on two engines.

Bennett designed a switch that would cut out all three engines at once. This was also a fire prevention device and one that later saved our lives, as I shall presently show.

We had a catwalk built from our fusilage leading to the outboard engines. By means of this a man could get out and work on a dead engine while the plane continued to fly. This was a new departure in plane design, and one we hoped that was a step forward.

Our radio set was devised especially for our flight by Malcolm P. Hanson and L. A. Hyland, in the Naval Research Laboratory at Washington, with a view to the greatest possible sending range for its weight. We wanted to prove that we could locate ourselves at sea with radio.

One of the most interesting features of our radio was the automatic sending device, by which call letters were repeated constantly, at the rate of about ten complete calls a minute on a prearranged wave length.

Then we carried a small water-proof set to use in case we should come down in the ocean. Surely the plane of the future would need such a set.

The next important matter had been the meteorology.

There was no suitable trans-Atlantic meteorological service and this had to be devised. Long ago Lieutenant-Commander Noel Davis and I had requested the Secretary of Agriculture to give us the cooperation of the United States Weather Bureau. This was granted. The bureau needed reports of conditions over the Atlantic, so we requested the Radio Corporation of America to procure radio reports from sea going ships, which they did magnanimously and patriotically.

The Weather Bureau assigned Dr. James H. Kimball, of its New York office, to make weather predictions for the trans-Atlantic flights and, for the first time in history, regular weather maps for aviation uses were made of the North Atlantic. This work, I think, undoubtedly is the beginning of a valuable meteorological service. I was further assisted by Mr. Roswell Barrett of New York, who received reports from Dr. Kimball and spent many nights with me studying weather conditions. Mr. Rossby, an expert of the Weather Bureau, also conferred with us.

We devoted some time to the study of a proper take-off field for a trans-Atlantic flight. The biggest field available around New York was the Roosevelt Field on Long Island. Mr. Grover Whalen leased it and we set about developing it for the heavy loads the long distance plane must carry.

Next to the plane, the take-off field was the most important consideration. It is the swinging of very heavy loads in the air that makes long distance flights difficult. A very long run and high speeds are necessary to get off the ground. The bigger and the more heavily loaded the plane, the longer the run.

René Fonck used a three-engined plane and one of the things that made for his fatal accident was the irregularity and shortness of the runway he had to use. We repaired this same runway and took out its worst bumps and soft spots. Day after day I personally went over every inch of the ground, striving for the same smoothness that we got on our Spitzbergen snow-way, and which finally had made the North Pole flight possible.

Even with a very smooth field and the biggest one within a radius of hundreds of miles, the field was not, we thought, big enough.

What could we do!

After many conferences we got the answer. Some one suggested building a little hill. Great! We had taken off going down hill with skis on the North Pole flight. Surely it would work with wheels. It did! We built the hill and got in effect at least 500 feet to the end of the runway by the fast initial start it gave us.

And this can solve the problem of cities that have small fields without chance of expansion.

With preparations as complete as this I felt that we would be hopping off equipped as nearly as possible for a practical commercial air travel between Europe and America. The next step would be to use pontoons instead of wheels. The reason we used land planes last summer instead of seaplanes was because, on account of the weight and resistance of the pontoon or boat, we could not quite make the necessary distance.

Things were going merrily along by the middle of March, when I ran into an altogether unexpected complication. Several other trans-Atlantic flights were being planned. Noel Davis, René Fonck, Charles Lindbergh, Clarence Chamberlin and nearly a dozen others announced their intentions of flying across the Atlantic Ocean from New York to Paris.

This was not exactly news. I knew they had been preparing. Each had his own ideas. We were working toward a workable commercial plane, while the others were no doubt interested also in that phase. Some of them were competing to be first to reach Paris to win the Orteig Prize of $25,000, which we were not. We didn't even enter our names.

As a result there was competition between them, but hardly between them and us. Mr. Wanamaker was very clear on this point; so were Bennett and the others attached to my camp.

Despite this, the first thing I knew I had been projected into what was euphemistically called by the press the "Great 1927 New York-to-Paris Air Derby." I admit it would have been gratifying to be first across; but that was only a secondary consideration with us. So we repeatedly said we were in no race, though the public insisted that we were.

On the surface, such a canard would seem to have no bearing on my work. But this country of ours is so large and its press so powerful that sway of public opinion can easily make a terrific difference. I think it may be compared to the swelling of the sea which carries the seaweed far below its surface to and fro.

My desire was to keep quiet our plans, do the best we could and then make the flight if possible. This would avoid hurting aviation if we failed. Now I found that my inclination to be quiet was looked on as a conspiracy of silence directed against my so-called competitors in the race who were really my friends whom I was rooting for.

Then there was another very important factor; in trying to point towards the trans-Atlantic plane of the future, our work was necessarily experimental—pioneering. We knew all about lifting heavy loads with single-engined planes but very little indeed about load lifting with a great three-engined plane. We knew we were taking big risks though, of course, we expected no recognition of this fact from the public. It was possible that we might find that we couldn't fly the distance necessary to go from New York to France. Should there be a great deal of publicity and then should we have to admit the plane couldn't make the distance, aviation would be hurt. We didn't want to hurt the game we were trying to help.

I was shadowed. Questions were put my family and friends about me to find out what I had "up my sleeve." Exaggerations and rumors flew about thick and fast. Caustic criticism of other entrants was attributed to me. Presently I found that instead of being a technical explorer I was some sort of frenzied political candidate. At least that was the impression I got.

As I would not speak, exaggerated things were published right and left, and so I was finally forced to break my silence. In dismay, I asked Mr. Wanamaker to employ a "public relations" man to get the "straight dope." I must add that I think representatives of the press, later on when I had a chance to explain things, sympathized with my position. But at that time their owners and editors had to get news. The public demanded it, due to its great interest in the forthcoming flight.

This passing phase of the venture is worthy of mention if only because it is one of the truly American phenomena that a man in public notice is forced to encounter and deal with as best he can.

On April 20, 1927, our plane was ready for the factory test. It was through no especial effort that we were many weeks ahead of all the others planning to fly the Atlantic. We wanted to make the flight in May when we would have the full moon. Our plan had no doubt gone smoothly because it was years old with me.

Having received word from the factory at Hasbrouck Heights, N. J., that the designer was ready to take his machine up for its first flight, I sent for Noville and Bennett to join me. Some of my friends tried to dissuade me from the flight. The plane was brand new and had not been in the air yet. But I did not want to accept the plane without personally observing its performance.

We got off all right. Fokker was at the controls; the other three of us were passengers.

So long as the engines were running everything went all right. But the moment they were cut off the plane felt nose heavy. Noville and I saw Bennett licking his lips. This is the only sign Bennett gives when he is nervous—which, I may say, is very rare. I nudged Noville and nodded toward Bennett.

Fokker brought the plane down for a landing. But when he slowed up to touch the ground again came unmistakable signs that the plane was nose heavy. He took her up again for another turn and to think over what we had better do.

As we had very little fuel we couldn't stay up long. And as there was no way to shift weights we could not help ourselves. We couldn't get aft on account of our great 1300 gallon tank— another experiment—that filled the fuselage aft of us. Fokker brought her down within a few feet of the ground. I caught hold of a steel upright just back of Fokker's seat—kept my gaze concentrated on the air speed meter. We were going a mile a minute. The wheels touched the ground. Instantly I saw Fokker rise and make frantic efforts to jump out. Bennett was trapped as Fokker occupied the only exit. There was no way Noville and I could even try to get out.

With all my strength I clung to the heavy steel upright. Abruptly the body of the fusilage rose under us. In a flash we knew she was going completely over. There came a terrific crash. It sounded as if every inch of the plane were being crushed to kindling. Something struck me a stunning blow on my head and in the small of my back. It was Noville thrown forward from the sudden stop. The impact snapped my arm like a match stick. Then dead silence.

"Look out for fire!" cried a strained voice. I learned afterward this was Bennett, caught in the wreckage. Noville and I, jumbled together with broken rods, frames, seats and other gear, scrambled to our feet to find ourselves trapped. With my broken arm and bruised body I was of little use. Noville wildly broke a hole through the fabric wall with his bare fist. Both of us were thinking of Fonck's similar crash in which his men inside the plane were trapped and burned to death before they could escape.

Noville dove through the hole and fell on the ground in great agony. He was injured internally. I followed.

There was no fire. Someone at the last instant had the presence of mind to pull Bennett's switch, cutting off all three engines.

I rushed to Bennett. He was hanging head downward, held by the wreckage of the pilot's seat. It certainly looked as if he had "got his" at last. His leg was badly broken and his face streaming blood. He was drenched with oil.

It seemed tough to get it on a trial flight after all we had been through.

I leaned over him and told him who I was. He tried to open his eyes but couldn't.

"Guess I'm done for, Commander," he said weakly. "I'm all broken up. I can't see and I have no feeling in my left arm."

"Nonsense, old man," I came back quickly, but was sure he was right.

Presently I noticed that his eyes were filled with oil. When I wiped the oil away he could see. It was a great relief.

However, for a week it looked as if Bennett might not pull out. But the fine attention he got from Dr. Sullivan and his own courage and grit saved the day. His leg took many weeks to knit. He was out of the ocean flight for good. That was heart-breaking for him and a very great disappointment to me.

Noville suffered a great deal and for a while was not expected to live. It was thought that he might have to be operated on. But it turned out that he had torn loose some of the muscles of his stomach. In several weeks he was up and back on the job again.

I set my broken arm on the way to the hospital. Two bones were fractured and there were many bruises. But beyond being something of a nuisance for a few weeks the injuries did not interfere with our plans.

We minimized the seriousness of our crash as much as possible, fearing that on account of the great amount of publicity our project had had, it would seriously hurt aviation. I felt like making a plea to the people of the country then not too let such pioneering accidents hurt the advancement of commercial aviation. Such an accident had nothing to do with regular commercial flights. The country was not yet sufficiently air-minded to distinguish the great difference.

We felt it our duty to go ahead with our flight—for the science of trans-oceanic flying.

The damage to our plane was serious. It took a month of day and night toil to get her back into shape again.

In the meantime others planning for long flights were able to go forward with their preparations and were ready to leave. While we were still working on the *America* installing instruments and mechanical appliances and making our tests at Roosevelt Field, before we could possibly have been ready on account of our crash, other trans-Atlantic planes were being tuned up and reports of the imminence of their hop-offs, *and ours too,* were in every edition of the daily papers.

That was tough, for the whole country looked upon us as feverishly active contenders in the great race. That crash—fate had indeed engineered me into a tight place. My stock was down to zero.

What was wrong with Byrd? What would the crossing of the Atlantic be with his great plane as compared to the other smaller ones in the race. Why was he delaying the hop-off?

I got thousands of letters, many of them reproving me unmercifully. Some of those fellows must have been betting on me in the race. I was called all sorts of ugly names. "Coward" one typical letter read. "I am sick of seeing your name. You are a disgrace to America. You have never had any idea of flying across the Atlantic."

Many were worse than that.

Our problem was somewhat at variance with that of others attempting to cross the ocean by air. I felt it important to go through a full series of scientific tests of plane and equipment, fuel and engine, in order that we should know exactly what our machine would do. To hasten this laboratory work for the sake of notoriety was to undermine the scientific character of our expedition. The others were using one-engined planes about which there was ample data available and they already knew about what their planes would lift. Bellanca's single-engined monoplane had already flown fifty hours.

No one knew just what a three-engined plane the size of ours could lift, or what its cruising radius would be. We had to find out.

Lindbergh and Chamberlin were on hand and ready to go. With much pleasure Mr. Whalen and I offered them our field. When Lindbergh hopped off early in the morning, we went down to the field to tell him goodbye and to wish him luck. It was a great moment when we saw his wheels just clear the telephone wire at the end of the runway.

Mr. Wanamaker had set May 21st as the date for the christening of the *America*. Many people had been invited to it. It was too late to call the ceremony off. Just as it began we received news of Lindbergh's arrival. Over 2000 guests were gathered around the *America* to hear us tell about the scientific aspects of our flight, and the goodwill we hoped would result from it. The French and American flags were hung side by side.

It was just a moment before I was to get up to speak that I

got the news of Lindbergh's arrival. I could of course think of nothing else but his magnificent feat. I realized what it meant to aviation and to international good-fellowship. I had seen enough of Lindbergh to know that he would make an ideal representative of our country. I knew also that his flight would create far more enthusiasm for aviation than ours could possibly do.

We promptly turned our christening into a celebration of Lindbergh's safety and success. The stage was well set with the French and American flags hanging side by side.

I found out later that the news of his arrival was premature and that while I was describing to the crowd his great take-off Lindbergh reached Paris.

The next day in addition to letters, I got telegrams from all over the country criticizing me for not getting away first. I'm afraid a lot of fellows lost bets on us. They were very peeved. One man from North Carolina wired me as follows:

"I just want you to know what you may not realize that you are the world's prize boob to get left at the switch as you did."

It did not seem exactly the right thing to do to fly immediately to Paris while Lindbergh was still there. To delay a little did not hurt our flight; while to have gone might well have done harm to the fine work he was doing in cementing French and American friendship. We didn't know. We simply didn't want to take a chance of lessening in any way the wonder of that which was going on in France.

So I took things a little easily until after he had come back to America. But again I was not allowed to pursue my course without criticism. Hundreds of letters poured in reproaching me for not having more backbone. Such is the capricious human nature.

However, having been projected into the "Trans-Atlantic Derby" this was all part of the game.

It was at this point that I had to thank the press for much heart-warming support. The great majority of the newspapermen assigned to cover my flight understood my plight; had seen the misfortune of our delay that had been caused by our crash.

They realized too, I think, that we were not racing—that we were making a very serious effort to point the way for the trans-Atlantic plane of the future. A few of those fellows knew that we were suffering from having kept from the people as much as possible the drama and seriousness of our crash so as to hurt commercial aviation as little as possible, so the people of the country did not understand that even if we wanted to race we were disabled and could not do so.

Fortunate had been those who had been able to make their preparations quietly.

But when I carefully explained to them day after day the difficulties of obtaining the then unknown facts about our very complicated piece of mechanism, the three-engined plane, they showed themselves to be among the best sports I have ever come in contact with. I owe them a debt of gratitude I can never repay.

This is an important point, because it is to the supporting press of America that advance in aeronautical interest in this country is largely due. American newspaper editors and publishers were among the first to see and believe in the future of American aviation.

Few people realize how difficult it is, with a plane like the *America,* to obtain revolutions of the engines for the various loads carried that will give maximum mileage per gallon of gasoline used, because these revolutions vary for every different weight carried. Of course, as the plane consumes gasoline, there will be an infinite number of ever-lightening loads. To calculate this we had to run over a course of known length, noting the speed over the ground and the fuel consumption for each number of revolutions. This had to be done for very many of the different loadings of the plane.

The calculations proved fairly accurate, but they were difficult to make because of rough air and winds blowing across the course, which affected our speed over the ground. We decided, after many tests, that we probably could fly to Rome. In the meantime Chamberlin and Levine made their epochal flight to Germany, breaking the world's record for distance. Again I took my hat off. They flew through two nights, and Chamberlin's wonderful success in locating their position after having been driven south by a storm was an astonishing feat.

After my return to Roosevelt Field from Lindbergh's reception in Washington and New York, we determined to make the flight at the first okay of the weather man.

Many times we sat up nearly all night hoping that the weather would be suitable for taking off next morning at daybreak.

At 1.00 A.M., June 29, 1927, Dr. Kimball phoned that, though conditions were not ideal, the weather was about as good as we could expect. I had determined not to wait, because I felt that the trans-Atlantic plane of the future could not wait for *ideal* conditions. Moreover, we probably could gain more scientific and practical knowledge if we met some adverse weather.

I now think that the *America* could conquer almost any storms that might be met in crossing the Atlantic. The only ocean weather conditions that need be serious for the planes of the future is a hurricane, which might exhaust the fuel supply.

Having decided to start, I telephoned my loyal crew to prepare the plane for the flight. I did not worry about the response I should get. For throughout this trying time three of my North Pole shipmates had stood like a stone wall: Tom Mulroy, Doc Kinkaid and Demas. Kinkaid had tended the engines for Lindbergh and Chamberlin as well as ours; and as a plane is largely its engine surely Kinkaid should go down in history. In the same category are Titterington and Goldsborough, representatives of the Pioneer Instrument Company who slaved day and night on the instruments and compasses of the *Spirit of St. Louis,* the *Columbia* and the *America.*

I had only about one hour's sleep that night, and I knew I had nearly two more nights to go through before I would be able to sleep. When I reached the field at 3.00 A.M. (standard time), June 29th, the plane was at the top of our little hill and, by the aid of powerful lights, the crew was applying the finishing touches. It was dark, dismal, and raining slightly, but even then a large crowd had gathered.

We felt that probably the most critical period of the whole flight was at hand, that of getting into the air with our load of over 15,000 pounds.

In order to get into the air with this terrific load we would have to get up to a speed of nearly a mile and a half a minute. If we should not quite make this speed we would crash as our great momentum would carry us over the end of the runway. All of the equipment we were carrying, four men, radio, the resistance of the radio generator propeller, pay load of 800 pounds, etc., would not only add to the take-off weight of our plane but would cut down our cruising radius as we would have to leave out a certain amount of gasoline.

And this too, in addition to the fact that originally our cruising radius was not as great as a single engine plane. So we had handicaps here which the public thought were an advantage.

Now let us review our preparations in so far as our plans to overcome whatever might be ahead of us.

First was the take-off with a very heavy load—an extremely hazardous undertaking with a field not more than a mile in length. The very smooth hard field would help and our hill would add to the length of the field, and, if that failed, our dump valve would lighten the load.

Having gotten into the air successfully, our next immediate great hazard would be from an engine stoppage and a consequent forced landing while swinging seven and one half tons in the air. A forced landing with such a load would smash the plane to pieces. Besides our dump valve to take care of this, we had arranged a cat-walk out to the engines so that if one should start to go bad there would be a real chance of repairing it in the air.

Another grave risk would be from ice forming on the wing. We anticipated this by placing thermometers about the plane so that we could keep a sharp lookout for the critical temperature. We were careful about our flashlights. We prepared to fly high so that should we get into the critical temperature and should we fail to climb out of it, we could dash down to a very low altitude and so change our temperature to a warmer one.

In case of an oil leak we carried extra oil and supplied a means of getting oil into the engines.

If our lights should fail we would be in grave danger of eventually going into a tail-spin without instruments. So we provided luminous substances to show them up in the dark.

There might readily be a leak in our great 1200 gallon

gasoline tank, as, of course, it had to be made of very light material. To meet this we carried a putty-like substance with which we could quickly repair such a leak.

We would undoubtedly be drifted off our course by the wind. We would use a wind drift indicator which could be operated through a trapdoor in the bottom of the plane. We carried bombs which would ignite upon reaching the water so that we could get wind drift even during the night. These same bombs would give us smoke in the daytime.

In case of good weather we carried a special airplane sextant that would enable us to get a line of position from an altitude of the sun. This instrument contained a special bubble in it that would enable observations of the sun to be taken at any altitude. Then the mathematics of the operation, which generally takes an hour or so, we had learned by short methods to make in a few minutes.

If, however, the plane should get in fog in the storm and clouds where it would be impossible to use the drift indicator or the sextant, there was our radio with which we could locate our position by getting lines of direction from ships or shore stations.

In case of strong adverse winds combined with engine stoppage, which would cut down our radius so that we would be in danger of not reaching our destination before running out of gasoline, we were equipped with instruments with which we could cut loose an engine and drop it into the ocean and so reduce down our resistance to the air. If a propeller should burst and cut a hole in the gasoline tank so that a forced landing into the ocean would be unavoidable, we would then dump all the gasoline before landing, then shut the valve of the great tank and stuff up the hole so that it would give as much flotation as possible.

We had two rubber boats, one large enough to more than accommodate four passengers and all of our emergency equipment—the other to use as a life boat in the larger boat. We carried along materials to repair these boats.

Our water-proof radio and a kite for the radio antennæ would get us in radio communication with passing steamers. The kite also would serve as a sail to pull us toward the steamer lane. Our three weeks food and water making apparatus, as well as water-proof tarpaulins to keep dry, would keep us in good physical condition. We also carried Very pistol lights to attract attention of passing steamers at night.

Another grave danger was from coming down in the night in a tail-spin in the dark clouds. We were O.K. there as we all had experience in night flying. It is very easy to fly at night when not in the clouds but night flying in clouds requires practice.

There is always a chance of a compass going bad. We provided three compasses to meet this danger.

The trans-Atlantic meteorological service that had been worked up would inform us, as nearly as was possible at that time, what weather we would be going to have.

We carried a medical kit that it took months to prepare.

We hoped that our attention to the details mentioned above would indicate something useful for the trans-Atlantic plane of the future.

In all of the years of thought we gave to preparations for the trans-Atlantic flight, the worst thing we could think of that ever could happen—and the only thing we felt that could prevent success after our thorough preparations—was to have the hard luck to reach our destination in the middle of the night during a storm with very thick weather making a low visibility.

XIII.

A Narrow
Escape

WE WARMED UP THE ENGINES gradually and took
our places in the plane. Lieut. George O. Noville sat with his
hand on the dump valve to release the gasoline in case we
could not get off the ground or should a crash threaten at the
end of the runway. Bernt Balchen, our young Norwegian relief pilot and mechanic, was working aft among the spare fuel.
We were taking off from the same spot and in the same direction used by Fonck a year ago with his three-engined plane.
They had crashed. Ours was the first three-engined plane to
make the attempt since then.

We put the engines on full; the plane strained at its leash
like a live thing. Tom Mulroy, our chief engineer on the North
Pole voyage, knife in hand, stood ready to cut the rope that
held the plane. The tug of the great engines suddenly broke
the line, as I learned later, and we started a little sooner than

we had expected. That was very bad. The engines were not warmed up as much as we had intended and it looked for some moments as if we might not get into the air before reaching the end of the runway. Once Bert Acosta at the wheel raised his hand to Noville to dump. It was a tense moment—everything hung in the balance. But just then the wheels left the ground and we set forth on the toughest air battle, I believe, that has ever taken place. I remember Balchen shouted with joy.

Slowly the great ship gained altitude with its tremendous load. This was a critical time because, should any one of the three engines stop or even falter until we could get an altitude of 400 or 500 feet, the dump valve would be of no value, and the plane would crash.

I made notes in my log and remarks in my diary, the same diary carried over the North Pole with me. I find this entry made a few minutes after leaving Roosevelt Field: "Altitude 300 feet, turning, after turn completed, altitude 400 feet." The *America* had climbed on a turn and was proving herself a very great plane.

With the engines roaring at maximum revolutions we went through the air at 100 miles an hour. Naturally, for the same wing surface, it was necessary to fly faster with a heavy load than it is with a lighter one in order to keep in the air.

Slowly we climbed. Shortly afterward I find the following note in my log:

"Raining, fog, clouds low, standard compass 83½°, wind

southwest on surface, drift 5° right, air speed 100 miles an hour, altitude 3000 feet."

We had to change the course of the plane five degrees to the left to allow for this drift. I had been taking our speed from the ground and found that at our altitude of 3000 feet we were getting probably the maximum assistance from the winds.

The air navigator of the future, I believe, will select the shortest route through the air by flying at that altitude which yields the maximum assistance from the wind. We wanted to prove the truth of this theory. The wind changes, both in speed and direction, at various altitudes. Greater speed and quicker time can be obtained by taking advantage of this fact, as we proved on our way to Newfoundland.

The rain continued for several hours and the weather was slightly foggy; but these factors did not bother us to any extent.

When we reached Nova Scotia the weather became clear. The air was very bumpy and rough. But we expected that. I had had the same experience over Nova Scotia on the first trans-Atlantic flight. We kept a sharp lookout for the plane of Nungesser and Coli, thinking it might have crashed on the rough land below. These two Frenchmen had heroically tried to fly from Paris to New York shortly before, and had never been heard from again. There were practically no landing places that I could see. At one time I thought I saw their big white plane beneath, but it was a curiously shaped, whitish rock.

The ground was covered with trees and rocks and we passed over many small lakes. When we passed near Halifax, we were flying over beautiful white clouds, but the sun was bright above us. The shadow of the plane was etched on the clouds, and around it was a rainbow. Here was an omen of good luck, following us on the white clouds beneath, at the rate of 100 miles an hour.

The plane was still cluttered with five-gallon cans of gasoline. Every now and then as I sighted the ground with our wind-drift indicator, through the trapdoor in the bottom of the plane, I could see a white object shoot down, glistening in the sun. These objects were gasoline cans that Noville was throwing overboard after he emptied them into our huge tank.

We were now near the air station I built at Halifax and there I was flying over territory that I had flown many times before. When we reached the beautiful Bras d'Or Lake, I looked down on the rough shore where Walter Hinton and I had once been washed ashore after a forced landing in 1918.

When we reached Newfoundland we found everything covered with fog. We had not expected such a tough break. Then for 2000 miles we saw nothing beneath us and it looked as if we would reach Europe without seeing the ocean and we almost did it. I hope no other pilots have that experience. It is not a very pleasant one.

There would be no chance to take a departure from St. John's and thus be entirely certain of our position before striking out over the ocean. We would have to fly "blind" for many miles over the land before hitting the water.

At 2 P.M. all the gasoline cans had been emptied and I asked Noville for a check on the gasoline consumption. This check showed that it had been greater than we had anticipated and I gave instructions to "lean" the mixture and to cut down the revolutions as much as possible. We had been going with almost a full throttle on account of the heavy load.

When we met fog, it was, we thought, advisable to fight our way above it, and so in climbing with our heavy load, we again had to run the engines at full speed. Slowly we got altitude and at 5.50 P.M. we found ourselves about a mile high, but in fog most of the time, and the plane was drenched. It would grow colder as night drew on and we would have to watch the temperature carefully, because, within 15 minutes, a plane so drenched could be precipitated into the ocean should the water freeze on the propeller and wings.

Finally we came to a point where we calculated that St. John's was beneath us, but we could barely see the tips of the wings, so dense was the fog.

I recalled the non-stop flight of Alcock and Brown from St. John's to Ireland. They accomplished that in 1919, when engines were not so safe as they are to-day. We must give England the palm for this great accomplishment, the first non-stop flight across the Atlantic.

I found myself thinking of Lieutenants Maitland and Hegenberger who were winging their way over the Pacific to

Honolulu. I wrote out a radio message for Noville to send them, wishing them good luck.

Little did we think, as we went into the fog, how many hours would pass before we could see the land or the sea. After we had left the land some hours behind, I again asked Noville for his gasoline consumption. I told him to be conservative. His figures indicated that it was much greater than we had expected. One reason for this, I thought, was our struggle in attempting to get above the clouds and fog. This had caused us to run the motors much faster than we had intended.

I made some careful calculations and showed Noville (in writing, of course, because the roar of the three engines prevented conversation) that, at that rate, with the slightest winds against us, we would drop into the sea from lack of fuel before reaching Europe.

I told him that I was responsible for the lives of all on board and that, regardless of my feelings, I wanted to know how they felt about turning back. He promptly answered that he knew of no landing place between Newfoundland and the States, except St. John's, that was now covered with fog, so that it was just as safe to go ahead as to go back. I was glad he felt that way, because I did not wish to retreat. We didn't mention our predicament to Acosta and Balchen—they had enough troubles of their own.

Here it was that we staked our lives on our theory that if we flew at the proper altitude we should have favoring winds. If I were wrong then we should fall into the sea and be lost before making a landfall on the other side.

I had studied thoroughly the velocity and directions of winds over the Atlantic. So far as I could learn, no reliable data had been procured upon the winds' strength at high altitudes, but several meteorologists of the Weather Bureau as well as I believed that a plane could fly high enough to get strong winds from the west, even though there might at the same time be easterly winds on the surface.

So that whenever any of us took the wheel we flew as high as possible. If we could have the winds with us, we should easily make Europe; if not, we should fall far short of it, if Noville's estimate of the gasoline on hand was correct. I also knew, from Dr. Kimball's weather map, which I had spread before me on the chart board, that I now was flying at first on the southern side of the storm area and later would be flying on the northern side of a high-pressure area.

We were now flying nearly two miles high. Above the ocean at night, bitterly cold, lost in storm clouds, so dark that we couldn't see our hands before our faces. It was not the pleasantest situation in the world.

I find notations made hour after hour in my log, as follows: "It is impossible to navigate."

Our safety depended upon winds behind us. It was a strain I must admit. Only an aviator knows what it means to fly 2000 miles without seeing the ground or water beneath. I doubt whether any other plane had ever flown blindly for half that time.

One notation in the log stated: "Ice is forming on the plane." We were at a dangerous temperature. That was to be expected, flying two miles high in fog, because the temperature decreases considerably with altitude. I passed a note to Acosta warning him to make every effort to get out of the clouds, which he very soon did.

Acosta and Balchen deserve great credit for their fine work during this critical period.

During the night, between turns at the wheel, Bernt Balchen had some sleep. As he moved restlessly in the restricted space from time to time, his foot nearly touched the handle of the gasoline dump valve. I watched him closely without awakening him, because if his foot should kick that, we should lose all our precious fuel.

Several times I took my turn at the wheel and realized what a strain Acosta and Balchen must have been under, steering for hours entirely by instrument.

Our night lights worked well. We also had powerful flash lights. We did not use the latter very much, because every time we flashed them we were blinded. The luminous dials and figures on our instruments showed up well in the pitch dark. I had a special portable light for my chart board.

I had left behind my rather heavy thermos bottle of tea, but during the night Noville gave me some of his coffee. It was only lukewarm, but it tasted good. We had plenty of drinking water. I ate a little roast chicken, but did not want to eat too much, because I knew it would be necessary to keep awake.

From time to time during the night we fought our way above the clouds. It was a weird sight to look down from the pinnacle of black masses we were skimming. Around us were ominous, towering peaks, some of which reached far above us. As we could not afford to go around those that lay in our path, we would dash through them in a darkness so intense that we could not see the wing tips. The fire from the exhaust pipes of our faithful engines, invisible in the daytime, shone vividly in the dark night. The 30,000 flashes of fire per minute through the exhaust pipes made a cheering sight against the black.

On one occasion in a thick cloud the plane got temporarily out of control. We must have been going downward at a terrific rate, judging from the roaring of the engines. Balchen, with great skill, finally steadied the ship again on her course.

Throughout the long night each man went about his duty efficiently and calmly, taking it as if it were all in a day's work.

I note in our record that I sent the following radio at 6.50 A.M. on June 30: "We have seen neither land or sea since 3 o'clock yesterday. Everything completely covered with fog. Whatever happens I take my hat off to these great fellows."

In those minutes between twilight and dusk we reached sufficient altitude to skim the tops of the clouds, and the spectacle was extraordinary. On the side of the sun, which, of course, was far below the cloud horizon, the clouds took on weird shapes and colors, but on the other side they were ominous and gloomy. During the day we had some terrifying views; there were fog valleys, dark and sinister, hundreds of feet beneath us. At times distant cloud peaks took on shapes and colors of rugged Arctic land and mountains.

I found myself again thinking of Maitland and Hegenberger. So confident was I that they would arrive safely I sent them a radio of congratulations. *They got both messages we sent them!*

I had another bad time when I discovered a leak near the bottom of one of the main gasoline tanks. We had provided against such an emergency by bringing along some of a patent putty-like substance. This nearly stopped the leak but a little of the precious fuel kept dribbling out. Along toward morning the leak stopped of its own accord. This I told myself could mean but one thing: that the fuel had got down to the leak. This meant further that we had only fuel in the four wing tanks. It checked up with what Noville had told me about over-consumption of gas, and confirmed the disagreeable fact that we should never reach the other side.

I was living over again now the same sort of time we had over the Polar ocean, from the bad oil leak, only this time I had the responsibility of three men's lives instead of one. That sort of thing makes a big difference.

I could have been saved much anxiety had I only known

that the leak was somehow stopped from inside the tank after all, and that the tank was far from empty at the time.

I find this note in my diary: "Went forward at 3.15 A.M. to pilot and got stuck in the passageway." I had to tear off a sweater to get forward.

For hour after hour we had seen no land or water. "I sit here wondering if the winds have been with us," I wrote. "If they have not been, we do not reach land. I take my hat off to the boys with me. Their courage is splendid."

From a study of the weather maps I concluded we were being drifted to the south.

From time to time we sent and received radio messages and it seemed miraculous that, flying two miles above the ocean, hidden in dense clouds, we could get messages from safe, comfortable places.

At one time Noville reported he had a message from a steamer somewhere beneath us and our signals were so clear that we must have been very near it. We were in dense fog at the time. He asked for conditions of weather at the surface and the ship reported fog. We got its position and a radio bearing. This showed we were on a certain line and indicated we had been right in judging that the wind had drifted us to the south.

A little later we had the position of another ship, the S. S. *Paris,* and this information put us somewhere on another line. Where the two lines intersected was our exact position. We were certain then that we had been drifted to the south, so instead of bucking winds to go to Ireland, we set our course directly for Finisterre, France. Indeed, by allowing ourselves to go with the wind we had made better speed toward our objective. I could now, however, allow for the wind to a nicety and knew exactly where we would hit land, although we were still several hundred miles away.

We must give Noville credit for this radio information. It was a remarkable feat and another triumph of science at which to marvel. Surely our whole flight was worth while, to demonstrate this one thing alone which we had been so anxious to prove.

Our position indicated that we had been assisted by the wind about 30 miles an hour all the way from Newfoundland. We had made splendid speed.

I wanted to find out the worst about the gasoline, so asked Noville for an exact estimate. He came to me in a few minutes and wrote: "I made a mistake in the first estimate. We have enough gasoline left to fly to Rome."

"Wish I had known that 18 hours ago," I wrote back.

The error was caused I think by the fact that the tail of the plane was somewhat down on account of the weight and the gasoline gauge did not register accurately.

Not long after that in the afternoon of the second day, we came out of the thick, solid cloud layers into broken cloud fields and we could see the water beneath us. Though it was fairly rough it was a most welcome sight. We could see it only every now and then, but that was enough to allow me to get my drift and to verify the fact that the wind was blowing from the northwest.

What a great contrast was our situation now compared to what it appeared to be a few hours earlier! We could get glimpses of the sun and water; by our navigation we now knew exactly where we were; there was enough gasoline to get to Rome, and all engines were hitting perfectly. When I squeezed up into the pilot's compartment to take a turn at the wheel, I could tell from the faces of my shipmates that they were much relieved.

Soon we were getting many radio signals. They began to increase rapidly in number and Noville reported to me that he thought the whole of Europe was calling us.

We hit land about the time and at the place we calculated and I am sure France never looked so beautiful to any one of us before. We passed over Brest and set our course for Paris.

We had flown nearly a whole day without seeing land. Since one's processes seem to quicken when flying, the period seemed more like two days.

We had fairly good weather, now, but it looked thick ahead. I asked Noville to radio to Paris to find out the condition of the weather there. It was reported thick fog and squally. Another battle was before us.

The worst that we had anticipated—fog at our destination—had happened.

In a way we welcomed the fight ahead. Here would be another test of aviation, and I felt we could conquer the elements with the gasoline we had left.

We probably could have flown on to Rome on the edge of the storm area and set the world on fire with this long distance record, but that would not have been "carrying the message to Garcia."

We were able to locate accurately our position by the cities beneath us and the coast line to the left. But before long darkness began to descend, and with it came thick rainy and ominous weather. Soon we got only occasional glimpses of the lights of the towns, and the thick, low lying fogs or clouds drenched the plane and again we were tossed about in the blackness without being able to see our hands before our faces.

It was so inky dark that every time we put on the flash light to give an order it blinded us temporarily, so that we could only dimly see the luminous instrument board. However, the personnel and the many mechanisms of the plane continued to function efficiently, and I had every confidence of hitting Paris.

If we hit Finisterre after almost 2000 miles of blind flying, I thought we certainly ought to be able to reach Paris, a few hundred miles off.

We were using the earth-induction compass and it had been excellent to steer by, better than the ordinary magnetic compass. The pilot had before him the pointer of the earth-induction compass, which was supposed to synchronize with a pointer in the navigator's compartment. A number of times I found my pointer considerably off and at first I blamed it on the pilot, but found that one of the pointers apparently was sticky. We would tap the dial and by checking with the standard compass we always managed to get on the course again.

I always take two or three compasses on an important trip to check for accuracy. In spite of a few minor mechanical difficulties, the earth-induction compass undoubtedly is the aviation compass of the future.

About the time we expected to hit Paris we got temporarily out of the thick weather. I saw bright lights ahead and a revolving light which I took to be Le Bourget. Our dead reckoning showed us to be just about at Paris.

Our troubles seemed at an end. It was a relief. I wrote out the following radio for Mr. Wanamaker: "Paris is in sight. It has been a great trip. I wish to tell you with enthusiasm that Noville, Acosta and Balchen have faced grave dangers with the greatest possible courage and calmness. They have been wonderful and we all send our best wishes to you."

That radio was never to be sent. I looked down and saw the revolving light flash for an instant on water. It was a lighthouse. I knew there was no ocean lighthouse near Paris. We were somewhere on the coast of France! I was astonished very greatly indeed.

The compass had gone wrong—had taken us in a great circle. By the flares of our flash lights, I conferred on paper with the pilots and concluded that we had made a circle to the left. There had either been some local affection of the compass in the plane, or the pilot's dial had stuck badly. The only way to get on again would be to lay some course and check up the compasses.

We tapped the dials, checked them with the extra standard compass we carried, and got them O. K. Again we set out for Paris and again were tossed about in the storm and darkness. It was raining very hard on the coast and visibility was bad. It was much stormier inland. We afterwards found that the centre of the storm was over Paris. I watched the course carefully after that and checked compasses every few minutes. I knew we were heading towards Paris. The inky darkness was broken occasionally by the flashes of our lights as we needed them temporarily, and the fire from the engine exhaust pipes. The rough air made it a little difficult to steer, especially in the darkness, but we kept a pretty good general course.

Then arose the necessity of watching the gasoline very carefully, for a forced landing in the darkness would not only have meant certain disaster for us, but also for some of those perchance beneath us.

Finally, our dead reckoning showed us to be at Paris but we could see nothing—nothing beneath us—nothing but the luminous lights of our steering instruments. We had got to the point beyond which, if we had continued, we could not have returned to the coastal waters, on account of the diminished gasoline. We knew that we would need a few gallons of reserve in order to cruise around for a landing place that we might not even then find. I believe at the moment we turned we were near Paris; our motors were heard by many people at Le Bourget through a sound intensifier, but I could not flirt any more with the lives of my shipmates.

The French trans-Atlantic flyer Lebrix twice said during speeches at his reception in New York, on February 15 and 16, 1928, that he and all the French aviators waiting for us at Le Bourget agreed that not only should we not have been able to land on account of the very thick weather but that we should have surely killed people had we attempted it.

In a flash it came to me that the compass needle taking us in a great circle right up to that lighthouse was an act of Providence.

A decision had to be made. My big job now was to try not to kill anyone beneath us and to save my shipmates. The only thing to do was to turn back to water.

It would probably be difficult for the layman to visualize our predicament, tossed around in the inky darkness of the storm, drenched by rain.

I doubt if any one could realize the strain of this part of the flight. We had no assurance that the plane could be landed safely on the water, but there was no chance of a safe landing on the land where we could see nothing.

Thus the decision to turn back did not carry safety with it. It meant that even should we find water we could not be certain of landing without disaster, because I never heard of anyone landing in the water when it was pitch dark and when the water could not be seen. We could not even be certain of landing a great plane like ours safely in the water in the daytime.

So, when we turned, we faced uncertainty ahead, but there was nothing else we could do under the circumstances that would give us any chance whatever to save the lives of the crew and to avoid endangering the people beneath us.

We set a course for the lighthouse we had seen. The wind might blow us off a bit in the darkness, but if the fog were not too thick there, we were confident of hitting it provided we were where we thought we were while over Paris. Much of the way we could see nothing beneath us, and we were flying so low that Noville had to pull in the antenna of his wireless to prevent it from hitting objects on the ground. Finally, when I thought we were near the lighthouse, I asked Balchen to get down lower. He was afraid of running into something but we had to take the risk. We emerged from the mists and there was the lighthouse ahead of us. That shows, again, I think, that we had not been lost—that we had been at Paris.

We cruised over it slowly, but in spite of the light the area around it was black, and we could only guess its topography. We could find no landing place. We had hoped there would be a beach and had written out a message on a weighted streamer asking the people to clear the beach and make some kind of light for our landing.

We then flew over the lighthouse and, by the quick flash of the revolving beacon, we could tell that we were over water and dimly distinguish the shoreline. We could not discern the character of the beach. It was still raining and dismally thick.

I wrote a note to my shipmates which I passed around with the flashlight which read: "Stand by to land." I knew there would be a hard bump.

We decided to land near enough to the beach line to swim ashore, if necessary, and to salvage the plane, if it were not too badly wrecked. At the same time we had to be far enough away to miss any rocks, should the beach be rocky. That, of course, we could not tell.

We had some navigation flares with us which ignite upon striking the water and give a light for a few minutes. We carried these to sight on at night, when over the ocean, to get the drift caused by the wind and to use in case of a forced landing. I had thrown half of them overboard to rid us of the weight, but had saved enough for such an emergency as this.

We now dropped a number of flares as nearly in a line as we could, about 100 yards from the beach line. They all ignited, and although they made a light in a pool of blackness, we hoped we would be able to judge the distance of the plane above the water as we descended. Of course, if we could not judge it, we should go into the water at flying speed, which would smash everything badly, since water does not give much when hit hard.

Those hours in the black storm had not been pleasant. I

felt myself entirely responsible for the lives of my shipmates. I don't believe they thought there was much chance of getting down safely, but still they faced gallantly, with steady courage, whatever fate lay ahead. In a few moments the story would be ended, but to the last they calmly obeyed orders.

The gasoline was running low, we must not wait for it to give out and be forced to land.

Balchen happened to be at the wheel. I gave the orders to land.

We were landing with the plane in control and the engines functioning perfectly. At that moment, in spite of our danger, I marveled at the three engines that for 42 hours had made some 1500 revolutions a minute without missing a beat. I thought of the Wright Aeronautical Corporation, that made the engines, and of my friend, Charles Lawrance, who had designed them.

Bennett and I had often wondered what would happen to a great three-engine plane landing in the water. Everyone thought the plane would turn over. Some thought the flyers would get hurt. Others thought not. Anyhow we were about to find out. Only we had the added difficulty of landing at night.

As we neared the water we could not see it; only the flares ahead of us and beneath us.

The wheels touched, and though the landing gear is secured to the plane with a tremendous factor of safety, it was sheared off, along with the wheels, with hardly a jar of the plane, as though a great knife had cut it, thus demonstrating the tremendous resistance of water when hit by a rapidly moving object. No one had predicted that.

It seemed just a second after that the crash came. I suppose I was dazed a little. I know I got a stiff blow over the heart that made it beat irregularly for many months afterward. I found myself in the water outside swimming around in pitchy dark and rain. I could hear Noville calling for me, but not another sound in the extraordinary stillness which contrasted so vividly with the roar of the great motors which had been pounding on our eardrums for 42 hours like tom-toms of Hades.

The plane instantly filled with water. Noville was getting out of the window. I yelled at him that I was unharmed and asked him how he was but he did not answer—just kept on yelling for me. I was a little worried about him, but I knew that he could not have been badly hurt. Hearing nothing from Balchen and Acosta and worried beyond measure about them, I swam to where they had been; the cockpit, of course, was under water. I yelled as loud as I could but got no answer.

I found Balchen slightly caught under water and trying to extricate himself. When he got clear I asked him how he felt. He didn't answer but asked me how I felt. He talked a blue streak but didn't talk to me. I couldn't make it out exactly but concluded that he, too, was somewhat dazed.

Thinking that Acosta must have been caught under the water in the cockpit, we dived down, but he was not there. I yelled for him, but there was no answer. A moment later he appeared, apparently from nowhere, swimming toward the wing, the leading edge of which was now down to the water. He must have been swimming around out there somewhere in the darkness all the time.

I asked Acosta the same question I had asked the others, but he too didn't answer—asked me how I felt. Bert also talked a blue streak but not to either one of us. In the course of his talking I found he had broken his collar-bone.

It was a weird sensation to have three shipmates there in the dark who would not talk to me or each other, but it was the most thankful moment of my life to find them still "kicking." The very worst thing we had anticipated had happened, and we had come through.

With grunts and groans we dragged ourselves upon the wing. The wing was down in the water by that time.

So it must have happened with all the land planes that landed in the ocean that summer.

Noville, still functioning perfectly, was carrying out his orders given before leaving the States, which were to rip open the emergency cabin in case of landing in the water and pump up the rubber boat. He was at his job, although he could hardly stand up and was falling every minute or two.

It had been with considerable difficulty that all hands got on top of the wing. I then found that the reason I could not get any answer from them was that the three engines roaring for 42 hours over their heads had temporarily deafened them. As

I had used ear protectors my hearing was normal. No plane had ever flown that long for a distant objective though endurance tests where the engine would not have to be run so fast of course had been longer.

The great question was solved at last. We could land without seriously injuring the personnel. The plane did not turn over, as many thought it would, and we had placed the emergency compartment in about the only situation in the ship where we could get our rubber boat and other emergency supplies when landing in the water.

My next thought was one of great admiration for Balchen's landing. My mind turned to Norway, which had produced this kind of a soul, cool and courageous in emergency.

We were stiff and bruised, tired and watersoaked, and it was with some difficulty that we pumped up the rubber boat. As the wing was almost flush with the water there was no difficulty in launching it.

We placed our most precious cargo, which included a piece of the original American Flag, in a compartment we had made in the great wing; this we thought was the safest place. After finding the things in there were only slightly wet, we shipped the oars in the rubber boat, and wearily made for the shore in the dark.

We were a mile from the village. Even after we reached it we spent much time going from house to house trying to arouse someone. But there were fences with locked gates around these houses and we were unsuccessful. Suddenly, a boy on a bicycle passed us. We tried to stop him but he took one look at us and kept on going. Wet and bedraggled, we certainly were not prepossessing.

Finally, we found the lighthouse keeper and his wife up in the lighthouse tower but they wouldn't come down. Noville could talk French but was deaf. My French wasn't much and seemed to add to their idea that we were a gang of roughnecks under the weather. But when at last they realized that we had landed at Ver-sur-Mer, having come all the way from America, their astonishment and excitement were intense.

Here began an experience with the people of France which was so remarkable that words fail me in describing it.

Balchen and I left Acosta and Noville there while we went back to the *America* to get the United States mail and to salvage what we could of our precious records. In the meantime the tide had been going out rapidly, and when we reached the plane it was nearly high and dry. Some of the villagers appeared and helped us carry our records and a few other belongings up to the village. So long as we live we can never forget the kindness of the people of Ver-sur-Mer, and before leaving France we motored back there to tell them "goodbye."

The wild scenes of joy and welcome which we received wherever we went in France are far beyond my power to describe. When we arrived at Paris, it was a long time before we could get away from the station. The entire city seemed to have turned out to welcome us. The people were mad with joy at our escape, though yet mourning the loss of their own beloved airmen.

The glass in one of our automobiles was broken, and the machine in which I was riding was almost upset several times by the crowds that surged against it. Some of the people must have been crushed and injured, but they did not seem to mind. We could not start the automobile engines, but were simply shoved along by the crowd.

My good friend, Herbert Adams Gibbons, finally rescued us and helped us through the balance of our exciting stay in France.

It seemed to us that if everyone in France had been our blood relatives we could not have received a more joyous welcome. If the reader thinks I exaggerate he has only to make a non-stop flight to France to find out the truth.

From the greatest statesmen down to their humblest citizens, we received warm expressions of admiration and friendship, but their words were not necessary to show us how they felt. The expressions on their faces were more eloquent than any words could have been. France gave us her very best. We were made citizens of three French cities. It would take a book to tell all they did for us.

There can be no doubt about the deep friendship of France for the people of this country. I vowed at the time to bring this fact back home. Since my return I have spoken of it publicly in more than half a hundred leading cities in the

United States. The response my word has received has convinced me that France's friendship is fully reciprocated.

France saw in us, from the moment of our great welcome, the embodiment and the spirit of America, and it was that for which they poured out their friendship and affection. They were saluting the Stars and Stripes which we for the moment carried.

XIV.

In Defense of
Spectacular Flights

DUE TO THE LOSS of thirty lives in connection with trans-oceanic flights during 1927, there has developed a strong public sentiment against spectacular flights, and the modicum of man's success in such flights was lost in an uproar of protest against the useless expenditures of so many lives.

I believe thoroughly in spectacular flights provided they are made after proper preparation and with a constructive end in view, and I have constantly decried such flights made purely for the sake of notoriety. Whether or not the failures of 1927 outweighed the good done to commercial aviation by the successes, I do not know.

But I wish to say with all the emphasis with which I am capable, that tragedy from a spectacular pioneer flight should not be laid to the door of, or in any way affect, the progress of commercial aviation. Commercial aviation, as I have tried to point out, can today be made as safe as a railroad train. The pioneer risks his life to bring the unknown into the column of the known.

I have always believed that no matter how hazardous an endeavor may be, it is justifiable when the end sought is human knowledge and augmented progress. Where would we be today if there had not been pioneers in the past who launched out into the unknown?

When my Grandmother Byrd was told of our proposed flight toward the North Pole she vigorously opposed it. She was eighty-seven years old at the time but had kept unimpaired an unusual keenness of mind. "What are you going to do with the North Pole when you get it?" she said.

I could not answer her. She saw eye to eye with thousands of our thinking citizens. Now that the flight is over she admits as do, I think, many of those citizens, that perhaps there was after all some reason for making our flight, though I doubt if they could define that reason. But she was delighted with our success and says it was written that the flight should have been made, for did not my great-great-great-grandmother prophecy that a Byrd would some day find the North Pole!

However, she was not the only one who expressed herself in no uncertain terms about our proposed exploit. At a formal dinner one night in Washington, a prominent young matron told me that she not only did not see any reason for flying in the "terrible Arctic" but she thought a man with relatives and responsibilities was thoroughly wicked and thoughtless to expose himself to such dangers. "Think," she said, "of the terrible anxiety he gives to his friends and relatives!"

The wickedness had to be admitted, but not the thoughtlessness, for one who deliberately takes risks must, if normal, worry considerably about the anxiety he causes and the chances he takes with others' future. That, I think, is much the hardest part of Arctic flying. We were rebuked by young wives who thought, it appeared, that we were setting their husbands a bad example. Of course, some of us have a great confidence in aircraft, and less dread than most people of the Arctic. However that may be, an Arctic flyer who has responsibilities feels more like a selfish sinner than an explorer going forth to conquer.

Another acquaintance, who had been approached for a donation, said: "I won't be guilty of subscribing a cent to your expedition before you go, to help you break your neck up there, but if you must go I'll help salvage the wreckage when you get back." He did not say "help *you* salvage the wreckage," and it occurred to me then, as I found out after our return, that he never expected to see me again. His was a good sporting proposition, but his attitude was typical of that of many people.

"Why," said another friend, "if you crack your machine up in your trial flights, as you are very likely to do, and so end your expedition before you get started, you will not only be a bankrupt, but you will make of yourself the world's greatest monkey!"

With all these powerful objections on one side, there must be something very strong indeed to outweigh them—to take a man on these pioneer flights in spite of them. What is the answer?—or is there no answer? Let us see.

We speak of our civilization as artificial, to distinguish it from life that exists in a state of wild nature, where animal eats animal and the struggle is for existence instead of for pleasure, where nature's favorites are the "strong and the swift." But civilization is just as much a product of the cosmical processes as is the beehive or the anthill, or the mountains and valleys. And the growth of civilization is as natural as the growth of a tree. We are just another product of the cosmos— the highest product we are taught to think—and so it would seem that we are subject to the laws that are immutable and that govern the whole organic universe.

I can not think then that our normal long-run tendencies, instincts, and urges are the results of blind chance, and so it would seem that they have their meaning—are part of the scheme of things. Civilized man's strongest and most prevalent instincts and desires appear to be for life and happiness. Primeval man had a great struggle for life alone. Civilized man finds easy the struggle for existence. His great struggle is for pleasures over and above his effort for mere existence. *Any one* could understand an act that would manifestly make for one of these two things.

Not so easily understood therefore are the urges to explore or to risk life for science. I am not prepared to say how prevalent these urges are, but it would seem reasonable to suppose that they are heeded only when they are very strong; for they must be so to compete with the instincts for life or pleasure. The race, however, from necessity produces some who have these urges and to them no explanation is needed as to why one will deliberately risk one's neck in a pioneer or stunt flight.

There are others who cannot understand the first thing about it, and perhaps no amount of discussion will convince them that such things are not entirely unnatural and useless. But these people's condemnation can be understood. For our view of life is too close not to seem made up somewhat of myriads of meaningless happenings that make the great procession of the race appear uncertain—disorderly—even chaotic.

The life of the individual is but an instant in that procession. How then could he be expected to know the meaning of all the great and small happenings that constitute that race's onward march? As is true with a great painting, too close a view will show a large number of meaningless dabs of color of different sizes and shapes, but from a distance, those dabs together take on form and meaning.

So it is with hazardous pioneer flights. May we not suppose that they are happenings, however small, that assist the great procession of the race toward its goal—though the meaning of these movements may be inscrutable? They would have their place in a painting of that procession—a small place that would none the less be a necessary part of the picture.

I suspect that there are few things that have survived the ages that are useless—that do not fit somewhere in the picture of life. The necessity for struggle renders ease a boon. Anger makes self-command a virtue. The fanatics counterbalance the conservatives. And so the procession goes upward, helped by contrasts and by contrary movements; energized here and there even by things of unsuspected worth.

Let us analyze then a few well-known flights in their relationship to the processes of progress, to find out how they fit.

When aviation was still a child—nineteen years ago—Bleriot hopped off from near Calais, France, for a flight across the English Channel, and landed 23 minutes later near Dover, England, having flown the then remarkable distance of 21 miles. He used a monoplane with a wing spread of about 20 feet and a 25 horsepower motor. Bleriot made his flight without a watch or compass, got into a mist over the Channel, but emerged and crashed upon landing. Shortly before Bleriot's hop, another Frenchman, Hubert Latham, tried the Channel flight, but fell midway and was rescued.

Bleriot's flight electrified the world and did much to attract attention to aviation, of which so many were sceptical. Now the Channel is crossed daily by passenger planes. Who can say that Bleriot's great feat did not hasten and help the initiation of these regular trans-Channel flights? Did not the interest he aroused draw men to aviation and make it easier for those men to finance their projects?

Next let us consider the navy N.C. boat trans-Atlantic expedition when the N.C.-4 made the first successful trans-Atlantic flight which I have already described.

In preparation for the flight the Navy did some very intensive work. The proposed expedition captured the imagination of the officers and employees of the bureaus concerned and some of them worked day and night with an enthusiasm and energy that no ordinary project could have called forth. Routine and red-tape were cut, and rules were broken, with the result that much was accomplished and some things were learned and developments made, that probably could not have been done without some similarly strong interest. In fact, the drift-indicator used, a difficult instrument to machine, was made by the Naval Gun Factory. Ordinarily it would have been entirely out of order for the Gun Factory to make a navigational instrument that the Bureau of Navigation would be responsible for.

Lives would probably depend upon the performance of the engines during the flight, and so something was learned of motor safety, precautions, and reliability. It was necessary that the planes should not run out of gas between bases, so accurate data was obtained relative to the cruising radius of large flying-boats. Commander Towers' experience on the rough seas in the N.C.-3 was valuable in that something was learned about the sea-worthiness of flying-boats.

The N.C. flight was the first where long-distance out-of-sight-of-land navigation was necessary and several new navigational instruments had to be developed—the old story of necessity. Two of these instruments, the most essential navigational apparatus—the artificial-horizon sextant and the wind and drift-indicator—are now, nine years later, standard equipment in the Navy. Even the war did not bring about the necessity for developing the artificial-horizon sextant for airplanes. Another benefit resulted. The success of that flight brought to the side of aviation, the Navy's new child, many of the older officers who had looked askance at it. It contributed to the formation of the Bureau of Aeronautics in the Navy Department.

The first non-stop trans-Atlantic flight was made by Captain Alcock and Lieutenant Brown, in June, 1919, flying from St. John's, Newfoundland, to Ireland, following practically the same route across the ocean that the other trans-Atlantic flyers have taken across the 1880 miles of ocean. They hit a bull's eye. On one occasion control of the plane was lost in a dense cloud while flying at an altitude of 3500 feet, and was not regained until within fifty feet of the water. I take my hat off to these fellows for crossing the ocean when engines were nothing like so reliable as they are now. Alcock and Brown were knighted by the British Government (as later were Ross Smith and Keith Smith, for their great flight of 11,060 miles in 28 days from London to Australia). The Alcock-Brown flight showed that an airplane could survive darkness, fog and rain, and strong and changing winds. There had been much discussion as to whether or not this could be done and the doubters were silenced in the only effective way—by a practical demonstration. Alcock and Brown staked their lives and won. They showed that the engine and structure could stand the dampness and buffeting of the elements, and the human body the great physical strain.

In October, 1919, First Lieutenant Belvin W. Maynard, making landings en route, won the first trans-continental race, flying from Mineola, L. I., to San Francisco and return, covering 5402 miles in a little less than 50 hours of actual flying. The Army Air Service reported many good results from this test from a technical standpoint but stated that "probably one of the greatest results of the test was the stimulus given to aviation in this country. The fact that public libraries en route were denuded of any book which dealt with aeronautics, and that many editorial headlines and comments were devoted to the contest gives a clear indication of the interest taken and the stimulus given to the public in general."

The first non-stop trans-continental flight was made by Lieutenant J. A. Macready and Lieutenant O. Y. Kelly in a T.-2 monoplane equipped with a Liberty 400 horsepower motor. They left Mitchel Field, L. I., May 2, 1923, and landed in California the next day, making the 2520 mile flight in 26 hours and 56 minutes, and so "linking the Atlantic and the Pacific in a non-stop flight." This extraordinary feat showed not only that a plane could be navigated accurately over long distance by landmarks, but also that the permanent lights of highways, railroads, towns and cities afford a means of navigating an aircraft at night.

The longest flight on record was the round-the-world flight made by Captain L. H. Smith, Lieutenants L. P. Arnold, E. H. Nelson, John Harding, Jr., Leigh Wade, and Sergeant H. H. Ogden in three Douglas transport planes with single 400 horsepower Liberty motors. Twenty-eight thousand miles were covered in 5 months and 24 days, the longest non-stop flight of which was from Iceland to Greenland, a distance of 830 miles. Here we had a flight combining both airplanes and seaplanes, for, when flying over water, pontoons were used in place of wheels. Again aviation received an impetus and a great deal of invaluable technical data was obtained. This flight of 28,000 miles had to be made over all sorts of regions and through all degrees of temperature and variation of meteorological conditions—over hot tropical jungle and deserts, and cold mountain tops and Arctic regions. And to top it all, both land and water landings had to be made. The preparation for this stupendous undertaking took intensive study and effort. The best types of planes and routes and landing places had to be selected, and then all three had a practical trial that made this flight of great value both from a commercial and military standpoint.

Let us consider the sensational flights that have been made for the Pulitzer Trophy and the Schneider cup—the speed classics. Without the spur of competition and the enthusiasm of the race it is probable that our army and navy planes would not have achieved the astonishing speeds of over 270 miles per hour—more than four miles a minute. It is either in preparation for these races or in competition to win the speed records that we have learned more about building fast airplanes than from any other one thing. It is largely its great speed that gives the airplane the advantage over other forms of travel, and anything that makes for greater rapidity of travel is contributing to the very essence of the game. An unofficial speed of five miles a minute has already been made, and we do not yet know the limit of airplane speed.

Nor must we forget the many notable voyages made by the great dirigibles from the time Count Zeppelin made his first flight in 1900 as a demonstration of his theory that a ship of that type could be flown. One of the greatest of these demonstrations to the public mind that the dirigible was suitable for long flights with several passengers was made in 1919, shortly after the first airplanes crossed the ocean. The British dirigible, R-34, commanded by Major George H. Scott and manned by a hardy crew, left England on July 2nd, and arrived at Mitchel Field on Long Island four days later.

She nearly ran out of gasoline in trying to evade a storm, but following winds came to her assistance and she made her landing safely. Then she turned around and flew the three thousand miles back to England in 75 hours.

Not only did that magnificent achievement catch the imagination of the world and thrill it, but it brought home to every man the fact that the Atlantic could be bridged by airships as well as airplanes and in lower flying time than the best time of the swiftest steamships. To some of those who gave it thought before the great achievement, it might have seemed a foolhardy stunt from which no good could result, but after it was all over no one could deny that those hardy pioneer aviators had demonstrated to the world that we were on the threshold of a great new epoch in transportation.

Five years later the ZR-3, now called the *Los Angeles,* was down from Friedrichshafen, Germany, to Lakehurst, New Jersey, for delivery to the American Navy, thus proving that the success of the R-34 was no freak of luck and that the distances between America and Europe were really conquered by a new kind of machine devised by man. That flight of 4060 miles was made in 81 hours and 17 minutes—a tremendous distance to cover by aircraft in a single flight in that remarkably short time. She was a larger ship than the R-34, and now both England and this country are building others twice as large.

Secretary Hoover, now following this pioneering, has announced that regular trans-Atlantic mail and passenger service will be instituted by one of these British airships the R-100 with the cooperation of the American Government.

Think what a long time has elapsed since the first crossing of the Atlantic by the *Savannah* in 1819 and then, by comparing in your mind that pioneer, steamship with the *Leviathan* or the *Mauretania* you may have some idea of what the airship might become in the next century. As a matter of fact, it was not until about 1837 that companies began to plan regular crossings of the Atlantic by steamships, and the *Sirius* and the *Great Western* crossed early in 1838. Financial difficulties, however, soon ended these first attempts to establish a line.

In reading over the history of these first steamship lines I am struck by two facts. The first was that the conquest of the Atlantic by aircraft seems to be proceeding with much more rapidity than did the conquest by steamships, which were built in a demand for swifter transportation over the ocean. To put it another way, the *Savannah* crossed in 1819; the *Royal William* in 1833; and the *Sirius* and the *Great Western* in 1838; fourteen years elapsed between the *Savannah* and the *Royal William*. But see how we have proceeded with aircraft. Alcock and Brown crossed in an airplane in 1919; Read and the N.C. boat also crossed in that same year, and Scott and the R.-34 flew over and back a few months later. And within five years after that the ZR-3, or the *Los Angeles,* was flown over from Germany. The around-the-world flight of the army planes called for an Atlantic crossing. Then we come to Pacific and Atlantic air crossings of 1927. All of this in eight years.

The second fact which strikes me was that one of these early ships was lost at sea with all hands, her fate to this day remaining a mystery as impenetrable as that of the recent loss of the American naval collier, *Cyclops.* Another ship, the *Great Britain,* was stranded in Dundrum Bay. Those who think that our pioneer aviation efforts are fraught with perils will see that the efforts of the early steamships also were fraught with perils, and thus far we have lost no great airships over the Atlantic.

Though they were not on stunt flights when they fell, we must think also of the ZR-2, the *Roma,* the *Shenandoah,* and other airships which met disaster amid the treacheries of the changeable skies, but should we be daunted by those losses, deeply as we feel the loss of so many brave and capable pilots—the very flower of their services? I am sure they would not have it so; I am sure they would have their companions complete the conquest of the air and that they would point to the long list of dauntless sailors whose death in great exploits failed to deter our great race from forging on in the conquest of the deeps.

The epochal flight of the *Norge* across the North Polar regions did much to wipe out some of the skepticism created by disasters among dirigibles. The Amundsen-Ellsworth-Nobile expedition not only accomplished one of the greatest non-stop flights on record, but also performed one of the greatest feats of exploration in all history. It is already apparent that the flight has had a profound and beneficial effect upon aviation in the lighter-than-air field, but when we think that plus that demonstration of the great value of air-craft, those hardy pioneers have performed a tremendous service in exploration, we must conclude that those men have accomplished one of the great feats of our age, which will shine through future ages as the feats of Columbus, the Cabots, Magellan, and other great navigators of the past shine through our age. Before the flight of the *Norge* was started, thousands upon thousands looked upon it as a "stunt," and it was freely predicted that those brave pioneers of the Arctic skies would never return.

As with the great flights of 1927, I am probably too close to the polar flight of our *Josephine Ford* to be able to tell with certainty what, if anything, it may have accomplished for progress. We are not concerned here with the exploration aspects of our flight, which were not far-reaching, having shown only that some thousands of square miles of polar sea did not contain land.

We *are* concerned with the other results of the expedition. It would seem that the polar flight, and eight other flights our Fokker made from Spitzbergen, showed that heavier-than-air craft can fly in the Arctic—can conquer it, at least at certain times of the year. But that fact was known before the flight and has no immediate value unless it becomes necessary to fly up there in the near future. Our flights made the previous year from Etah, 700 miles from the Pole, where 6000 miles all told were flown by the three planes, had proved that seaplanes can be used in the Arctic in midsummer.

The flight of both the *Norge* and the *Josephine Ford* demonstrated that in spite of the queer things the compass does in the Arctic regions, it is possible under certain conditions to navigate an aircraft accurately up there. The sun compass is not only a contribution to aviation, but will probably be useful on all sea-going ships for steering when the sun shines and for quickly and accurately obtaining the error of the magnetic compass.

Then, too, after breaking up two sets of airplane skis on the Spitzbergen snow we think we have learned something about skis that may be valuable for winter flying over the snow. As to the engines, Lieutenant G. O. Noville worked out a method of starting them in cold weather, which is, I believe, a contribution to science. He covered our Wright air-cooled motors with a fire-proof canvas hood, and by placing a gasoline stove beneath them, heated the motors to any desired temperature.

Whether or not the recent long flights of 1927 and 1928 have helped the aviation game, and in what way, I must leave to the future to judge, as we are too close to the picture. We *had* hoped, however, to give some added confidence, by showing that even the cold frozen North could, without too much difficulty, be traversed by aircraft. There is one thing that we can say with some certainty has happened in connection with spectacular flights. The interest and the imagination of the youth of the country has been captured. We have thousands of evidences of this fact. I gave a talk to a number of Boy Scouts recently and I was not surprised that practically every one of them seemed to know all about our flight. When I asked how many of them would volunteer to go with me to the South Polar region, all answered in the affirmative. Floyd Bennett tells me that far more youths recognize him from his photographs than grown-ups. I have had the same experience.

It seems fair to conclude then that spectacular flights are more than just circus stunts made to satisfy a morbid appetite for excitement, or to make money, for expeditions have nearly all developed fair deficits. The urge to go adventuring, to try that which has never been done before, appears to be not just a product of blind chance, but has its meaning—is a part of the scheme of things—and is entwined in the roots of progress. Our records show that a spectacular flight, for any unusually long or hazardous flight, must be sensational until it becomes a regular thing.

Bleriot's flight preceded regular flights across the English Channel. Maynard's flight preceded regular flights across the United States. Read's trans-Atlantic crossing was followed by other similar crossings. The trans-Atlantic flight of the airship R-34 and *Los Angeles* will as we have seen probably be followed by regular airship flights next summer. It is simply a matter of economical evolution.

Spectacular flights accelerate progress, for when the flight is decided upon, then necessity in some cases produces inventions and developments which, in the ordinary course of events, would tend to be very slow and uncertain. Man needs this spur of necessity—a powerful impetus due to the risk of life involved. The deep instinct of self-preservation comes into action. The material and instruments are therefore improved, and the science of aviation is benefited.

Then again, nothing will progress far unless it is the will of the people. The attention and interest of the people is best directed toward aviation by the outstanding spectacular flights that take hold of their imaginations. Sensational flights are the italics in the story of aviation's progress.

Some of these flights are said to be epochal and to bring prestige to the country. If that is true, then there is another value in them. At any rate, certain it is that the United States is specially adapted to aviation by its great distances, and specially favored for it by the temperament of its people.

As regards international good fellowship that has resulted from spectacular flights there seems no argument. As time goes on, aviation will be shown to be more an instrument of peace and progress than of war. For the trans-Atlantic and trans-Pacific flights will bring us closer to the nations of the world both in distance and in sympathy.

XV.

The Last Challenge

AFTER I CAME BACK from the North Pole I had six good offers to go into business. One of these was from a successful advertising man who was a partner in a great manufacturing plant.

"But we can give you $25,000 a year!" he exclaimed, when I politely refused to show any enthusiasm about his business. He acted as if I had been impertinent.

"But I don't want to go into business," said I.

"Why not?"

"Because I have still some exploring to do."

He reached out and patted my shoulder in a kindly way, as if to say, "You poor misguided man." Actually he said: "But, Byrd, there isn't anything left to explore."

Luckily I was equipped to dispute him. I unrolled a chart of the world which I had brought along with me and showed him some of the things that are left for man to do and see and find out about on this globe of ours.

When we got on the subject of the huge unexplored South Polar Area the man became fascinated. For two hours we pored over this great white wilderness never seen by eyes of man.

While on our way back from the North Pole flight Bennett and I made plans for the Atlantic flight, but in moments of mental luxuriation we used to let ourselves dwell upon the big task of conquering the Antarctic by air. Now the Navy has again coöperated, as it has done so generously in the past, by giving me leave. Again the Navy is helping me to the limit the law allows.

Aviation cannot claim mastery of the globe until the South Pole and its vast surrounding mystery be opened up by airplane.

The South Pole lies at the center of a huge and lifeless continent as large as the United States and Mexico combined—a continent eternally buried in ice and snow—or is it a continent? We do not know. The Pole itself is on a vast plateau nearly two miles high at about the center of this area, which is in the throes of an ice age, a glacial period just as existed ages ago when this country was largely covered with a sheet of ice and snow. I must confess that ice age has fascinated me; and now I hope to see an ice age in full swing.

In the winter of 1911–12 two expeditions, one British and one Norwegian, based on opposite sides of Ross Sea—a deep, wide inlet in the New Zealand sector of the glacial fringe which abuts on all sides of Antarctica—set out for the South Pole. Both leaders, Amundsen and Scott, reached it; Amundsen's party got there first and got back successfully, the triumph of two long years of preparation; Scott and his men also stood at the Pole but perished of cold and hunger on their return.

It is my plan to sail south in September, reaching our base in Ross Sea sometime after Antarctic midsummer, which is December 21st, probably the first week in January. If we are unusually fortunate we may do much flying and get home before June, 1929. But we may have to winter and stay an extra year.

A winter in Antarctica is not as easy for personnel as in the North. Most of those with Amundsen were old timers; Scott also had many with him; yet both parties felt the deathlike isolation of the regions about them. North Polar expeditions have always tempered their loneliness by hunting bears, caribou and musk oxen as well as by intercourse with friendly native tribes. There is none of this life down there. It is unlikely that we will be able to obtain more than three or four trained Arctic men among the two score members of the party.

Conditions of weather, distance and terrain that govern a South Polar flight are surprisingly different from those met in the Far North. Superficially the polar regions are cold and stormy during a major portion of the year. Both have many months of darkness and of light. In both men find mechanical work most trying. Life itself suffers from the depressing effect of long-continued hardships. Specifically there is a vast difference between the two ends of the globe.

Weather, which means so much to the airman, is notably more severe in the South than in the North. This is easily explained because the Antarctic is still in the throes of an ice age. The Antarctic continent is a lofty and nearly circular dome on which rests a smooth ice shield. Air rising at the Equator flows toward the Poles, where it cools and descends. Upon striking the South Pole's ice-cap it rolls in all directions toward the circular coast, gaining momentum as it falls.

This theoretical flow is disturbed by local storms that move from Southern oceans. But it is distinct enough to give steady character to the pitiless tempests that rage for weeks beyond the great ice barrier. *Home of the Blizzard,* Sir Douglas Mawson called his narrative of an expedition to that wind-tormented tract. Both Scott and Mawson speak eloquently of the howling gales that thundered about their stoutly built Winter quarters.

When Columbus set out across the Atlantic he did not even dream that he had a great unknown land ahead of him, but we shall know when we set sail for the South that we shall have a chance to take off the maps for the ages to come, a part of that great blank white space at the bottom of the world. And a hundred years from now what will be there in place of that white space in Antarctic maps in our school geographies?

"And how does it happen," I have been frequently asked,

"that there is such a large area in the world that still remains unexplored?" And others will ask: "What is the use in bothering with it at all? What is there down there that could be of value to the world?" To me the answer to the latter question is obvious, and yet I always find myself hard put to it to answer convincingly.

It has always seemed to me that science is the loser so long as there remains a large unexplored area left in the world. To quote Sir Douglas Mawson: "Science is a homogeneous whole." Final knowledge is reached only by putting together a large number of facts. For example, there are meteorological data to be gained from the South Polar regions, the gaining of which alone justifies the hazards encountered. Weather conditions depend upon an equalizing tendency between the two poles and the equator. The Antarctic has even more influence on weather than has the Arctic.

The comparatively small part of the Antarctic that has been explored has been covered with snow and ice, even in the Antarctic summer time (which is, of course, our winter time), but, owing to the powerful effect of the twenty-four-hour sun, it is in the realm of possibility that there may be some areas in that immense region that are uncovered by snow in the summer. In the North Polar regions, for example, we know that if low land were found at the pole itself, some of it would be bare of snow in the summer. If such areas are found in the Antarctic, the most conservative scientists would say that it would not be unreasonable to expect that new

species of plant and animal life might be found, or that secrets of the past might be revealed by the signs that mother
earth may give, and the fossil remains that may be embedded
in her bosom.

With airplane cameras we should be able to get photographs of rocky peaks the sides of which, owing to their
vertical position, are naked. This will give an accurate geological section, even more accurate than could be obtained
by the foot traveler. It is possible that mineral deposits might
be located. It is an interesting fact that the only known cryo-
lite in the world is at Ivigtut, in ice-covered Greenland.

Seal, penguin, or other birds, sojourn on the rim of the
Antarctic, and carnivorous killer-whales and various species
of fish swim around its borders, but there is almost no life in
the interior. The land life is limited to the lowest in the organic
scale, like protozoa and minute insects. Of course there are
bacteria there, but I believe the largest living creature found on
the land was a spider. Is it not possible that land life existed in
the Antarctic and that the ice-cap which now covers the region has exterminated it all in comparatively recent geological
time? If this is true, cannot the fact be disclosed by investigation? Will it not teach us more about the geological ages into
which the past of the world has been divided?

At any rate, the primary object of the expedition is scientific. I wish to stress this point. There will be plenty of work
for the dozen specialists we will take with us. The more we

can unfold of the past and the unknown present, the better we shall know what to do for the future.

Southern explorations began in 1773, when Captain James Cook got as far south as 71° 10′. He discovered the ice bulwark, but it was left for Capt. John Wilkes, U. S. Navy, in 1840, to discover the Antarctic continent. In 1899, Brochgrevinch reached 78° 50′. Great Britain opened up a new chapter in Antarctic exploration when, in 1920, Captain Robert Falcon Scott made the first real explorations on the land. He reached a chain of mountains surrounded with gigantic glaciers "and proved first-hand that the climate was the coldest on earth, its winds insufferable, and its glacial crevasses incredibly hazardous." In 1907–1909, Sir Ernest Shackleton attempted to reach the South Pole, and for this he deserves the immortal fame because he jumped the farthest south record from 82° 17′ to 88° 20′, and was forced to turn back when only ninety-seven miles from the Pole. Indeed, he paved the way for Amundsen and Scott, who reached the pole sixteen years ago.

There is probably no more inspiring story in the history of exploration than that of Sir Robert Scott and his brave men who gave their lives in the cause of human knowledge.

Since that time Sir Douglas Mawson has done fine work down there. He is a great expert on Antarctica, and is the author of *The Home of the Blizzard,* a very valuable work on the South Polar regions.

It is with the inspiration of all these great men that my shipmates and myself will tackle the problem where they left off, and it is because this is the most hazardous region in the world from an aviation standpoint, that we are determined to prepare as far as possible for whatever dangerous situations may arise. On long expeditions in cold and unresponsive countries, such as the Antarctic, untoward characteristics appear in the individual that we never dreamed of in civilization. The selection of the personnel is, therefore, of the utmost importance. My old and tried shipmate, Floyd Bennett, who flew with me over the North Pole, will be second in command. Hardships in the polar regions seem to bring out the best and the worst in a man. Of the thousand or more men who lost their lives in the attempt to conquer the Arctic, many of the deaths were caused by disloyalty or mutinies. I can, therefore, say nothing better for Bennett than to state that there is no man in the world I had rather go into the Antarctic with than him.

We shall attempt to put our base on the opposite side of the Antarctic continent from the Weddell Sea, on the great Ross ice barrier, which is at the southern end of the Ross Sea. There will be an ice pack to force our way through before we get to the barrier and we must be as certain as is humanly possible that we get through this pack without getting caught in it. That, of course, would end the expedition. When we were getting our plane through the ice at King's Bay, Spitzbergen, for our North Pole effort, we might easily have had our frail raft, containing the personnel and the plane, crushed—and so would have ended our expedition almost before it had started.

We plan to use a ship especially made to withstand ice. Her hull is slightly wedge-shaped so that she will rise under ice pressure. Her bow is a powerful solid ram built to strike hammer blows against the floes that bar our way. Strong crosstimbers are placed from end to end to stand the enormous squeezing of the merciless ice fields.

Since we shall be gone so long from our last port of call that the coal bunkers will not be able to hold anything like the quantity of coal necessary, we shall have to arrange several of the cargo holds of the ship to carry extra hundreds of tons of fuel. It is extremely hard work to move this coal from the hold to the coal bunkers and that job alone will give our fifty-five adventurers plenty of exercise. In the case of our Polar flight, the moving of this coal was an "all-hands" job from the Captain down to the mess attendants. The result was that when we reached the Arctic every one was in good physical condition.

There will be one big monoplane for our serious work. It will have three engines and the wing spread will be about seventy-six feet. It will contain all the improvements we have made as a result of our last three expeditions. Then there will be two smaller monoplanes with single engines, similar to the plane Chamberlin used in crossing the Atlantic. All of these planes will be equipped with interchangeable landing gear so that they can fly from the water with pontoons, from the snow with skis, or from the land with wheels. We found on the Polar flight that these skis should be made with a great factor of safety for the rough snow work and that they should be bowed in the center like the Norwegian foot skis. We shall experiment with snow flying this winter with the planes we are going to use.

The ship will be equipped with powerful modern radio, both short and long wave, with which we shall make an effort to keep in constant touch with civilization. We shall use short wave radio during the six months' daylight. There will be a year and a half's supply of food on board in case it should be necessary for the personnel to spend the Antarctic night before returning.

Before we get to our last port of call about 8500 miles away—the expedition should be broken into harness and the landlubbers should have their sea legs. After leaving New Zealand we shall hit for the Ross ice barrier, which is 2300 miles directly south. We should have our first battle with the ice pack in the Ross Sea during November, 1928, or the first part of December. Then, there will be more or less open ice-strewn water for several hundred miles, until we get to the ice barrier; we shall be fortunate if we reach our main base before the first part of January, 1929. It now appears that we shall place our main base at the Bay of Whales, near where Amundsen based; or Discovery Harbor: Scott's base was on the eastern side of the Ross ice barrier, Amundsen's on the western side, and Discovery Harbor is between these two bases and may be a desirable place to embark on to the ice because the ice is low enough at that point to enable us to get our planes and equipment up on the barrier. It is thought that as weather conditions are better on Bay of Whales side we are more likely to put our base there. At other places the ice barrier ranges from 30 to 230 feet in height at its precipitous edge, making it impossible to get our equipment ashore with any such altitude as that to scale.

Our base, then, will probably be established on snow-covered ice. This will be about the same thing as camping on a stationary iceberg. It does not seem a practical thing, but I believe it is. Amundsen did it successfully. It will even be an advantage in one way because we can dig down in the ice and make ice rooms for some of our work shops and supplies.

There is no place where one can get so far from human life. Our base will be at least 2300 miles from the nearest human dwelling. We shall have in effect a small village. It must be a self-sustaining unit capable of maintaining itself indefinitely without outside help, because if we should have to spend the Antarctic night, or if our ship should get injured in the ice, there is no telling how long we might have to stay down there. It is wise always to be prepared for such an emergency. I was a member of one expedition which came very near getting caught in the Arctic for the winter without sufficient food to last until summer.

We should, in case of an emergency, be able to supplement our food supply with seal and birds, which abound at certain times on the fringe of the Antarctic continent. As soon as we arrive we shall begin sending out parties to kill seal to lay by for possible use during the winter months. This would be important as a scurvy preventative. There will never be any scurvy as long as there is plenty of fresh meat. We shall have four or five portable houses, and for heating and cooking purposes we shall use coal, gasoline, and oil. It is very likely that we shall take an electric plant with us for lighting.

We expect to take with us at least seventy-five Eskimo dogs, which will be used to haul loads near the base and to assist in establishing sub-bases on the route to the South Pole. Arthur T. Walden, of Wonalancet, New Hampshire, a veteran of the Arctic and a great dog-team leader, has trained a special dog team. The majority of the dogs, however, will probably be procured from Greenland or northern Canada. In addition to the dogs we shall use, for transportation about the base, caterpillar tractors. This will be especially useful for hauling the plane around. We discovered on our North Pole expedition that it is extremely difficult to handle a great plane equipped with skis by hand alone.

Of course, we hope to finish the mission of our expedition during the Antarctic summer, which will last until about March 1st. That would give us about two months for operations. I should say that chances of doing this would be about even. But I don't know. It is an unknown quantity. If we have to spend the Antarctic night, our ship will have to be sent back to New Zealand, or possibly to the States because it probably could not stand the winter ice.

So much for the main base itself. We expect to put down several sub-bases towards the South Pole about one hundred miles apart. The number of bases we can put down is another unknown quantity. There are several reasons for doing this. First, because it will be impossible to predict the weather conditions that will exist on a flight from our main base to the South Pole, and the winds in that region may come up suddenly and blow violently, frequently with very thick snow, which would bring about a situation much worse than fog for the flyer, because he would not only be blinded, as is the case in fog, but would also have a terrific wind at the same time. With bases every one hundred miles the flyer would have a chance to land near one of these bases and survive the storm. In such a case, he would have to carry along some special apparatus and use some special methods to prevent the plane from being blown over.

In a forced landing in any kind of weather, within 500 miles from base, there would be a chance of getting back with bases down every hundred miles. Without them, there would be no chance, because (as has already been explained) there is no animal life that would enable one to procure food, as in the case in the Arctic. Then these bases could be used for flights to the right or left for scientific exploration. For example, suppose we should establish our main base on the ice barrier near the Bay of Whales. Then our line of flight towards the Pole would be on the very edge of the unknown. When we reached an altitude of 5000 feet anywhere along this line of flight we should be looking into regions never before seen by a human being. Probably we should be able to fly out in an easterly direction a hundred miles or so with our mapping camera. We plan to do that. In that way we would be able to photograph a considerable unknown area, at the same time running the minimum risk from sudden violent gales. But no matter how carefully we might plan our expedition into this largely unknown region, it is impossible to say ahead of time exactly what can or cannot be done or exactly how far apart we shall be able to put our bases, or how far towards the Pole.

The principal supplies we shall leave at these bases will be food and fuel and repair material for sleds. Three methods will be employed to put them down—airplanes, dog teams, and our air propeller sleds. It is probable that the dog teams will play the largest part in this work. Dog teams should supplement the airplane in getting minute scientific details.

On the final flight to the Pole, the flying done after the last base is passed will be hazardous, of course, because should there be a forced landing with the plane out of commission, our ability to return to the nearest base would be very far from a certainty. In such an emergency we shall have to depend upon radio and the reserve planes. If our bases are far enough along we may be able to hike back to the nearest one. But here is another unknown quantity. We shall take a kite with us in order to send messages back to the base and receive them. The Navy has already offered to assist with the radio work as much as the law will allow. We shall use on our plane a set similar to the one that did such fine work on our trans-Atlantic flight. This, a regular Navy set modified for our use by W. E. Hansen and Hylan, very capable Naval radio engineers, used a wave length of about 600 meters. It was Hansen who made the radio set we used on our North Pole expedition. We shall have also on the plane a small auxiliary high-frequency, short wave set of about forty meters, with a storage battery or a hand crank generator so that we can get back to base in case we have to land on the ice. The short wave, high-frequency sets are generally preferred in the Arctic, for they can carry great distances with small power and an aerial of a few feet in height. Captain S. C. Hooper, U.S.N., one of the greatest radio experts in the world, especially on radio equipment for planes, is giving the expedition the benefit of his expert advice and help.

As the South Pole itself is on a plateau over ten thousand feet high landing on it is going to be difficult, because it is likely to be very cold, but what is more important, the air at that height of nearly two miles has lost so much of its denseness, that it will require more power to take the plane off the snow. The landing speed also will be faster. It is clear that this matter must be worked out with the utmost care because it would be impossible to get back to base from that distance should the plane for any reason be unable to rise after landing.

There are some planes that cannot even reach that altitude. Our plane will need a ceiling of twice that altitude. This landing will be further complicated by the fact that we must have on board when we land at least twelve hundred gallons of gasoline and a thousand pounds or so of emergency equipment. This weight, of course, will make the landing speed faster. We do not know whether we shall be able to land there but we are extremely anxious to do so in order to take scientific observations.

Reaching the pole itself is only a part of the work to be done by our expedition. The total unknown region is an area of 4,600,000 square miles, the circumference of which area is about 9000 sea miles, more than one-third of the distance around the world. As the ice barrier has prevented ships from reaching the land, no one knows just where the land begins. Airplanes can fly over this ice pack with ease where the ordinary ship would meet with certain disaster, but the flying would be hazardous in case of a forced landing.

It must not be thought that even one or two expeditions can disclose very much of the secrets of the Antarctic.

In the plane itself on the final dash, it is possible that we shall carry a small team of light dogs and a sled. The plane will be capable of carrying the necessary load. That is why we prefer a large plane for this work. In addition to that equipment, there will be carried in the plane a primus stove, reindeer sleeping bag, two months food supply including pemmican (the great Arctic food), chocolate, tea, and hardtack, together with dog food; also a special tent such as we carried on the North Pole flight, medical kit, skis, snowshoes, extra shoes and clothing, rifles, ammunition, and hunting knives.

This equipment will be used in case of a forced landing, when we should have to hike back to base. I am not prepared to say just what chances we should have of getting back. That would depend, of course, on our distance from the coast line.

The Antarctic can be conquered because a permanent base can be established that will not float away, as would be the case when putting down bases on the moving ice fields of the frozen polar area. Were it not possible to place these permanent bases, the frightful meteorological conditions would make the conquest of Antarctica by air well-nigh impossible.

How great it will be, looking down into tens of thousands of square miles of regions never before looked upon by a human being, so far as we know. I must admit, too, that although the primary object of the expedition is scientific, it will be most gratifying if we succeed in planting the American flag at the South Pole—at the bottom of the world.

XVI.

Behind
the Scenes

THE PUBLIC LOVES THE DRAMA of dangerous adventure—as described on the printed page. The perilous part of exploration is also the adventurer's greatest joy. Of the toil and the anxiety that now go into the organization of a big expedition the public hears but little. Of the anguish the leader must suffer in this preparatory phase none can know who has not been through it.

In my big library of Arctic books I find that one poignant similarity joins them all as a class. On the final field map of each thrilling expedition one fatal spot is usually denoted as that at which came the climax of the leader's grim success or galling failure.

I choose at random: "X marks the spot where our brave men died after six days of howling blizzard and bitter cold."

But, alas, like styles on the boulevard, so have styles in exploration changed. How profound has been the change can be indicated in no better way than by the fact that the X that used to mark the spot where the dying explorer ate his last morsel of pemmican now marks the office where he collected his last dollar of backing.

Exploration has always been a battle between man and the elements. It is now; except that chilblains and thirst have given away to creditors and thrift. Sixty below zero still makes the brave leader quake. But his zero isn't on the thermometer, but on the credit side of his expeditionary ledger.

It cost Columbus $2,115 to discover America. It cost the world $200,000,000 and hundreds of lives to discover the North Pole. I don't intend to argue that either was worth more or less than it cost, but the overhead of polar work hasn't gone down since the date of Peary's discovery.

My North Pole expedition in 1926 was made just about as cheaply as possible. We spent hours and hours trying to get things done economically. It had to be. Yet it cost in cold cash about $140,000. Nor does this take in a very large sum represented by men and material which were given at cost or donated. For a few weeks at sea and a few hours in the air such expense is high.

Our trip to the South Pole will cost above $450,000. As we have to be ready to winter on the Antarctic ice barrier and cover about 24,000 miles in the round trip from New York, the cost rises much beyond that of a North Polar party.

There was much hue and cry a few years ago over the ease

and economy air travel would bring to the explorer. It looked as if so much time would be saved and so little work have to be done in the hard winter seasons that one of my dollars would now do the work of four or five of Peary's.

But we were all wrong. The first thing that happened was that the expedition ship had to be bigger in order to carry an exploring plane to the base of operations. A larger ship meant more men, more fuel, more repairs.

Another costly item was the mechanical extravagance of the new vehicle. The old explorer never made 100 miles an hour, but his hour-mile cost more than 100 times less. There was nothing of the prima donna in the sledge. It could be pushed or pulled until it fell to pieces. Its only fuel went into the leather-lined bellies of its draft animals and its lubrication was Nature's own snow fields. The whiplash was its throttle, and all the overhauling one did after a trip was to tighten up a sealskin lashing and hammer a bent runner into shape with a granite bowlder.

There are something like 2000 integral parts in a modern airplane. At any time some 300 of these may get out of commission. At least 800 of them have to be replaced if broken. Repairing one part may mean the readjustment of fifty others. With the nearest airplane factory more than 2000 miles away, one has to take plenty of spares. The old proverb read, "For want of a nail the shoe was lost," and ended by blaming the rider's demise on this tiny item. Exploration by air can be equally fatal for the want of a part a good deal smaller than a horseshoe nail.

The old explorer never faced complete failure so steadily as does the modern flying leader, who literally has all his eggs in one or two very expensive baskets. By sledge or back pack it was always possible to accomplish at least a part of the original plan. But let one serious crash come to the aeronautical side of a modern expedition and there is nothing left to do but go home and face the music.

On our North Pole trip Bennett and I were not half so worried about breaking our necks on the polar ice as we were about smashing our plane on the take-off. Our big three-engined monoplane was equipped with skis which we hadn't yet learned to use. Three times we came within a hairbreadth of cracking up before we got away for the top of the globe. Had we done so, the expedition would have ended then and there. My news rights and films and lectures with which I hoped to stave off a small army of creditors wouldn't have been worth a backstay's bight.

It would have given some of these same creditors St. Vitus' dance to see us bring our expensive plane ashore through half a mile of loose ice between the ship and the shore. We made a raft that did the trick, after some hair-raising setbacks when the big floes started out with the tide. This time X marked the spot not where we were cold and wet and in imminent danger of drowning among the growlers, but where we escaped by our teeth from nearly plunging into a financial abyss from which I personally might not have emerged for many years.

An explorer has always been a geographer. He was also expected to be on speaking terms with the flora and fauna of the region which he was to penetrate. He had to have medical knowledge in case of emergency, and be prepared to deal with any form of crises from putting down a mutiny to considering an offer of kingship over a savage tribe.

When the twentieth century opened with primus stoves and percolators, electric generators and spectroscopes among the essentials of an explorer's kit, the professorial aspects of his job began to weigh heavily. When another decade brought radio, with its tubes, counterpoises and condensers, the successful adventurer was less a two-fisted leader than a six-cylinder physicist. With the introduction of flying into the exploring field, no outstanding explorer could equip his party economically without knowing most of the principles of aeronautical dynamics in addition to all the burden of other sciences under which his predecessors labored.

Naturally an outdoor man, the modern explorer has now to learn to be an indoor man. He must attend numerous functions and ceremonies where he generally has to make a speech. He is expected to be able to talk well on any subject. He must lecture to raise funds for his expedition. For the same reason he writes for newspapers, magazines, and every now and then he produces a book. He therefore must be able to write. But the last straw has come in the past few years with the terrific financial complexities which have changed exploration from a species of research to something resembling a stock-market manipulation. If he does not administer the business affairs of his expedition economically, he is likely to go on the rocks a bankrupt. History proves this point only too poignantly. Columbus died penniless. Scott, perishing on the Antarctic ice, penned a message to the English nation pleading that his family be cared for. Shackleton, dying in harness, left an estate too slight to keep his wife and child. Amundsen, Rasmussen, Stefansson, Capt. Bob Bartlett and a dozen others who have devoted their lives to the spread of human knowledge through the medium of exploration are all poor men.

The paradox of the whole thing is that the true explorer usually has ideals enough not to want to commercialize his work.

There are several legitimate ways to raise funds that cannot logically be condemned. Lectures are a medium through which many conservative people may be reached who otherwise would have some difficulty in following first-hand an explorer's work. Films, magazine articles and still pictures are of more or less value, depending on the skill and perfection with which they are produced and distributed. The expedition leader's newspaper stories, when properly handled, bring good prices and give the public well-directed information of an expedition's progress in the field. Such stories cannot be given away. They must be exclusive to be of any value.

The radio has introduced another consideration—the spot news; that is, the day-by-day news of the expedition. Formerly the Arctic explorer could not give the daily happenings of his expedition to the world. When I go to the Antarctic I shall have my base 2300 miles from the nearest human dwelling. But I hope to get back interesting reports of how we are progressing.

These legitimate fund-raising methods are by no means assured profits. A newspaper story worth $30,000 if an expedition is dramatically successful, may be worth less than $3000 in case of unavoidable failures. Contracts are drawn in advance, making price contingent on results. The same applies to lectures. If there be no story to tell or no film to portray the story, a tour may well shrink to half a dozen friendly engagements given with little or no profit.

It is clear then that the modern explorer cannot force his burden of debt on other shoulders by simply discounting his news, film and lecture success. Were he able to do so, the wilderness would be populous with fantastic expeditions. Little does the public realize the widespread craze to explore today. What holds most amateurs in check is purely the problem of where to get the money.

Almost the only way to finance a modern expedition is to get subscriptions from private citizens, institutions and associations altruistically interested in pure science. It is easy to picture Mr. Millionaire giving a big sum to applied science. In such an investment he always has a chance of making a killing if the research be a success. But contributions to Arctic exploration are generally made unselfishly, without any chance of dividends.

But before the leader can approach a prospective contributor he must have established on one hand his ability to do the job and on the other the authenticity of his plans.

In my own case I struggled through a maze of red-tape in 1925 before finally emerging with Secretary Wilbur's approval. Officialdom was kind enough individually, but for complexity, the mills of the gods that grind so slowly give a modern printing press a puerile simplicity. What I wanted to do was to command the naval aviation unit of the National Geographic Society's expedition, then bound for North Greenland.

"I will go to the President," the secretary told me, signifying I had reached the last barrier.

But I was none too sanguine. President Coolidge's ideas of economy and his natural reluctance to let his military personnel take undue risks made me feel that my chances of getting away were none too bright.

When the secretary took the matter to him the critical moment had been reached, the moment of which I had been dreaming for years. If only I could go on this one expedition, I knew I might have a chance in the following year to realize my cherished hope of some day flying to the North Pole.

The secretary told me later about his interview with his chief. He went thoroughly into detail.

"There is still a great deal of blank space on our polar map, Mr. President. Don't you think we ought to let Byrd go?" he concluded. In complete silence the President had listened, yet with attentiveness.

After a moment of thought the President nodded to his cabinet officer and said "Why not?"

No discussion, no questions. Just that pair of words which for prodigious consequences in my life compare favorably with the other well-known couple: "I do."

The President's tacit approval of my plan enabled me to get prompt orders to go north. Between these orders and the press announcements I had something sound on which to base my collection of equipment. Luckily I needed no money, since the Navy was going to let me have my men, equipment and planes. We got away in the early summer and, as previously stated, managed to fly with the three machines more than 5000 miles—the first extensive Arctic aviation up to that time.

I might mention here that, like wars, expeditions into polar regions are won by preparations, though it is of course natural that the zero hour—the final dash—gets the spotlight. Yet behind the scenes there is frequently the more interesting drama, and even zero hours unwritten and unknown may be found there. It is not in order to go into the infinite detail connected with a polar expedition, but I will touch briefly on some of my business experiences.

The year after our 1925 expedition Bennett and I

launched our plan to conquer the North Pole by air. The first man I tackled was Edsel Ford. He was near my own age, a big man with ideals, and son of a father who thought in terms of America's tomorrow.

It was a big moment. Should he deny a subscription, there would be no 1926 expedition for me. There were then four or five North Pole expeditions underway. I laid my cards on the table.

I told him frankly the plane I wanted to use, knowing that this was a machine in competition with the new Ford design. My reason for using that plane was that the particular plane I had in mind had been flown 15,000 miles—long enough to get the usual kinks out of it. It was a ticklish moment, asking a big man to finance a scheme that would be an advertisement for his competitor. He nodded gravely, but did not reply.

"And if we crack up on taking off our great plane with skis," I confessed, "that's the end of the party."

It is significant of the man's tolerant, broad character that when I finished he said simply:

"Certainly I will help you. I believe your expedition will do a lot to increase popular interest in aviation in America."

Not only did Mr. Ford promptly give me the generous sum I asked for but he wrote a friend, urging him also to come in.

I was now in a position to condition the ship which the United States Shipping Board had so kindly put at my disposal and to order the provisions we had to have aboard in case we were forced to winter. But though I figured as carefully as I could, I soon found myself again in financial straits. Well I knew that almost regardless of expense my equipment must be of the very highest order. A tainted can of pemmican, a poorly sewed ice boot, a mitten without a lanyard, an oversize screw thread on some insignificant airplane part, might well spike my guns long after I had left the nearest civilized base of supplies.

More money had to be got. I had gone ahead too far to turn back; yet my credit was strained to its breaking point. Putting my pride in my pocket, I called on the president of one of our great corporations, a Crœsian cliff dweller on Broadway. In my pocket I fondled a warm letter of introduction from an old friend of the great man.

From nine A.M. until after noon I cooled my heels in the magnate's plush-lined outer office. Painful waiting it was, too, with a thousand details of preparation clamoring for my attention. And there was none of the consolation that my men could sympathize with my apprehension as they could when later we faced the hazards of field work. I scarcely dared tell my best friend how thin my funds were for fear an adverse publicity might leak into the papers, which for years had been captious about the undue risks of Arctic work.

By a side door my quarry slipped out to luncheon, leaving word that he would see me in the afternoon. I waited. As the sun was sinking over the Hudson I got my final word—of dismissal. A colored messenger came out and told me that Mr. Blank had decided he couldn't see me at all.

How different were my relations with John D. Rockefeller, Jr. The sequestration of great wealth in this country may infuriate demagogues; but whatever be its defects, the social system that makes rich men possible also makes possible the promotion of scientific endeavor that would scarce be thought of under a more general diffusion of wealth. I soon found that Mr. Rockefeller had made just as much a business of giving as the modern explorer must make of collecting. I believe that to give in such a way that progress will be helped instead of hindered is one of the most difficult and elusive things to accomplish. Being of a scientific turn of mind, Mr. Rockefeller has developed into a past master in the art of giving. But he is broad enough to value and heed advice from specialists, so he has hired some of the best brains in the country to help him decide what enterprises promise results and human profit, and what do not. Mr. Rockefeller came to my rescue by matching Mr. Ford's contribution.

The thing that astonished me about these men, as well as others of their class with whom I have come in contact, is the wide disparity between the public's picture of them and the men themselves. Edsel Ford, for instance, is the real directing head of the mammoth enterprise his father has built. He keeps longer office hours and works harder actively managing the Ford Motor Company than the average business man, yet he goes about it all so quietly and efficiently that the public knows scarcely anything about him.

Then take the young Mr. Rockefeller. Even fiction writers

are chary about giving their heroes such a fortune as the Rockefeller estate. To the average man this wealth suggests a sort of Sybaritic solitude, full of gilded joys made sweet by a quintessence of ease. In contrast, John D. Rockefeller, Jr., slaves away daily just about like any other business man. He isn't working at making money, but at the far more difficult task of supervising its scientific spending for progress. He is an excellent speaker. And his athletic prowess, on which any man can build a sane philosophy, he probably prizes higher than his fortune. He is a man of very high ideals and he lives up to them.

As the day of my departure north approached once more, I saw my liabilities outdistancing my assets. Perhaps there is something in telepathy, for about this time Vincent Astor sent for me and wanted to know how I was coming along.

"I'm worried about your finances," he said, throwing down the guard that all rich men must wear. He had already made a substantial contribution to the expedition.

He offered to go on my note for any amount that I needed, asking no more than my signature. It was a strong temptation to accept. If things broke right in the north I should have no difficulty repaying the loan. But I admitted that my name had nothing back of it now that the expedition was already in debt. As with Edsel Ford, I further explained that a crash on our take-off in Spitzbergen would likely precipitate bankruptcy proceedings when we came back.

"What difference does that make?" he asked. "I'm simply betting on you, am I not?"

Again I saw how quickly and completely a big man can make up his mind on occasion.

Nine men and one woman subscribed for my polar flight. I know that all gave for unselfish reasons; but some went so far as to refuse to let me even publish their names in connection with the enterprise. Among others who subscribed were Captain and Mrs. John H. Gibbons, U.S.N.; Thomas Fortune Ryan, a Virginian; and Richard Hoyt of New York.

I remember paying a call of pure courtesy on a rich citizen of Virginian descent two months before we sailed north. As I got up to leave he said quite unexpectedly:

"Byrd, I want to donate something to your expedition. But I will do it only on the condition that you do not mention me."

I recall one night lecturing in Washington before the Massachusetts Society of the District of Columbia. To my surprise a Congressman I know hurried up and insisted that I let him give something toward my new adventure, as he put it. There is more than altruism in that sort of enthusiasm. I think it reveals a little of the love of romance lurking in the hearts of most people, far beneath the sleek enamel of civilization.

This fund raising goes on generally until the day of departure, for the explorer nearly always leaves with a deficit facing him. When I left on our North Pole expedition I had a deficit of nearly $30,000, which, before our expedition was disorganized, swelled to nearly $40,000. The Amundsen-Ellsworth-Nobile expedition had a much larger deficit after the flight of the *Norge*.

Peary returned from his first expedition with a deficit. To pay off his debts he went on a lecture tour, giving 168 lectures in 96 days, and had enough funds left over to help finance his next expedition. Peary told some of his friends that he had never made a trip that was harder on him than this one.

When our North Pole sailing day finally came the expedition was only partially built by the dollars that had passed through my bank account from the hands of generous friends. For instance, we had procured the 3500-ton steamer *Chantier* for the charter price of one dollar a year so long as we should need her. That we owe to the United States Shipping board. Armour & Company gave us meat. The Pioneer Instrument Company gave us instruments and experts. The Weather Bureau sent along William Haines, one of its most experienced meteorologists. Johns Hopkins University loaned us Dr. Daniel O'Brien, as agreeable as he was able. The Wright Aeronautical Company donated Doc Kincaid, noted last summer for having nursed the engines of all three planes that succeeded in flying the Atlantic. The Vacuum Oil Company donated oil; and the Standard Oil Company of New Jersey, gasoline. Of the fifty-one men on the ship, I paid only five their accustomed salaries. This shows in some measure the untrammeled eagerness behind such a venture.

Indeed, the success of my North Pole expedition was due far more to the patriotism, unselfishness and loyalty of a great many people than to any peculiar competence on the part of Bennett and me, who simply had the divine privilege of riding the winning horse. A dozen times the half hundred volunteers with me, by super-human effort up in the bitter weather of the Arctic, saved the day for Bennett and me. I believe this wide diffusion of indispensable support is one of the chief peculiarities of a modern expedition.

Few people seem to realize that one in my position has to support his family in between times. His mail is mountainous, yet he must bear the secretarial expense of handling it. And he is considered "high-hat" if he does not answer promptly and satisfactorily everything from a demand for an autograph to an application for membership in his next expedition, both of which come in daily by the hundred. Telegrams become a prodigious item of expense as time passes.

Then there is the so-called public service which the hardworking explorer is called upon to shoulder. This includes being present at innumerable ceremonies, many of which have not the remotest connection with him or his work; charities, conventions, civic drives, political shindigs and scores of other kinds of log-rolling.

At all times he is being called upon to use his nicest judgment about accepting business offers. One offer would have given me $5000 a week to talk at a string of moving picture theatres for fifteen minutes every time my polar picture was shown. Some of my enterprising friends urged me to send our North Pole plane around the country, taking up passengers at ten dollars a head. Since we could have held ten at a time, that meant a profit of almost $100 every ten minutes, or close to $10,000 a day. That was most tempting, but had we done that we would have been commercializing our expedition in such a way that we would have defeated one of our main purposes, which was to help aviation. Instead, we chose to arrange with the Department of Commerce and the Guggenheim Fund for a tour around the country on behalf of aviation. Bennett piloted the plane successfully to forty-four cities. Bennett's batting average was high, not missing a single engagement on his list. I talked on aviation in more than fifty cities. Had we commercialized the expedition instead of doing this, we would not have been worthy of support.

I find it a toss-up as to whether the explorer has a harder time with his complications before or after an expedition. It is a heavy strain to get ready; but the aftermath of a successful trip is in some ways worse. Crossing the Polar Sea and the Atlantic were fatiguing flights. Yet both times I had to get busy the moment I landed and write long articles for syndicates that had bought my story of the flights. When civilization is reached there springs up an unavoidable round of social engagements. At such periods only the hours between midnight and three A.M. are available for answering wires and cables, drafting instructions to personnel, making important decisions of policy, considering invitations and attending to innumerable other items of business. I have averaged only three or four hours of sleep a night after both my polar and Atlantic flights, despite the fact that I have never felt so much the need of rest as I did at those times.

The legacy of troubles bred in days like these is a long one. I am still receiving bills which came out of the confusion of our North Pole flight.

"Of course a reporter wrote your story, didn't he?" so many people say to me.

Frankly I don't believe in having some one else write one's statements to the newspapers. Occasionally it can't be helped. After our landing at Ver-sur-Mer, when I had had a total of only about two hours' sleep over three days and three nights, I found myself under contract to produce copy for the papers. Pure physical exhaustion and an official delegation from Paris led me to dictate my first installment to a journalist. I did not see his version until I returned on the *Leviathan*. It was well done and, in the main, true. But had I written it myself I should not have repeatedly declared, as the reporter did, during my flight that I was completely lost. We weren't. While over the ocean, three hours before we reached France, we knew our position and course very exactly. When we found Paris smothered in fog we were able to navigate back to the coast, the only place we could make a safe landing and save our lives. A small point in the layman's mind, but a vital one in the aeronautical record.

Yet an explorer must live up to his press contracts or forfeit his profit, the life blood of his expedition.

Lecturing is a vastly overrated way of raising money for explorations. It is the most trying work I know. With its one-night stands, receptions, banquets, irregular hours, disordered regime, long periods of standing and general nervous strain, it can well break the strongest man in a few months. In addition to all this, the active explorer is generally carrying on much correspondence in connection with the preparation for his next expedition.

The order of the lecturer's day is fairly similar in each city. Usually he is met by a delegation of friendly citizens. Luncheon that is really a daylight banquet follows. There are speeches of welcome, culminating in an address by the distinguished visitor. Sights of the city come next—a vague method of pseudo entertainment that may mean anything from a series of cocktail parties to a hundred-mile motor trip over the local parkways. Often there is an afternoon reception, engineered by the ladies. Then the big banquet and lecture of the evening. The explorer is lucky if he gets back to his hotel by midnight and is free to plunge into the pile of telegrams, letters and long distance telephone calls awaiting him.

My attitude may seem captious and ungrateful. But I am only trying to give a dispassionate picture of what men in my position go through. In fact I find that, when fully aroused, the generosity and hospitality, the civic pride and the innate kindness of the average American city transcend those of any race or nation in the world. I have felt humble and grateful for the wonderful kindness and hospitality I have received.

I wish I had space and words to emphasize more strongly the priceless experience I have had in the incredibly warm friendliness I have met everywhere. I wouldn't take anything for that experience. I can only say that I do not accept this tribute for myself alone but also for the fine young Americans who have helped me to succeed.

Just when the explorer is trying his best to be a hardboiled business man and get the threads of his mountainous debts unraveled, he often finds himself tangled up in an altogether new set of complications which I believe the average business man is rarely called upon to face. I mean personalities—personalities of men and of women; of men and women who write letters; of men and women who want to give money; of men and women who compose audiences, and so on.

For example, each audience has its own personality. One of the warmest I ever faced was that collected by the Junior League in a conservative northern city. One of my coldest was far south of the Mason and Dixon Line. I am a Southerner, too. One audience will have little sense of humor, another a lot. Some are serious and detached, others are gay and responsive. The speaker must guard against succumbing to the mass mood of those who face him.

School children are irresistibly enthusiastic. Thousands of my letters are from boys and girls in their teens.

In this connection it is significant that girls outnumbered the boys ten to one in asking to go on my Arctic flight, whereas applications for the South Pole come in now at a rate of 100 boys to one girl. Looks as if the girls want to keep warm—or else get to Paris—doesn't it?

Probably the most personal, surely the most insistent thing that keeps cropping up through all the explorer's business, through all his lecturing and writing, amid all his money gathering and on all his travels, is a question. Strange to say, this question is unanswerable. No, let me modify that: it is not satisfactorily answerable to the average person. This question is:

What is the sense of Arctic exploration anyway?

And the more the questioner knows about this question, the harder it is to answer. But let me frame my own reply:

The Antarctic continent, our next destination, is save on a tiny fringe at one or two spots where seals and penguins abound, this white wilderness is, so far as we know, lifeless as space and nearly as cold.

It does at first sight seem unreasonable to spend large sums of money and face great hazards in order to know more about so uninviting a part of the world. The only thing its exploration can promise is a tithe of abstract scientific information, though our expedition will be purely a scientific one.

What then is the good of adding to man's store of abstract knowledge?

The answer to this must come ultimately in material results, if at all. For example, as a result of centuries of apparently aimless research we now have the telephone, the telegraph, radio, airplanes, anæsthesia, antitoxin, illuminating gas, electric lights, X-rays, automobiles, and a thousand other devices that make life safer and happier. Every one came suddenly and seemed to be the work of an inspired inventor. But that was not true. Each was the culmination of generations of plodding abstract inquiry into the unknown, and more often than not the inquirer was jeered or feared for being a necromancer.

Exploration is just such inquiry after abstract knowledge. We anticipate no immediate gain, unless it is from our meteorological investigations, no application of our discoveries to commerce. The expedition's scientists can perhaps only unfold something of the past. For my South Polar trip our justifiable incentive is that we shall add to man's store of knowledge in the abstract if only by gazing upon and photographing a portion of the 4,000,000 square miles of Antarctic territory as yet unseen by human eye.

XVII.

A Glimpse into the Future

THE TEMPTATION to speculate about the future of flying is very strong. For likely, when posterity looks back upon this amazing age in which we live, flying will be seen to have done more to promote human welfare than any other human agency.

Yet it is wise, I believe, for some of us flyers to "keep our feet on the ground," figuratively, at any rate, and to be conservative, and not to let ourselves be carried away by our enthusiasm so that we picture a so-called "air age" so exaggerated that it may never come.

Aviation has already been much hurt by air enthusiasts whose predictions have not panned out. Others have condemned the art without fair consideration. I try to steer a middle course between these two extremes, though I am confident that flying is going on to heights as yet undreamed.

A Glimpse into the Future

The limitations of aircraft are several and serious. A large percentage of the power plant of an airplane must be used to overcome gravity, to keep the plane and its load in the air. In contrast, the weight of an automobile and its load is carried by the earth.

Throughout its progress aviation has had the handicap of contending every flying minute with the force of gravity, life itself the cost of failure. The railway and the automobile have not had this handicap. This is the chief reason why the plane must evolve more slowly than the automobile. However, this same slow evolution indicates an ultimately great stature.

Another limitation is that the cruising radius of an airplane does not increase in the same relation to increase in size as does the steamer and the airship. Airships will, I think, be the freight carriers of the air.

Air transportation is relatively more costly than the automobile as to construction and application. However, cost of the plane itself is gradually getting down to a reasonable figure as production increases. An up-to-date six-passenger plane can now be bought for $12,500, a figure based on production of 50 airplanes. A small two-seater for family use can be purchased for $2000.

Operation is still expensive. Gasoline consumption of the $12,500 plane, with a 200 horsepower Whirlwind motor, is about 11 gallons per hour and one pint of oil per hour for a speed of a mile and a half a minute. Yet we must not forget that there are no rails to lay in aviation; no roadways to construct; no bridges, tunnels or snow-sheds to provide.

Aviation is fortunately entering the most controversial stage of its brief life. The ranks of designers and builders and pilots are being swelled every day both from the college class-room and from the workshop. As a result, its development is, in the sense noted above, slower than it was ten years ago; but it is far more real.

Development in aircraft design will, of course, slow up as the limit of their possibilities is approached. I am one of those who think that that limit is a long way off.

I gather from talking to the layman that the thrill that comes to him when he contemplates the progress of flying is twofold: he feels a shudder at the pilot's peril and a twinge of wonder at the possibilities of the future. The future of aviation and the dangers of flying are intimately associated. There can be no future for any forms of transportation that is not safe. As I said in the beginning, the public will never fully patronize the plane in preference to the railway until, as in the case with the latter, inter-line rivalry is on the grounds of comfort and not on the score of safety.

In the last two years we have made several great steps forward. One is, we have learned that a gas engine can be counted on for many hours of performance in the air. We knew some time ago that we could mount it "on the block" in a test shed and run it without stopping for two days. But with the polar, European, and Hawaiian flights behind us now we know that a pilot can at last depend on his engine in all sorts of weather for from thirty to sixty hours' unbroken running. I believe the 100-hour reliable engine is at hand.

Further, these long-distance flights have established beyond a doubt the practicability of a multi-engined plane for use over areas where there are no landing places. This gives us another factor of reliability. Over France in the *America* our fuel was reduced to the point where two of our three engines could have held us aloft. It requires no flight of imagination to see that the large passenger plane of 1936 will likely have four or five engines (housed in the wing out of air resistance), not all of which will be required to keep their pilots in the air. Engines so housed will probably have to be water cooled.

To increase the factor of safety still more there will be special emergency devices for lightening the load which the engines have to carry. As I have related, we had such a device on the *America.* It permitted us to empty our fuel tank in about a minute and a half. In a huge ten-engined airplane such a mechanism might well make up the difference between what eight and seven engines could carry by an operation lasting less than half a minute.

It is conceivable that this matter of lightening the plane may be carried to the point of dropping other weights. One designer has suggested an emergency cabin to which all passengers would be brought when it became necessary to let go the main under-body so that surviving engines could keep the plane aloft. This does not mean that I favor resorting to such devices. It merely goes to show the direction in which we are moving to make passenger air service as safe as that on the ground.

Another great step forward I believe we are soon to make is the reduction of landing speed. The early Wright machine could land at 30 miles an hour. With a fair load our big planes of today require a landing speed of from 45 to 65 miles an hour. At such speeds the slightest misjudgment on the part of the pilot may lead to a serious or even fatal accident. Perhaps it is in this phase of airplane design that some of the most startling changes of the near future will come.

I think it not unlikely that there will be developed some practical forms of braking devices. These would be attachments to wings or fuselage that would permit the plane to have more supporting and wind-buffer surface during the moments just prior to touching the ground. A bird gains this effect by arching its wings and turning them up to the wind, so that it can hover for a second or two before it alights. Probably our stiff plane wings will always prevent exactly this being done. But extra surfaces that can be momentarily extended will accomplish the same result with slightly additional weight. Planes are now being built with wheel brakes so as not to run so far after landing.

On a large and well-prepared landing field under normal conditions this matter of landing speed is not so important.

But now that cross-country flights are becoming more and more frequent the pilot must be prepared to land in almost any sort of cleared space. Furthermore, we are already beginning to get ready for the day when we shall have to come to a stop on the roofs of skyscrapers and high landing platforms built up like wharves. I think this day is but very little in the future.

Another point about which the layman thinks little, but which is one of the designer's milestones of progress, is the size of the normal gliding angle of the plane. Roughly, this is the angle to the horizontal which a plane can assume and still keep maneuverable speed. In one set of tests set forth for progress along this line the object was stated as "to demonstrate the ability of the aircraft to glide for a reasonable distance in case of engine failure and alternately to glide at a steep angle in order to facilitate the approach to a possible landing ground." In a stalling emergency nothing could be more important to the safety of the passengers. Requirements of the test were:

First, flattest glide: The aircraft shall be able to glide with all power switched off so that the angle between the flight path and the horizontal is not greater than 8 degrees.

Second, steepest glide: The aircraft shall be able to glide with all power switched off so that the angle between the flight path and the horizontal is not less than 16 degrees. During this test the air speed shall not exceed 45 miles per hour. In both cases the aircraft must demonstrate that all the controls are definitely effective throughout the test, and that it can land safely out of this glide from a useful altitude.

All this sounds very technical. But that is true of nearly any present-day discussion of aeronautical details. Engineers have been going ahead with this new science for more than twenty years now and we are well out of the primer class. The important point I want to make is that while this business of gliding angle and landing speed may be obscure to the layman, it is in just this sort of details that our next aeronautical advances are coming.

I predict that we shall follow the example of Europe in popularizing the art of gliding without engines. I can conceive that in the next ten years there will be put on the market engineless gliders that will cost less than four hundred dollars. They will be in a class with canoes. Our young people who now go boating on the lake will then spend part of their time gliding from the hillsides. We may expect to ring the dinner bell only to find that Sally or Jim is half a thousand feet over our chimney tops where the morning breeze has taken her or him in the new glider. As a result of such a fad we should not only rapidly recruit our ranks of pilots throughout the country, but the improvement of design would naturally be helped. Closely following these two items is the matter of ascent angle. With more and more obstructions over the ground we are finding it increasingly difficult to get off with our big planes unless there is wide latitude for running before the hop. I feel sure that devices fashioned for braking on landing will also be used to help the plane get quickly clear of the ground on the takeoff.

Stability has been a mooted question since the Wrights first made their historic glides at Kitty Hawk. Designers have been working toward automatic stability for years. There are now on the market several planes in which the pilot can momentarily in smooth air leave the control while in the air and walk back among his passengers. Such stability must in the future be obtainable not only when weather is perfect, but when the plane is being thrown about by gusts of wind striking it from any direction.

A startling discovery has recently been made in England. Slots in the wing of the plane open automatically when the plane starts to stall, and so by cutting down the resistance, prevent the plane from falling into a tail-spin.

We have been over the same hurdles with craft that travel on the sea. Early boats of the Nile dwellers were flat-bottomed. They had no keel or bilges. They drifted about at the mercy of every breath of air unless the oarsman was continually on the job. Now we have automatic stability in our ships that is gained in several ways. Bilge keels steady them when rolling and yawing. A large deep rudder aft prevents sudden swinging. A heavy keel, or keels, governs their leeway to a large degree. The helmsman has but to touch his wheel or lever occasionally to keep the huge *Leviathan* on her course.

Besides the items already listed there are some immediate handicaps to safe and efficient passenger air service throughout the United States that I believe will be overcome in the next few years, judging from the rapidity of aeronautical progress today. First, and in some ways most vital, is the fact that we are overloading our planes today when we want to make a long flight. Lindbergh's plane was overloaded; poor Noel Davis's was; mine was. By "overloaded" I mean carrying so much that there is great difficulty getting off the ground, as well as considerable risk in landing, if necessary, in the early stages of the flight.

Had we been forced to land the *America* in a restricted area during the first six minutes of our ocean flight until we could get altitude I think she would have been smashed to kindling wood. To reduce overloading we must first increase the cruising radius of the plane. This can be done in a number of ways. We are continually improving our streamlining and so cutting down resistance. We can increase the efficiency of the wing-lifting power, of the engine, of the fuel, and of the steering surfaces which with the equipment add materially to the total weight of the plane itself. We can decrease the weight of our engine per unit of horsepower. But this will come slowly from now on as we are near the limit now. Minor items such as radio and other auxiliary mechanisms are being made lighter and lighter all the time. Over-loading may dangerously increase strain on the wings; it reduces materially maneuverability of the plane when it is near the ground.

I have already spoken of the value of a reliable engine. Failure of motor at night over land and at any time over sea or rough land, is one of the most pregnant causes of accident in all flying. I am convinced that if we can once reach the point where an engine never stalls in flight we shall not average 5 per cent of the tragedies we have today. There are as many causes for stalling as there are parts in an airplane engine. The entirely foolproof engine has not yet been built; it never will be. But we are working toward that end rapidly; and when men can hop into a plane with confidence that they will run regularly on a set air-mail schedule such as we have today, we are pretty close to the theoretically perfect power plant.

In the next ten years I believe that our big transoceanic radio companies will organize a complete system of air radio. Ships crossing will periodically fix the positions of planes to which they have been assigned. Powerful radio stations on both sides of the ocean will keep a continual stream of radio emanations pouring out over the dark wastes of the sea like beacons of light now visible near the shore. When this sort of system is in force, a plane need scarcely use her compass at all. She will simply start off in the right direction and depend on those ashore or on the surface of the sea to provide her with course corrections as she flies.

The next problem is one that trans-Atlantic flights last summer made the first great attack upon. This was the problem of knowing weather conditions in advance of getting under way for a long hop.

When we were getting ready to hop off in May, 1927, the first regular ocean weather maps for the upper atmosphere were issued by Dr. Kimball of the New York office of the United States Weather Bureau. This was the beginning of what in a few years may become the most extensive and important work of our coastwise weather service, supplementing the land service towards which we have made considerable progress. Most persons will remember how bad conditions were during the periods immediately prior to our hop-off. The trouble was that just when one zone of the ocean route would be reported clear of fog and storm another zone would be very bad. Had we been able to get reports over a larger area, or had our plane boasted of a longer cruising radius, we might have dodged the rough spots and hopped off much sooner. In order to prove the reliability of air-craft we did not await ideal weather.

When we finally did go visibility conditions were such that we were lucky to escape with our lives on the other side. For about twenty-four hours we saw neither sea nor land. This sort of thing need not happen once regular passenger service starts. There will eventually be in operation a perfected system for knowing every hour of the day or night just how the weather is over any spot of the entire globe.

One more difficult air problem that is still unsolved is navigation of the plane. Of course, with perfect weather conditions and a good radio directive system working, the plane doesn't have to be navigated. Over the land in daylight and a good visibility the pilot guides his machine by known landmarks.

But here we reach an impasse with which oceangoing steamships long ago were faced. The steamship pilot can pilot and depend on soundings or radio for a great deal of his cruising. But the law requires that he protect his passengers by constant proper navigational checks of his position at sea. This is done so that if other means of fixing his spot on the chart at any moment suddenly fail him he can still steer an accurate course to port. I am positive that the long-distance plane of the future will be navigated by her officers in much the same way that a ship is navigated at sea. We now have a sun compass for daylight flying in high latitude and reliable airplane magnetic compasses. But neither instrument indicates to the pilot how much his ship is drifting to one or the other side of the course as a result of the wind.

We have instruments to tell how high a plane is, and in clear weather how much she is drifting, and approximately how fast she is going through the air and over the ground. But the figures obtained are still somewhat crude. And the longer the flight in bad conditions the worse such errors become.

One of the greatest inventions yet to be made in aviation is an instrument to be used on the plane itself that will give the drift of an airplane caused by the wind when flying in thick fog or above the clouds. There are those who say that it is impossible to develop such an instrument; but I don't believe it.

Wherever there is a radio beacon available at some nearby station the wind drift can be calculated. But there should be such a fog drift indicator on the plane itself. This together with sensitive altimeter and amber colored light beacons should ultimately conquer this last foe to safe flight.

The pilot of tomorrow must be so secure in his navigation that he need not wait for perfect conditions, or depend for his results on unusual skill. He must have instruments of such accuracy and methods of such simplicity that he can achieve the same results as we did near the pole whether the weather be good or not.

Summing up, commercial aviation of the future need not be subject to any of the accidents that have made aviation thought of as dangerous. The commercial company will have the best modern equipment; highly trained fliers and mechanics; careful and competent inspection; sufficient landing fields along the route or multi-engined planes until there are sufficient landing places; adequate night lighting of fields; efficient meteorological service; perfect radio communication between field and plane; radio beacon to direct the plane on its course, etc.

There are some very special problems in addition to those listed above that project us somewhat farther forward into the future when we consider them. One is the likelihood of landing in midocean on some sort of anchored way-station. Such a device has been suggested time and time again. But an investigation of the architectural difficulties entailed is discouraging. Besides such a landing place is not practicable unless fog is entirely conquered.

No doubt there will be a period of rivalry between the airship and the plane which we scarcely foresee today. Certainly the huge investments several governments are making along the line of lighter-than-air vessels is significant. When I was in Europe last year I investigated the new British air-ship, the R-100, which will be 720 feet long and have a gas capacity of 5,000,000 cubic feet. This will make it about twice the size of our own air giant, the U.S.S. *Los Angeles*. Such a ship can cruise over 5,000 miles without taking on additional fuel and she will be able to carry more than 100 passengers. Germany is building the LZ-127 which will be 774 feet long with which the Germans hope to circle the world in twelve and a half days.

In passing, it is well to mention that our new American airship will be even bigger than the German one. Its capacity will be about 6,000,000 cubic feet. Once we are confident in our weather predictions over the area of the United States such a vehicle will certainly bid for wide use as both a passenger and a mail carrier.

There is still a feeling against increasing the speed of our planes beyond what we are doing with them today. Terrific speed records of about 300 miles an hour which have been made in the last three years suggest equally terrific accidents.

On the other hand, it is quite conceivable that we may soon combine our high altitude exploration with high speed flying. A figure of 500 miles an hour is, I think, in sight.

The great boon for the future of aviation is public sympathy. I do not believe that government subsidies will help it much, if at all; aviation had better stand on its own feet. What we need is private capital and individual enthusiasm. Once these two great forces are available the meteoric rise of the automobile will surely be duplicated in the coming decade by the plane.

IN CLOSING let me go back for a moment to the stirring days in France that followed our arrival there by air in the *America*. While sorrowing for their own gallant fliers, Captain Nungesser and Coli, the French were not inclined to be envious of our success but met us with a joyful spirit of celebration.

May it not be that aviation in the future will in much this same way become the world's strongest instrument for peace?

Surely it brings mankind closer together, knits the interests of the world, and helps spread knowledge and an understanding without which there can be no lasting peace.

If this some day be so, then the men who have given their lives for aviation will not have died in vain.

Appendix

CHRONOLOGY OF BYRD'S LIFE

BY RAIMUND E. GOERLER

1888, October 25	Born at Winchester, Virginia, son of Richard Evelyn Byrd and Eleanor Bolling Flood.
1900	Travels the World alone at twelve years old.
1904–7	Attended Shenandoah Valley Academy and Virginia Military Institute.
1907–8	Student at University of Virginia.
1908–12	Cadet at U.S. Naval Academy.
1912	Assigned first to USS *Kentucky* on July 12, then to USS *Wyoming* on September 25.
	Accident aggravates earlier athletic injury.
1913, September	Reassigned to USS *Missouri*.
1914	Assigned to USS *Washington* during Mexican War.
	Rescues two seamen from drowning. (Awarded Congressional Life-Saving Medal in 1922.)
	Takes first flight on an airplane.

Appendix

1915	Assigned to USS *Dolphin,* yacht of the secretary of the Navy.
1915, January 20	Marries Marie Ames of Boston.
	Assigned to Presidential yacht, USS *Mayflower.*
1916, March	Requests retirement from active duty.
1916, May	Appointed administrator of Rhode Island's naval militia.
1917	Appointed, as a retired officer on active duty, to Bureau of Naval Personnel in Washington, D.C.; serves as Secretary of the Commission on Training Camps.
1917, August	Becomes a naval aviation cadet at Pensacola.
1918, May	Receives pilot's wings and becomes assistant superintendent at Pensacola, with responsibility for instruction in navigation and for investigating plane crashes.
1918, July	Proposes flying NC-1 aircraft across Atlantic; goes to Halifax to establish refueling stations for transatlantic crossing. (Experiment ends with the end of the war.)
1919, February 6	Assigned to newly created Transatlantic Flight Section.
1919–20	Involved in setting up Navy Bureau of Aeronautics.
1921	Navy rejects Byrd's plan for transatlantic flight and sends him to England to help navigate a dirigible to the United States. Byrd misses train and loses his space on the airship, the ZR-2, which exploded.
1922	Becomes responsible for creating an air station in Massachusetts to train reserve pilots.
1924	Travels in Midwest to organize naval reserve units.

Appendix

1924, January	Ordered to assist in planning the flight of the dirigible *Shenandoah* over North Pole (*Shenandoah,* damaged in storm, does not make flight).
1924, June	Receives congressional promotion to rank of lieutenant commander, inactive.
1925, August	Participates in Arctic expedition with Professor Donald MacMillan, with planes from Navy and Navy volunteers and financing from Edsel Ford and John D. Rockefeller.
1925, August 22	Expedition, which did not cross North Pole, returns. (MacMillan opposed to Arctic flights.)
1926, April 3	Byrd's expedition to fly across North Pole begins.
1926, May 9, 12:30 A.M	Byrd takes off for North Pole, with sun compass, wind-drift measure, and bubble sextant as navigational aids; claims to have reached pole at 9:02 A.M.
1926, December	Congress promotes Byrd to rank of commander and awards him the Congressional Medal of Honor.
1927, April 20	Crash of the *America,* which Byrd later used for his transatlantic crossing, on its first test flight.
1927, June 29–30	The *America* takes off from Roosevelt Field, crosses the Atlantic, and makes a successful water landing off the Normandy coast.
1928, September	Byrd's first expedition to Antarctica begins.
1929, November 29	Byrd flies to South Pole.
1930	Expedition returns to the United States from Antarctica; Congress promotes Byrd to rank of rear admiral.
1933	Byrd's second expedition to Antarctica begins.

Appendix

1934, February 3	CBS Radio broadcast from "Little America" in Antarctica.
1934, March 28	Byrd begins nearly fatal winter stay at Bolling Advance Base.
1934, August 10	Party rescues Byrd at Advance Base.
1935, February 7	Expedition departs from "Little America."
1935–36, October–May	Byrd makes lecture tour to 156 cities throughout the United States.
1939, July 7	Official announcement of U.S. Antarctic Service expedition.
1939, November	Antarctic Service expedition (Byrd's third) begins.
1940, March	Byrd leaves Antarctica.
1942	Byrd reassigned to Navy Bureau of Aeronautics.
1942, May–July	Byrd assigned to tour Pacific islands looking for sites appropriate for wartime air bases.
1943, September–October	Byrd tours islands in the east Pacific in search of suitable locations for postwar commercial airports.
1946	The U.S. Navy runs Operation High Jump in Antarctica, using thirteen ships and 4,700 men. Byrd is officer-in-charge but does not exercise actual command. (Byrd's fourth trip to Antarctica.)
1947, April	Return of Operation High Jump forces from Antarctica.
1955–56	Byrd makes fifth and last trip to Antarctica in conjunction with Operation Deepfreeze and the upcoming International Geophysical Year (1957–58).
1957, February 21	Byrd is awarded the Medal of Freedom.
1957, March 11	Byrd dies in Boston at the age of sixty-eight.

A Legacy of
Richard E. Byrd:
The Byrd Polar
Research Center
Archival Program

WHEN A HERO DIES, what remains? Boxes. Four hundred ninety-one contain the original documents of the adventures Byrd described in *Skyward*. The records of Byrd's five expeditions to Antarctica and his personal papers form one of the largest collections of historic documentation of any polar explorer.

Today, Byrd's papers reside in The Ohio State University Archives, where they are fully cataloged and available to researchers. The most controversial item in Byrd's papers is the diary of his flight to the North Pole in 1926. Byrd wrote extensively about this accomplishment in *Skyward,* but doubts that he actually reached the North Pole have remained.

A Legacy of Richard E. Byrd

In *Skyward,* Byrd acknowledged that he carried this diary to the North Pole in 1926 and across the Atlantic Ocean in 1927. The diary contains not only daily entries but also notes from Byrd to his pilot, which have been published in *To the Pole: The Diary and Notebook of Richard E. Byrd, 1925–1927* (Columbus, Ohio: The Ohio State University Press, 1998).

The archives also contain the historic documentation of other polar explorers and scientists. They include Sir Hubert Wilkins, the first to fly an airplane in Antarctica and a rival of Byrd, and Dr. Frederick A. Cook Society, the polar explorer who claimed to have reached the North Pole in 1908, a year before Robert Peary.

For more information about the Byrd Polar Research Center Archival Program, contact The Ohio State University Archives and/or visit its website at http://www.lib.ohio-state.edu/arvweb.

—RAIMUND E. GOERLER, PH.D.

ASSOCIATE PROFESSOR/CHIEF ARCHIVIST

THE OHIO STATE UNIVERSITY

ABOUT THE AUTHOR

ADMIRAL RICHARD E. BYRD became the first person to fly over the North Pole on May 9, 1926. Graduating from the United States Naval Academy in 1912 and later serving in the battleship fleet until he won his wings in 1918, he became Naval Aviator 608. After his historic flight to the Pole in 1926, he organized the Naval flight expedition to the Arctic with the National Geographic Society. On November 29, 1929, Byrd became the first person to fly over the South Pole.

Throughout his life, Byrd organized a total of five expeditions to Antarctica and became the most highly decorated American, receiving the four highest medals available from the United States government and military: Congressional Medal of Honor, Congressional Life-Saving Medal, Distinguished Service Medal, and the Flying Cross. He was recalled to service in the Pacific during World War II and remained an influential figure in polar exploration and flight safety until his death in 1957.